Computing Horizons

Computing Horizons

Tony Durham

Addison-Wesley Publishing Company

Wokingham, England · Reading, Massachusetts · Menlo Park, California
New York · Don Mills, Ontario · Amsterdam · Bonn · Sydney
Singapore · Tokyo · Madrid · Bogota · Santiago · San Juan

Cover design and part-title illustrations by Crayon Design of Henley-on-Thames.
Text design by Lesley Stewart.
Typeset by Colset Private Limited, Singapore.
Printed in Great Britain by The Bath Press, Avon.

First printed in 1987.

British Library Cataloguing in Publication Data

Durham, Tony
Computing horizons.
1. Electronic data processing
2. Computers
I. Title
004 QA76

ISBN 0-201-18046-4

Library of Congress Cataloging-in-Publication Data

Durham, Tony, 1948–
Computing horizons.

Bibliography: p.
1. Computers. 2. Artificial intelligence. I. Title.
QA76.D836 1988 004 87-14981
ISBN 0-201-18046-4

Preface

This book is a selection of articles originally published in the *Over the horizon* column in the weekly newspaper *Computing.*

The articles are about computer science and artificial intelligence. They are also about mathematics, biology, music, language, learning, emotion, secret codes, games, the fourth dimension, and the nature of the universe. These are some of the subjects you get drawn into when you start talking to computer scientists.

Most people in information technology over the age of 30 (and many under that age) did something else first. This means that they have looked at the world from more than one point of view. Also, they like what they are doing and they believe in it. They chose to do it. They were not steered into the subject by teachers who thought they saw a talent. They did not drift into it through inertia.

The other incomparable advantage of the outsider is to see the subject with fresh eyes. To question the way things are done, and suggest simpler, better ways. Whoever discovered water, it certainly was not a fish.

I do not dispute the need for proper, professional courses in information technology and computer science. But too narrow a training will turn out people who know everything about how computing machinery works, and nothing about the way the world works. Such people are unlikely to achieve anything worthwhile in information technology or any other sphere. Some software houses pass over the computer science graduates, except for a few specialized backroom jobs, and recruit arts graduates instead. They can easily be taught to program.

Some computer books begin with hardware and work up to 'difficult' subjects like artificial intelligence. The plan here is different. Computers appear first as intelligent helpers for human beings. Peeling away the layers, we touch on artificial intelligence, software engineering, and finally the physical machinery itself.

Computers exist to help people work, play and learn. People ('liveware' in the jargon) are the most important part of any system. Their needs should dictate the form of the software (programs) and the hardware (machinery). Everything else – artificial intelligence, software engineering, and microchip technology – flows from these needs. In all these areas, a crucial issue is the understanding and control of complexity. An interlude at the mid-point of the book looks at complexity from several angles, including cryptography, mathematics, physics, biology and game-playing.

(The term 'mindware', used as a heading for the section on artificial intelligence, is not original. Though not part of normal computer parlance, it has been seen in *Byte* magazine's advertising, and as the name of a range of products from Intelligent Environments Ltd.)

The text of the articles is generally close to that which appeared in *Computing*. Sometimes material which was cut for lack of space has been restored. Headlines have often been changed. References to other issues of *Computing* have been removed and replaced, when appropriate, by a reference to a chapter in this book. Titles such as Doctor and Professor have been omitted. A few statements which were factually incorrect or misleading when first published have been amended. Statements which have merely gone out of date are allowed to stand. When up to date information was available, I have given it in the material which accompanies each article. However, in many cases even this material is not totally up to date. The book would never have been finished if I had indulged the journalist's desire for up-to-the-minute topicality.

In connection with British research projects, there are frequent references to the Alvey Directorate and the Alvey Programme. For readers unfamiliar with the UK research scene, I should explain that the Alvey Programme of advanced information technology research is Britain's response to Japan's Fifth Generation Computer Systems initiative. It is a joint venture of three Government Departments (Trade and Industry, Defence, and Education and Science) with British industry and academia. The five-year programme began in 1983 and will cost £350 million, of which £200 million comes from public funds and £150 million from industry. Most Alvey projects involve both academic and industrial researchers; a large Alvey project is nearly always a collaboration between several companies and several institutions of learning. Doing research this way has not been without its frictions, but it has been educative for all parties.

Acknowledgements

For once an author can say with total sincerity that many people helped to create this book. I would like to thank all those who patiently explained their work and their ideas to me and whose names punctuate the text. This book is also enriched by those, too many to name, who were interviewed for the many *Over the horizon* articles which I have been unable to include. There are many others I would like to thank: Richard Sharpe, for offering me a column in his paper, and not changing his mind when I told him what I wanted to write about; Caroline Shaw, Lesley Wright (now Bolton), Caroline Berman, Candice Goodwin, and Jenny Mill for their trust, support and editorial skill; Donald Michie, Jean Michie and Judith Richards for the four days which generated six chapters; Joanne Peters for taking care of the children while I tried to finish the book; Vega Roberts for her wonderful cottage where I finished it; Joe for letting me play my computer games when he should have been playing his; Ben for accepting fatherless evenings; Pam.

Illustration acknowledgements

The author and publishers wish to thank the following for permission to reproduce illustrations and for supplying photographs and colour transparencies:

Thomas F. Banchoff, David Laidlaw, Hüseyin Koçak and David Margolis for Plate 1; Douglas R. Hofstadter for the illustrations on page 140; John Milnor for the illustration on page 165; Heinz-Otto Peitgen for Plates 2 and 3 from *The Beauty of Fractals* by H.-O. Peitgen and P.H. Richter (Springer-Verlag, Heidelberg, 1986); Tommaso Toffoli and Norman Margolus of the Massachusetts Institute of Technology for Plates 6 and 7; Stephen Wolfram of the University of Illinois at Urbana-Champaign for Plates 4 and 5.

Trademark notices

Contents

PART 1

Liveware

1

Soft robots people the human interface

'Computing as if people mattered.' This is not my phrase, but Alan Kay's.† The importance and subversiveness of this innocent-sounding notion cannot be overstressed.

Kay is one of the few individuals in the computer industry who has consistently stuck to his belief that computers should be adapted to people, and not vice versa. This is not how most of the industry has worked. The general attitude seems to be that people should wear square shoes, because square shoes are easier to design and manufacture than foot-shaped shoes. If the shoe industry had gone the way of the computer industry it would now be running £200-a-day courses on how to walk, run and jump in square shoes.

'They say the best way to predict the future is to invent it,' Kay observes. He has worked at inventing the future for three computer companies: first for Xerox, then for Atari, and latterly for Apple. Some would say he is a dreamer because he has never trimmed his ideas to fit what is technically possible at a given moment. There is a very important issue here, which probably has no universally valid solution. How does one do what is feasible today, without losing sight of what is desirable tomorrow? A computer company which solves that one will find the secret of eternal youth. So far, none has.

Many of the best ideas about computers, and how they could help people live their lives, are surprisingly old. Kay cites the visionary article 'As we may think', written in 1945 by Vannevar Bush. Bush was a professor at the Massachusetts Institute of Technology in the 1930s, and later President Roosevelt's science adviser. Most of the article is about a desk-sized machine called Memex, with multiple screens and pointing devices, and an information store the size of a small town library. Today we would call Memex a personal computer, and one day there may even be real personal computers with Memex's capabilities.

†Echoing E.F. Schumacher's book *Small is Beautiful*, which was published in 1973 with the sub-title, 'a study of economics as if people mattered'.

'There were three or four multi-million dollar projects funded in the 1960s to try and do something like Memex,' Kay recalls. The money for these far-sighted projects came almost entirely from the Advanced Research Projects Agency of the US Department of Defense. Doug Englebart's project at Stanford Research Institute, usually known as AHI (Augmentation of Human Intellect) was one of them. The pointing device known as the mouse, later taken up by Xerox, Apple and others, was invented for that project in about 1963.

For those unfamiliar with the mouse: it is a little box with one push button (or sometimes more) on top of it. As you roll the mouse around on the table top, a pointer on the computer screen copies your movements. If you want the computer to do something with one of the things displayed on the screen, you use the mouse to point to it, and push the button.

At MIT in September 1984, Alan Kay talked about some of his current interests. He spoke of machines specifically designed to communicate and cooperate with human beings and raised the question: should we try to give such a machine – outwardly at least – a human-like personality?

---

18 October 1984

At opposite ends of the United States, two contrasting visions of human-machine interaction have evolved.

Strangely, it was hip California that produced the efficient, easy-to-use office machines. While 'stuffy' New England witnessed an exuberant mingling of art, entertainment and computer technology – so much for stereotypes.

Xerox Palo Alto Research Center (PARC) gave us the 'desktop metaphor', the crisp black-on-white display, the icons (common sense graphical symbols used for menu selection), the overlapping screen windows, and the mouse as a pointing device.

Under the surface was the Smalltalk programming system, based on the ideas of data objects which send messages to each other; and the Ethernet network to hook the desktop machine into a powerful 'information utility'. It was a brilliant synthesis of ideas from many sources, and it was influential. Most of the PARC ideas did eventually emerge in Xerox products. They strongly influenced the design of Apple's Lisa and Macintosh personal computers. The same ideas have appeared in diluted form in many other products.

On the other side of the continent, Nicholas Negroponte's Architecture Machine group (ArcMac) at the Massachusetts Institute of Technology turned the desktop metaphor inside out. Arcmac's version of the electronic office resembled a flight simulator or an all-enveloping video game. The user sat in a soft black chair straight out of *Mastermind*, using joystick controls to 'fly' from one data item to another. The spatial information environment known as Dataland was back-projected on one wall of ArcMac's womb-like Media Room.

Other ArcMac projects have aimed to let humans communicate with machines in the same way as they communicate with fellow human beings. That is to say, by speech, gesture and facial expression. People are actively encouraged to see machines in anthropomorphic terms. A personal computer, even a telephone answering machine, acquires a façade of humanoid personality.

Xerox has lost many of its leading researchers. But ArcMac's star seems to be in the ascendant. This winter the Architecture Machine group will at last lose its incongruous name as it merges into MIT's prestigious new Center for Arts and Media Technology.

Nicholas Negroponte is the centre's director and one of his star recruits from the computer world is Alan Kay. Kay now splits his time between MIT and Apple, the company he joined in April. Before that, he was chief scientist at the games and personal computer company Atari. Before that Kay was one of the leading lights at Xerox PARC.

Kay tends to emphasize the many ideas that PARC and ArcMac shared, but he agrees that there are important differences. 'When I was at Atari,' he recounts, 'I realized that a lot of the things that Atari was interested in as a consumer company were rather better suited by Negroponte's stuff than they were by the PARC stuff.'

Before former Commodore boss Jack Tramiel bought Atari from Warner Communications, the company was working on robots, computer music and artificial intelligence for the next generation of electronic consumer goodies.

Kay hired ArcMac researchers to work at Atari. And Atari funded projects at ArcMac. Kay himself sketched out the designs for two ArcMac projects: a personal electronic newspaper, with items selected automatically to match the reader's interests; and a 'phone slave' or smart answering machine. The slave answered calls in a human-sounding voice. In the ensuing dialogue it asked the caller's name and number, the subject of the call, when to call back, and what message, if any, the caller would like to leave. It did not understand what it heard, but it asked its questions with uncanny timing. And people were prepared to talk to it. This, according to Kay, was an attempt to find an interface that could deal with a person in anthropomorphic terms without having to be intelligent. The phone slave was an 'agent', a semi-autonomous extension of its owner's goals and desires.

The idea of the agent, Kay says, is an old one. He traces it back to the 'advice taker' described in a 1956 paper by artificial intelligence pioneer John McCarthy. The term 'agent' was coined in the mid-1960s. But agent systems are not easy to engineer, and in Kay's view 'an agent is harder than an expert system'.

Agents were never part of the Xerox PARC approach. There, says Kay, the user interface was seen as a tool – 'a better way of massaging text, a better way of getting pictures, a better way of dealing with mail, a better way of seeing all the different things that you have'.

The Xerox work assumed that the user builds an illusion or myth about the system and uses it to predict how the system might behave. 'The perception of user friendliness is directly concerned with how often the system confirms that myth,' says Kay. 'So we did the designs at Xerox by thinking about what kinds of myths people would think up, and then ruthlessly simplifying them.'

The famous overlapping screen windows were 'designed so you could understand what they were in five seconds'. From this it is a bold and potentially dangerous step, to deliberately set up the myth that the machine is human. 'As soon as you stick your toe into the anthropomorphic arena, you're setting up a user illusion that is almost certainly going to be shattered time and time again. Talk to something in English, and your illusion is that this is an intelligent entity. Because the only entities you can talk to in English right now are people. So you're setting up the user for a fall.'

Kay admits that as yet, nobody can build an agent which fully lives up to people's expectations, but there are tricks. The phone slave uses psychology. 'It gets a good model of the hesitation rate of people's speech,' Kay explains. 'It uses that to decide when a pause is actually a pause, and then it just jumps right in and redirects the context back to something that it can actually deal with.'

'The particular insight in that system is that if you can do that, and ask the question in a solicitous manner, almost every person will in fact derail whatever it is that they're doing and try and answer that question.' Quite simply, the phone slave mastered the art of polite interruption.

Did people think they were talking to a human being? Surprisingly, the researchers never tried to find out. 'The interest,' says Kay, 'was in whether they would talk.'

In another ArcMac experiment, Richard Bolt's Put-That-There, the user could point at a large, distant screen and say things like 'put a blue triangle there.' A blue triangle would appear on the screen in the indicated position. Saying 'make that a circle' would immediately turn it into a circle. The pointing gesture was measured with an electromagnetic sensor made by a company called Polhemus.

'Put-That-There uses a very nice trick, which is another defuser of anger,' Kay observes. 'The thing that makes you most angry is when somebody asks you, repeat the whole thing. When people ask you, "What did you want to do?" or, "What colour was that?" you will answer right away.'

Put-That-There never directly asked anyone to repeat what they just did. Apparently it managed to keep its users unruffled, even though its speech recognition was only 60 per cent efficient.

Kay believes that many people are unwilling to learn new skills such as the use of a keyboard. They will want to use the communication skills they have mastered already, including speech and body language. 'Every time you use one of those things you're getting much closer to anthropomorphism,' he says. 'You're basically thinking about the user interface as kind of a soft robot. It's a robot that lives inside the computer, and the mouse or the Polhemus sensor is a sense organ for the robot to know where certain things are.'

Kay expects that future 'agent' projects will use fewer tricks and more real intelligence. But he sees no harm in using tricks to get started. You don't try to do a James Bond film as your first experiment in interactive movie making, he points out. You choose something simple like a Saturday morning cartoon.

At Atari, Kay and his team distinguished 'hard robots' or physical agents from 'soft robots' or software agents. There were, he says, half a dozen agent projects at Atari. 'One of the things we did was to have the agent appear on the screen as a cartoon character.' This created an anthropomorphic myth without leading people to expect great intelligence from the agent.

Kay has believed passionately in the importance of networks since his Xerox days. But how to find the item you want, from the wealth of information that the network makes available? Perhaps a quasi-human agent could help. 'You would like to have an oracle, but nobody knows how to do an oracle. And the next best thing to an oracle is a librarian, which is yet another agent, the guide. Networks require guides.'

Machines will also tune in to the non-verbal signals we all send out unconsciously. 'It will only be two or three years,' Kay predicts, 'before there is a television camera in your console that looks at your face to try and register facial expressions.'

Further reading

Bush, V. (1945). 'As we may think' *Atlantic Monthly*, July.

Kay, A. (1984). 'Computer software' *Scientific American*, September, 41–47.

Press, L. (1983). 'Personal computing: where did it come from?' *Abacus*, **1**, no. 1. New York: Springer-Verlag.

2

Machines with feelings

Many people believe that emotions are a very important part of what it is to be human. Many also regard emotion and reason as opposites. The television series *Star Trek,* always a good textbook of twentieth-century folk philosophy, has a long-running joke which concerns the character of Spock, the human-like alien who is second-in-command on the starship *Enterprise.* Spock is supposed to have a perfectly logical mind, and Captain Kirk regularly takes him to task for displaying 'illogical' emotions. The implication is that logic and emotion are incompatible, and that of the two, emotion is the more essentially human.

No doubt one reason for this emphasis on our emotionality is the awareness that machines are actually rather good at logical deduction, and that logical ability no longer differentiates reliably between people and machines. In a show with a bigger costume budget, Spock could easily have been made a robot.

Perhaps the folk philosophy will need to be readjusted once again, if the emotional behaviour of machines becomes as convincing as their performance in logic. Even those who are happy with the proposition that machines can think, may be a little uncomfortable with the idea that they can have feelings. Yet this is a possibility that we may have to confront soon. Machines designed as if people mattered may begin to resemble people themselves.

This article does not attempt to settle the philosophical question of whether machines can have feelings. It merely points out that emotion is already on the agenda for the designers of computer systems. Some people refuse to mention emotion and computers in the same breath. As Spock would point out, that refusal is not entirely logical.

16 February 1984

Does emotion have a place in computer systems? George Kiss believes it does.

Kiss (the name is Hungarian and rhymes with dish) is engaged in an unusual three-year project at Warwick University. His aim: to model human emotions in a machine.

While Kiss clearly enjoys entering philosophical minefields, he treads with due caution. The first year of the project has been spent refining concepts and looking for an intelligent way into the problem. 'We are getting to the stage now,' he says cautiously, 'where we could probably sit down and have a shot at programming something.'

As a psychologist Kiss hopes that computer models will throw light on the nature of human emotions. But his interest in the subject goes much further than that. He believes that emotion will be a valuable and, probably, an unavoidable attribute of intelligent computer systems. 'Intelligence is intimately tied up with motivation and emotion,' he says.

Psychological research on motivation and emotion was held back for a time by the influence of behaviourism. Behaviourists such as B.F. Skinner denied that emotion and motivation have any role in scientific explanations.

It is ironic, then, that artificial intelligence (AI) researchers, working with supposedly unfeeling machines, found that they had to reintroduce the concept of motivation. The General Problem Solver, an influential computer program written at Carnegie-Mellon University around 1960, was designed to work systematically towards an explicitly stated goal.

Most of the AI community now accepts that goals or purposes are an essential component of intelligent behaviour. But George Kiss goes beyond the prevailing AI view that a goal is something purely intellectual. 'Many people say we need cool, calm intelligence. They contrast reason with emotion,' he says. 'I am opposed to that view. Emotion is there for functional reasons. It is not a vestige of something primitive. Normal healthy emotional reactions to situations are necessary.'

Kiss sees emotion as the product of an evaluation process. Fear, for example, is the result of a process which evaluates a situation as dangerous. In a rather simple way, machines already perform this kind of evaluation. 'Error messages are the primitive forms of it already,' says Kiss. 'The machine has done some evaluation of what you have done and judged it inappropriate. If you think of systems controlling plants or nuclear reactors, the idea of danger seems an important concept for the machine to have.'

It is easy to imagine a sense of danger being programmed into, say, a nuclear power station. It is much harder to believe that it would have anything in common with the human emotion of fear.

But George Kiss has an answer to the objection that 'fear' in such a system would just be another numeric variable like temperature or pressure. He points out that human fear, too, has physiological indicators such as the heart rate. But there is more to the phenomenon of fear than that. To merit the name of 'fear', a variable would have to be linked both to an intelligent process which evaluates the degree of danger in a situation, and to processes which take appropriate, intelligent action.

Like many (but not all) other AI researchers, Kiss takes the functionalist view that you do not judge something by what it is but by what it does. You do not decide whether something can think by looking to see whether it has a brain. You do not insist that it has a heart, before you admit that it can be frightened. Asked whether the machine will actually feel fear, Kiss replies, 'My position is that it will. The system for most purposes, both practical and theoretical will feel genuine emotion.'

Consciousness will be explicitly represented in the hierarchical model of emotion that Kiss is developing. 'The overall architecture has to be a kind of multi-level system, of which the top level is consciousness,' he says. Kiss manages to make this sound unsurprising. 'Current information processing systems have things which already are analogues of consciousness. The central processing unit had been compared to consciousness.'

He argues that something analogous to consciousness also appears in the 'blackboard' model which was used in the Hearsay speech recognition project of the US Department of Defense. A number of subsystems worked separately on the problem. All chalked up their results and suggestions on a central 'blackboard'. The blackboard can be seen as the focus of the system's 'awareness'.

At last year's International Joint Conference on Artificial Intelligence a poll found that 75 per cent of the delegates at one symposium supported the 'strong AI' hypothesis. According to the philosopher John R. Searle (who himself rejects it) strong AI says that 'The appropriately programmed computer really is a mind, in the sense that computers given the right programs can be literally said to understand and have other cognitive states'.

There is a view that consciousness is something that suddenly switches on like a light when living things, or machines, reach a certain level of development. But George Kiss believes there are many degrees of consciousness. If one builds increasingly sophisticated models of consciousness, they will gradually approach the human level of consciousness. There is no magic moment at which the model ceases to be a model and becomes the real thing.

Though he does not feel obliged to be kind to microcomputers, Kiss insists that 'there are ethical problems and they need to be taken seriously. They cannot just be ignored.'

He rejects the suggestion that there is an enormous gap between what we can actually build, and machines which model aspects of the human mind. He believes that two things have deterred research in this direction. One is the argument, forcefully presented by Joseph Weizenbaum in his book *Computer Power and Human Reason*, that it is socially and morally wrong to try to build machines like human beings. The other obstacle, according to Kiss, is that the possibility is just not taken seriously. 'There is a kind of snobbishness, even in AI, in not tackling problems which smack of philosophy,' he comments.

Only the wildest optimist would expect anything more than a very simple model of human emotion to emerge from a three-year research project. But George Kiss believes that even a simple model could be valuable in commercial computer systems.

In the area of research which the Alvey programme designates 'man–machine interface', it is now generally accepted that computer systems must provide appropriate assistance both to beginners and to expert users. This leads rapidly to the idea that the machine should have an internal representation of the user's knowledge.

George Kiss believes this is not enough. A person's reaction to a machine may run through anger, boredom, frustration, contentment and sometimes even delight. To handle such a temperamental thing as a human being, a machine will need an internal model of human emotions. It will have to guess how its human partner feels about things. Perhaps 'user-friendly' computer systems can be raised above the level of inane chumminess, to something more like empathy.

Further reading

Weizenbaum, J. (1976). *Computer Power and Human Reason.* San Francisco, Calif.: W.H. Freeman.

3

Breast-pocket Britannicas

The idea of the 'Dynabook' is still fascinating, perhaps because it seems only a little closer to realization than it was in the early 1970s. Anyone whose life or work depends on information has dreamed of such a gadget, small enough to take anywhere, as direct and simple to use as pencil and paper, as rich in knowledge as a library, as helpful as a personal assistant.

It did seem, at the time when this article was written, that the personal computer was beginning, slowly and painfully, to evolve towards this glorious goal. The hardware pieces were falling into place. But that made the lack of Dynabook-worthy software all the more conspicuous.

---

5 July 1984

Most 'portable' computers are plonked on a desk and never budge from it, a salesman confided. But customers still buy the idea of the go-anywhere computing machine and the lifestyle it stands for, the post-industrial blend of work and play that is caricatured in the TV ads where the executive lounges by the pool toying with the diminutive micro on his lap. That, of course, is very much an American vision. An equally simple-minded caricature of Japan might show us images of manager beavering at micro while sardined in traffic jam, commuter train or capsule hotel.

The marketeers hark back to these crude scenarios because nobody can yet predict with any certainty what kind of machine the portable computer is destined to become, or how it will fit into (or disrupt) the lifestyles of East and West.

Alan Kay's concept of the Dynabook has proved remarkably durable. Kay worked at Xerox Palo Alto Research Center from 1971 to 1982. He had a long-term vision of a high performance notebook-sized computer with a high-resolution display, which could tap into shared information resources.

The entire Smalltalk project at Xerox PARC has been described as the software part of the Dynabook. The software ideas surfaced in the Xerox Star workstation, and also influenced Apple products.

Kay himself joined Atari a little while before the Warner subsidiary's fortunes took a dive, but he is reported to have got a Dynabook-style research project going at the company's Sunnyvale think tank.

Physically, computers are beginning to catch up with Kay's vision. Machines like the Grid Compass, the Husky Hunter and the Epson PX-8 have flat displays of sufficient resolution to allow some real graphics. Most of the 'enabling technologies' for the Dynabook are developing fast.

Displays Liquid crystal displays are the front runners at the moment. They use little power and, like a printed page, give good contrast over a wide range of lighting conditions including full sunshine. Both these advantages can be traced to the fact that LCDs reflect incident light – rather than emitting light of their own, as plasma panels, cathode ray tubes and electroluminescent panels do.

The main problem is to address something like half a million pixels without running a separate wire to each dot. Everyone from Epson to GEC is trying, one way or another, to make what amounts to a faultless semiconductor chip the size of an A4 sheet of paper and as complex as a 512-kilobit random access memory (RAM). Amorphous silicon is one of the favoured materials.

Microprocessors Many are now made in the low-power complementary metal oxide semiconductor (CMOS) technology. The telecommunications business created the main demand for CMOS, but it has proved very useful for all kinds of devices which have to work away from a mains supply.

Memory The arrival of 256-kilobit read-write RAM chips means that a system with the power of, say, the BBC Microcomputer can be built with a single memory chip. 1-megabit RAMS are being planned, for production late in the 1980s.

Already there are handheld machines with more memory than existing microcomputer software can use. One way to cope with this abundance of memory is to treat it as a 'silicon disk'. Thus the Husky Hunter runs CP/M, a disk operating system, even when no real disk drive is connected.

Packaging The insect-like dual-in-line package is a relatively gross object in comparison to the silicon die which is its active heart. There are more compact ways of packaging chips, and what IBM does in mainframes today may be done in handheld micros tomorrow.

One neat package is the so-called 'smart card', a microprocessor sealed into a plastic credit card. Casio now sells a calculator, complete with solar power cells, keypad and display, which is as thin as a credit card. Toshiba has developed a paper-thin lithium battery for self-powered smart cards.

Conceived as a way of identifying yourself and paying for things, the smart card also has potential in quite a different direction, as a form of removable storage for very small computers. Software could be distributed in read-only smart cards.

Mass storage Optical devices, such as the Drexler laser card and various optical disks, offer very large data storage capacities in a small space. They tend to be read-only or at best, write-once, so their prime use would be as a medium for publishing software and distributing copies of large databases.

Sony and Philips are investigating the possibility of storing 550 megabytes of data instead of music on the 5-inch diameter compact disc. And from an early stage Sony has talked of still smaller laser disks, perhaps only two inches in diameter, to be played on a Walkman-style personal stereo. It seems almost inevitable that if a tiny audio disk is manufactured, someone will try recording computer software on it.

Batteries Advances in this area have been hard-won. There is much less theoretical scope for increasing the amount of energy supplied by one gram of battery than there is for decreasing the amount of energy used in processing one bit of information.

The high energy-to-mass ratio of lithium batteries has attracted the interest of the electronics industry. But a book-sized computer can run for a long time on conventional batteries unless it has moving parts such as disk drives or a printer.

Speech Speech is attractive as a means of communicating with very small computers, if only because the transducers (loudspeakers and microphones) are inexpensive, and smaller than screens or keyboards. The people walking down the street wearing headphones in ten years time may be listening not to disco or Mahler but to their personal computers.

Communications The modem is increasingly seen as an essential part of a personal computer. But a 'go-anywhere' computer should not need a telephone line to communicate.

Cellular radio will increase the number of people who can have in-car telephones, but its uses need not be confined to the transmission of speech.

Racal is taking part in an Alvey project on the possible data services that could be provided via cellular radio.

Motoring information services are one likely application, but in theory cellular radio could give the Dynabook user access to the world's electronic databases.

Databases Hundreds exist already for specialists in various professions. Only a few, such as the Source (owned by *Reader's Digest*) draw their subscribers from the general public. It may take major changes, both in technology and in public attitudes, to reverse this ratio.

Software In the 1970s this was the first aspect of the Dynabook to be investigated; but it remains a weak point, especially in Japan where the hardware technologies such as LCD screens are developing so fast. Epson, for example, is well equipped with these technologies, but its managing director Susumu Aizawa has admitted the existence of a 'software gap'.

A handheld CP/M business machine may be what the market needs today, but this is surely a temporary phase. Early motor cars looked like horse-drawn carriages, but not for long.

Smalltalk and its offspring foster a style of interaction which depends heavily on graphics and makes minimal use of the keyboard. This is especially relevant to a machine which will not, in general, be used at a desk. The increasing research activity on the general principles of human-computer interaction should yield insights which can increase the friendliness and power of handheld machines.

Knowledge based systems Expert systems and other 'intelligent' knowledge based systems are likely to figure strongly in Dynabook software. People will turn to their portable computer for help and advice when other sources are not at hand.

Apart from fully-fledged expert systems, there are now a number of techniques for structuring and animating information so that relevant facts can be found quickly or even automatically.

Applications Many of these may be unexpected, just as many of today's personal computer applications were unimagined five years ago.

The book analogy may be relevant, but the databases consulted via a Dynabook are likely to be more richly interconnected than those found in books.

Already companies like Wang Electronic Publishing are beginning to publish books such as Roget's *Thesaurus* in software form. Reference books are an easy starting point. Manuals and training material cry out to be converted from dead paper into living software. And of course we shall hear more of that old favourite, the computerized novel which allows the reader to choose either a sad or a happy ending.

Two years on, there are really only two types of personal computer: desktops and laptops. Some of the desktop machines are 'luggable' as an additional feature. Laptop computers are becoming more powerful, but they are still seen as machines for people with special needs, such as roving journalists. Physically small computers are not comfortable to use. Nor will they be, so long as using a computer consists of hitting keys and looking at a screen.

Flat screens (in LCD or other technologies) can now give a picture good enough to be used with standard personal computer software. But one important conclusion of the Xerox research was that a Dynabook needs a high resolution display. Otherwise the tremendous information-gathering capacity of the human eye goes to waste. For displaying detailed pictures made up of very large numbers of dots, the bulky cathode ray tube remains unchallenged.

Getting information out of online databases is still not easy. There is still no simple and uniform method of retrieving information from a database. Even the problem of establishing communication or 'logging on' is non-trivial with today's equipment and software. Most of the systems are designed for an expert, regular user with a 'dumb' terminal. Clearly what the inexperienced or occasional seeker after information requires is the help of an intelligent information-hunting 'agent'.

The CP/M operating system is in decline, with MS/DOS the current standard for personal computers, and many people now looking for something more sophisticated than MS/DOS.

The Smalltalk programming system is becoming available on a wider range of computers, including the IBM PC. But Alan Kay believes Smalltalk has strayed from its origins and become too complicated. It is a fine environment for programmers, but not for children. Those programmers, of course, may yet use Smalltalk as a tool for building real Dynabook software.

Cellular radio has enjoyed great popularity in the UK since the service was launched in 1985, though it still costs upward of £900 to acquire a mobile telephone. Neither the market nor the technology appears to be quite ready for a computer, modem and cellular telephone bundled into a single device, but this will come sooner or later.

There has also been a wave of enthusiasm for laser disks, in the burgeoning electronic publishing industry. But as with cellular radio, the equipment is still a bit too bulky to be tucked away (with everything else) inside an A4-sized electronic book. Little has been heard about two-inch diameter laser disks. For read-only disks, the most popular size is the 4.7-inch CD-ROM. Write-once disks are available in 5¼, 8 and 12-inch sizes.

One-megabit RAM chips have reached the market. Four-megabit and larger sizes are reported to be under development.

Further reading

Byte (1986) **11**, no. 5, May. (An issue devoted to mass storage, with several articles about optical disks.)

4

Driving software design from the front end

This chapter and Chapter 6 describe research at Leicester Polytechnic. Britain's polytechnics have been teaching degree courses for more than 20 years, but their status remains markedly and often unjustly lower than that of the universities. They are financed out of local rather than national funds, under a system which was not designed to support research. But some excellent research teams have been built up by such individuals as Ernest Edmonds at Leicester, and Agnes Kaposi at the Polytechnic of the South Bank.

The SYNICS project began at a time when people designing computer systems were much less willing than they are now, to recognize the human-computer interface as an issue in its own right. The idea of separating the human interface or 'front end' from the main body of a system leads on to more ambitious ideas, including interfaces which automatically adapt to the user's skills, experience and preferences.

But every front end is the front end of something. The front end should reflect the nature of the application. And no matter how sophisticated the user interface, the underlying application program should be able to carry out what the user requires, reliably and with reasonable speed. The separation cannot and should not be complete, if humans and machines are to cooperate effectively.

27 September 1984

Software is no longer judged by the standards of the old-style computer priesthood. What makes a package tick now matters less than what it is like to use. To a large extent it is the user interface, the front end, that turns a bright idea into a useful and marketable software product.

Treating the front end as a separate module within the program has obvious advantages. It shifts the priorities from software that is easy to write, towards software that is easy to use. It makes it easier to redesign the front end later if necessary. And to the extent that the front end is left 'soft', users can configure the package to their own hardware and their personal tastes.

Where this is not possible, or where the desired changes are more drastic than the designers envisaged, there are software tools which can be used to build a new front end onto an existing package. The same tools can be used, of course, to build a front end for a program which does not yet have one. It is even possible to create a front end for a package which does not yet exist.

SYNICS, a front-ending toolkit of this kind, is being developed by Leicester Polytechnic's Human–Computer Interface Research Unit. The unit, headed by Ernest Edmonds, was set up with a Science and Engineering Research Council grant in 1982. Work on SYNICS began, however, in the early 1970s.

SYNICS can be used to design human-machine dialogues, from the grand outline down to the individual keystroke.

Seen at low magnification, such a dialogue can be imagined as a road map of the country. Towns and cities correspond to 'events' of which the user is aware; for example, when something new appears on the screen, or a choice is made from a menu.

To see what happens in detail when the user types in a sentence or hits a single key, we need the equivalent of a large scale map of a single town. But as far as SYNICS is concerned, there is no real difference between large scale and small scale maps. Both can be represented in the same way.

The Leicester team believes that the road map or transition network picture is the one that is likely to be in the mind of a programmer designing the overall structure of a dialogue. It so happens that a transition network can also be used to define the grammar of the language in which the dialogue takes place.

Internally, however, SYNICS uses production rules to represent both dialogues and grammars. Given a description of a transition network, SYNICS translates it into production rules consisting of a condition (IF such and such) and an action (THEN do so and so). This is done partly for SYNICS' own convenience. Production rules contain less redundant information and make the computations easier. But there is nothing secret about the rules. A programmer who wants to examine the rules can call them up on the screen.

'SYNICS includes a powerful parser and translator,' says Edmonds. The function of a parser is to determine the grammatical structure of sentences in a natural language such as English, or a formal language such as a programming language. But the concept of parsing is also applied more generally. For example, a front end can be said to parse the action sequences of the user. SYNICS literally does this.

The SYNICS parser is really an empty shell, waiting for the programmer to supply a set of grammatical rules. In theory, someone who knew all the rules of English grammar (and there are many more of them than appear in textbooks) could set up SYNICS to parse any English input whatsoever.

In practice SYNICS has been applied to somewhat less ambitious tasks. One application takes the 'metafile' output from GINO graphics software and translates it into a set of facts in the logic programming language Prolog – or rather, in a graphics extension of standard Prolog.

Designed primarily for interfacing software to human beings, SYNICS has also proved useful for interfacing software to software. 'We've found we can use this system as glue between packages,' says Edmonds.

Programs which were never designed to be used together can be integrated. Edmonds also sees opportunities for fast and inexpensive software prototyping. Prospective users could try out a skeleton system glued together with SYNICS, while some of the modules were still unwritten. 'It might be that some of the modules would have to be humans sitting at another terminal,' he says.

SYNICS' own user interface has perhaps been neglected but it is now moving to the style of the 1980s, as the system is implemented on a workstation with mouse and high-resolution display.

The move to workstations has also brought the possibility of logging, in detail, the user's interaction with the machine. This was difficult under a multi-user operating system. 'The log not only logs all the information about the keystrokes,' says Edmonds, 'it logs where you are in the dialogue.' Design can then be based on an analysis of the way people actually use a program.

Underlying this whole approach is the assumption that the front end can be treated separately from the rest of the program. Edmonds explains, 'What we're talking about is what's happening to the user. There may be big things happening to the data, which may be hidden in a dialogue-event description.'

But, of course, what happens to the user and what happens to the data are not unconnected issues. 'A thing that we're currently very interested in is ensuring that the front end has a model of the back end within it,' says Edmonds.

This would not be a literal copy of the back-end code, but some high level representation of what the back end actually does. At the moment it is up to the programmer to ensure that the front-end design reflects what happens in the rest of the program.

SYNICS is not a general purpose programming language but it is moving in that direction. One could write the entire control structure of a program in SYNICS, dropping into FORTRAN for the occasional burst of number-crunching.

Instructional and interviewing programs, for example, spend most of their time interacting with the user. In a sense these programs are 'all front end', and could reasonably be written on a front-ending system.

More and more software packages (databases, spreadsheets, even word processors) have a general purpose programming language, or something very like it, lurking inside them. Front-ending systems are no exception.

But you don't choose a car for its engine, you choose it because it suits the kind of driving you want to do. A front-ending system must have the right algorithms ticking away inside it, but ultimately it will be judged by its aptness for purpose and the quality of its own front end.

In October 1985, Ernest Edmonds and the Human–Computer Interface Research Unit moved bodily from Leicester Polytechnic to Loughborough University a few miles away. He said at the time, that despite his long-standing support for the polytechnics, it had become impossible to continue the work of his team in the polytechnic system. Good research can certainly begin in a polytechnic. It is sad when it cannot continue there. Maybe the purpose of polytechnics is to teach; one wonders how well they can fulfil that purpose if their best staff leave to pursue their research in the more favourable environment of universities.

A microcomputer implementation of SYNICS called MicroSYNICS has been marketed by the National Computing Centre as part of the Alvey Directorate's successful expert-systems starter pack. According to *Alvey News*, October 1985, there are versions for IBM and Apricot personal computers. The other three programs in the starter pack are Micro Expert, ES/P Adviser, and Expert-Ease. We shall return to the subject of Expert-Ease and similar programs which induce general rules from examples.

5

Guidelines for a universal human interface

SYNICS is a tool for building front ends. Like any good general purpose tool, it does not dictate the design of the finished product. It is for the designer to decide how an interface will be attuned to the user on the one hand, and to a particular application on the other.

One cannot expect to separate these two issues completely. But it is interesting to ask how far the human interface can be made independent of the application. Are there certain features that will always help people to work comfortably and productively with computers, irrespective of the task in hand? And if so, could these features be built into a universal, reusable interface?

If a universal interface is too much to hope for, it may still be possible to devise a general purpose interface for applications belonging to some wide class. This is what Xerox did with its desktop metaphor. To control a program by means of little icons of folders and waste paper bins makes sense so long as the task in hand bears some relation to ordinary office paperwork. But there is nothing about the idea of icons that restricts them to deskwork and the office. In very different contexts, once could still use icons, but they might have to be different icons.

The Warwick man–machine interface (MMI) proposal skilfully pinpointed some of the key issues in human–computer interaction. It would have been extremely interesting to see the outcome of the proposed research. The Alvey Directorate turned the proposal down – surely not because there was anything second-rate about it. However, there were other excellent research proposals in the same area, which may have fitted better into Alvey's general plan of MMI research. One other project, in particular, has subsequently taken up some of the ideas that would have been explored in the Warwick project. That project is discussed in Chapter 7.

29 March 1984

'Good human interfaces are going to be *the* factor, I believe, that decides whether people buy information technology products.' This is the opinion of Edmund Furse, who was seconded from a job at GEC Telecommunications to Warwick University, and is now in charge of the Warwick MMI project.

Warwick's industrial partners in the proposed £2 million research project are GEC, STC and ICI. The participants have applied to the Alvey Directorate for funding.

The project is based in the University's psychology department. Its human-centred priorities can be traced back to the work at Xerox's Palo Alto Research Center which led, eventually, to the 8010 (Star) workstation and its artificial intelligence-oriented clone, the 1108.

'Xerox really paved the way by employing all those psychologists,' says Furse. He quotes a Xerox contribution to the *Byte* magazine issue on human factors engineering: 'reduced cost will allow people to *buy* computers but improved user interfaces will allow people to *use* computers.'

'We believe the heart of the problem is cognitive,' says George Kiss, the Warwick psychologist whose interests outside the MMI project include the computer modelling of human emotion.

The seven-phase plan for the project leads, somewhat unconventionally, to a specification via an implementation. This makes sense once you grasp that the plan represents one and a half iterations of the usual specification, design, implementation cycle. Along the way there will be real hardware and real software and real people tangling with it. The lessons learned will go into a final specification on paper. It will then be for industry to use the specification, or parts of it, or ideas from it.

The aim is to define a universal human interface which could be implemented on a wide range of hardware, and used with equal success in an office, a factory or a software house. Crucial to this vision is the concept of the MMI or intelligent front-end as an independent entity, not tied to any application program. This has advantages both for the system builder and for the user. 'You don't have to keep rewriting the code,' says Furse, 'and the user doesn't have to keep learning a new cognitive style.'

Apple's Lisa and Macintosh computers exemplify this approach, as do a growing number of third-party software packages. But the desktop metaphor used by Apple and others is matched to the special needs of office workers. The Warwick project will be looking for an interface which can be applied to a much wider range of environments including real-time computing.

Another aim of the Warwick project is to raise the level of interaction between user and machine. The idea is that instead of telling the machine what to do, you should be able to tell it what you want. That is to say, the interaction should be in terms of goals, rather than action sequences.

Better, they argue at Warwick, to be able to type 'I want my expense form filled in' than to have to spell out every boring step of the process to a gee-whiz speech recognition system. Not that they have anything against speech recognition. Voice input and output, and sophisticated graphics, will all almost certainly have important roles in the project.

Much of the classic work in artificial intelligence was on this very problem, the problem of getting a machine to perform an appropriate series of actions when given only a broadly stated goal. Furse, Kiss and their colleagues intend to use the best of the existing AI work.

The Warwick project will explore a number of properties which are seen as desirable characteristics for an MMI. One of them is 'cognitive matching'. The idea here is that the human being should be able to express things naturally and should not feel cramped by the machine. The cryptic commands of, say, the Unix operating system clearly fall some way short of this objective.

Another goal is to make the system adaptive. 'We feel a machine should adapt so that it knows what you know, and it knows the level at which you want to interact with it,' explains Furse.

Some commercial software offers a choice of 'novice' or 'expert' mode, but an uncharitable person might dismiss this as the equivalent of the skill level switch on a Pac–man game. The idea now circulating in MMI circles is that the machine should contain a model of the user's knowledge. George Kiss envisages a three–fold intelligent knowledge based system (IKBS), containing knowledge of the user, knowledge of its own capabilities, and knowledge of the application domain.

The IKBS approach is dictated because the system must be able to cope with unforeseen situations. The exact form of the knowledge base is still undecided. But it could be a rule-based system. The full set of rules would be formulated by picking the brains of an already expert user of the system. When a less experienced user took the controls, the interface would switch to a simpler set of rules.

'You might delete rules if that is appropriate,' suggests Kiss. 'Or you might introduce simpler rules.' But which rules to delete? Kiss argues that the system must deduce, from the user's behaviour, which rules are missing from the user's mental picture of how the system works.

The machine would begin to formulate its model of the user's knowledge by parsing the user's action sequences, interpreting their structure in terms of some kind of 'grammar' in much the same way as sentences are parsed in machine translation or natural language programming.

An inexperienced user is likely to make errors, of course, and the machine could be left wondering what the user was really trying to do.

Kiss's answer is that the machine should seek clarification by firing questions or suggestions at the user.

That would be an example of a 'mixed-initiative dialogue'. This is another of the Warwick project's guiding ideas: the idea that the machine should question, suggest, or even act on its own initiative, instead of always leaving the initiative with the user.

One other guiding idea is that of 'appropriate modality'. Ed Furse offers an example: 'If you are asked where you want your desk, you want to be able to point and say "Here!". You do not want to have to say "Left a bit, right a bit . . . " '

This example actually came in the form of a cartoon, drawn by a friend of Furse's who is a professional cartoonist. The example loses something in the telling. Perhaps a cartoon, rather than an article, is indeed the appropriate modality for this particular information.

These then are some of the ideas that are waiting to be explored if the Alvey Directorate stumps up its half of the project's cost. The plan is to run fieldwork and theoretical studies in parallel, with the two streams converging halfway at the completion of an initial MMI specification, and again at the end of the project when the full specification takes shape.

The fieldwork will initially look at three application areas: the office was chosen for the richness of its activity; computer-based training was chosen as a natural testbed for machine modelling of the user's knowledge; the third area is software engineering. The needs of today's software specialist may be the needs of tomorrow's non-expert user if, as Ed Furse believes, 'The only real way to solve the software crisis is for users to do their own specification and their own programming.'

It will certainly not be easy to write a specification for an advanced human interface which is truly 'domain-independent.' One computer fits in a coat pocket, another controls an oil refinery. There will be an ever richer variety both of hardware and of application software. The variety is obvious. It is much harder to identify those features of human–machine dialogue which are, or could be, universal.

Edmund Furse and George Kiss have both left Warwick. Furse went to the University of Sheffield's psychology department, to do research on learning in mathematics. Kiss moved to the Open University, and has acted as a consultant to Alvey's Adaptive Intelligent Dialogues project (Chapter 7) which, of all the Alvey-funded MMI projects, is perhaps the closest to what the Warwick project would have been.

6

An image system for creative doodlers

Here are more intriguing ideas from the research unit that Ernest Edmonds has built up, first at Leicester Polytechnic and now at Loughborough University. This particular project tackled a problem – picture understanding – that will not be solved easily or at one stroke. The concept is a little different from the more familiar idea of computer vision, where the aim is to interpret real three-dimensional scenes. A picture is two-dimensional, it need not be a geometrically faithful representation of reality, indeed it need not represent anything physical at all. The picture may be a diagram, using symbols and conventions that humans understand instantly.

If we are to work successfully with computers, it is important that they should be able to make some sense of the pictures, diagrams and doodles that are such an important part of human communication. The task is related to that of optical character recognition and could be said to include it.

The work raises several important issues. For example, everyone who uses a personal computer must have discovered that pencil and paper are still essential; many will have wondered why. They will also be accustomed to the precision and decisiveness that is generally required when dealing with computers. Yet there are times when one wishes to be vague. One of the greatest gifts of the computer is the freedom to postpone or rescind decisions. Inflexible software often denies us this gift.

It can be particularly difficult to handle objects which begin their lives as one thing and smoothly change into something else which requires not only a different description, but a different type of description. The people who do animated computer graphics for film and TV, for example, have to plan every metamorphosis in advance. What is so often missing is the quality that Douglas Hofstadter calls 'slippability'.

Picture understanding or computer vision is the inverse of computer graphics: instead of transforming structured data into an image, the task is to extract structure from an image that is given. Computational problems often fall into pairs – speech generation and speech understanding, deducing facts from rules and inducing rules from facts, computer graphics and computer vision – and the harder of the two problems is often described as the 'inverse problem'. Inverse problems often require methods based on search, and knowledge must be used to direct the search in the most profitable directions. In other words, inverse problems are the classic problems of artificial intelligence. Inverse problems were a recurring theme of the early *Over the horizon* columns, or so I concluded one week in April 1984 when, at a loss for a subject, I decided to sum up some of the themes of the series so far. That article is included as Chapter 17 of this book. This one appeared the following week.

The proposition is that if machines are good at one set of problems and people are good at the 'inverse' problems, then the human and the computer must work as a team. To bring unaided computers up to the human standard of performance on inverse problems is a long-term project of uncertain outcome. For the time being, computers need us as badly as we need them.

---

26 April 1984

An old envelope is still, for many people, the favoured tool for sketching out new ideas. And that includes many individuals who have expensive personal computers on their desks. This is surprising, since one of the supposed virtues of word processors, computer aided design systems and similar electronic aids is that they allow you to try out alternatives and to change your mind.

Ernest Edmonds believes that computer systems should give the user greater freedom to be vague. 'In human problem-solving,' he says, 'there is always tentative decision making and backtracking, especially in the early stages.'

Ten years ago Edmonds observed some textile designers using a newly installed computer aided design system. He discovered that they were still drawing their designs on paper, before entering them into the computer. 'The reason for that,' he says, 'was that the computer was not being very helpful during that tentative, early stage of the design process.'

Edmonds runs the Human–Computer Interface Research Unit at Leicester Polytechnic. With a £700,000 grant from the Science and Engineering Research Council, the unit is developing tools such as the SYNICS 2 language for the design of human–machine dialogues. The unit also has projects on speech recognition and picture handling, both of which are seen as important future methods of communication between humans and machines.

An amalgam of graphics, image processing and knowledge-based systems, the Leicester work on picture handling may lead to an intelligent sketchpad that even diehard envelope-scribblers could use with pleasure. Techniques are being developed for manipulating raw images which have no underlying data structure. They could be images from a television camera, or they could be images created with a computer painting system which uses a mouse or light pen as its brush. The important thing to understand is that, initially at least, the system has a brightness and colour value for every picture point, but no other information about the picture.

This contrasts with the pictures produced by a typical computer aided design system. Here the computer contains a high-level description of, say, a chemical plant or a gearbox. The software uses that description to generate various views of the object concerned.

Human beings perceive structure in pictures so naturally and unthinkingly, mentally filling in what they cannot see, that it can actually come as a shock to realise that the computer does not share this perception. With a little assistance, however, perhaps the machine could begin to see pictures as we do.

All the Leicester unit's work demonstrates a strong belief in the positive value of cooperation between humans and machines. 'A lot of artificial intelligence problems, that are almost intractable for automatic solution, are quite approachable if you approach them with human–computer cooperation,' says Edmonds.

If images are being handled as part of a human–machine dialogue, then obviously human assistance is available if the machine needs it. There are situations where fully automatic image analysis would be required – for example if a robot had to find its own way around on the surface of Mars – but this is not one of them.

The current Leicester system begins by dividing the image into regions of uniform colour and brightness. Already, machine-vision purists will object that this presupposes the picture has been 'cleaned up'. However, little cleaning up or noise removal should be necessary if the picture originates from a computer painting system.

The system then numbers each region and measures various attributes for each region. These include area, perimeter, length, width, orientation, and centre of gravity. Up to this point, the operation resembles that of the commercial image analysis systems used in medicine and metallurgy.

Further analysis is performed by a program in the logic programming language Prolog. The influence of Prolog is subtle. It encourages an approach to image analysis which is, at all but the very lowest levels, knowledge-based.

The Leicester researchers draw a distinction between knowledge which is specific to an application, and that which seems to be intrinsic to visual perception. They would like to automate, as far as possible, the recognition of certain 'perceptual universals'.

Complete success in this task would mean that the machine, faced with some unfamiliar kind of picture, would see the same things in it that are seen by an equally naive human being. Complete success is unlikely, in the short term at least, but no matter. The aim is to crack the problem by combining human and machine capabilities. This is not a virtuoso exercise in unaided machine intelligence.

Beyond the perceptions that all humans share, there may be meanings in the picture that can only be extracted by applying some additional knowledge. A doctor studying an X-ray, or an engineer a printed circuit layout, will bring expert knowledge to bear. A machine could share some of this knowledge.

Indeed, the engineer's or doctor's specialist knowledge may be easier to codify than the universal knowledge that we all apply unthinkingly whenever we look at anything. The expert's knowledge is more accessible to introspection and, it follows, likely to translate more readily into Prolog.

How would such a system help the human creative process? Programmers are taught to design from the top down, but artists (and there are two of them on the Leicester team) do not stick so rigidly to this precept.

You may start developing one idea, and after you have started another quite different idea may emerge. To take an artificial but familiar example: you start off drawing two black silhouettes of human faces. You end up with a picture of a white candlestick. Even if you were using a computer system which held a high-level description of the two faces, it would have no explicit description of the new entity, the candlestick.

An image analysis system might spot the candlestick for itself. More likely, you would have to give the system a few hints. But once you had formed a new, high-level description of the candlestick you could go on developing your picture in terms of candlesticks rather than faces.

Other possibilities are perhaps more realistic and useful. Many computer programming methods begin with diagrams, including the familiar flowchart. How convenient if you could sketch your flowchart freehand with a light pen or graphics tablet, and then have it 'coded up' semi-automatically or even automatically.

Hardware engineers might sketch a circuit diagram, again freehand, and proceed straight to a simulation of its electrical behaviour. They can already do this with computer aided design systems, the only difference being that CAD systems will not accept a freehand sketch.

Some will probably see this as a retrograde step. Why go back to the electronic equivalent of the blunt pencil when, with a CAD system, you can have neat, machine-drawn pictures from the start?

The answer you would get from Edmonds and his colleagues is that the very neatness and precision are inhibiting. An architect planning the interconnecting spaces of a building may start by drawing vague overlapping blobs. A CAD system would probably draw precise rectangles which cannot represent the architect's uncertainty about the final layout.

But how does this deliberate vagueness fit into a world where there is increasing stress on formal specifications and on design methods which guarantee that the specification is met? Edmonds has often run up against the objection that 'You should know what you want to do before you start.' His answer is that you should know what you want to do, but you need not know in advance exactly how you will do it.

Until there is an equally flexible electronic alternative, old envelopes will fulfil the deeply felt need for creative doodling.

7

User-shaped software

Software that adapts to your likes and dislikes, your skills and your weaknesses is on the way. Efforts to build programs which learn about people in order to serve them better are under way in the United States, West Germany, Canada and no doubt also in Japan. This British project suggests how it might be done, and in the process it pulls in a number of the powerful ideas that are in the air of the 1980s.

There is that intriguing symmetry between the user and the machine – each regarding the other as a black box to be investigated and understood. The computer becomes a student, a scientist indeed, as it forms hypotheses about this mysterious animal which is tapping its keys, as it tests those hypotheses and confirms or rejects them. An adaptive interface is a striking example of machine learning and inductive reasoning.

There is the knowledge-based style of software design which runs through the whole project. The system contains several distinct inference engines and a variety of stores of knowledge. Some of the knowledge may be used in more than one way, which is easy when the facts and rules are kept separate from the logical machinery which manipulates them. Among the proposed knowledge stores is one which contains knowledge about the application program. Looking on the interface and the application program as a whole, here we have an interesting phenomenon: a program which knows about itself.

Does not every program know about itself? No – most programs press on blindly from one instruction to the next, and cannot stop to think about them. In any case, there are things to be known about a program which may not appear explicitly in the program text. Well written programs generally make more of these things explicit than badly written ones. But they do so for the benefit of humans who may wish to read, understand and alter the program. The computer does not need this background knowledge in order to execute the program. The traditional role of the computer is like that of the soldier who is given orders but no explanations.

If you ask someone 'What does that program do?' you do not expect to be walked through it line by line and told where the bits and bytes go. You expect a broader, more abstract description, which bears some relation to the purpose of the program and its use in the world. You expect to be given an informal *specification* of the program. The details of how it satisfies that specification are generally of less interest.

What is proposed here, is that the adaptive interface should possess a kind of specification of the application program, and the means of reasoning about that specification. Thus one part of the system would be able to survey the actions of the other part from an almost human perspective. This would be a major step away from the artificial stupidity of programs which do not know what they are trying to achieve.

Equally fascinating is the idea that a program might be able to work out what *you* are trying to achieve, even when you express yourself badly. How many humans bother to do that?

---

25 July 1985

For most of the history of computing, the crunching of data was seen as the priority, and there was little or no computer power left over to give the user an easy life. Now, after years of neglect of the human interface, everybody is furiously making up lost time. No effort is spared to make computer users happy, productive, and well-disposed towards their machines. Technology has made this possible, and the growth of the packaged software market has made it commercially necessary. A customer faced with two packages which do similar things will choose the one which looks good and feels right.

We all know what we like (or like what we know), but it is not so easy to state precisely what makes a good user interface. There are dozens of theories, some compatible and some conflicting. One possible answer is that a good interface adapts to its user. Just how clever can a program get, in tailoring itself to regular and occasional users, novices and experts, and to people who simply like to do things their own way? And if software can do these things, what, if any, are the practical benefits? The companies and universities participating in one of the Alvey Directorate's biggest man–machine interface projects intend to find out.

Nearly £2.7 million, out of Alvey's £32 million MMI budget, was awarded last November to a consortium led by Standard Telecommunications Laboratories – the research laboratories of STC – for the four-year Adaptive Intelligent Dialogues project. STL's partners are Data Logic, British Telecom Research Laboratories, and Heriot-Watt, Strathclyde and Essex Universities.

STL's Phil O'Donovan, the overall manager of the project, reports that the collaboration is working well. He has felt 'from very early on' that the project will succeed. He attributes this, in part, to a shared feeling that the project has picked on the key issue. 'It seems now,' he says, 'that adaptiveness is coming to be seen as the thing that makes a good MMI.'

On this, however, the project participants are trying to keep an open mind. Adaptive interfaces developed in the course of the project will be carefully evaluated in real working conditions. British Telecom will take the main responsibility for the evaluation work. An experimental interface for the Telecom Gold electronic mail service is now under development, and in a later phase of the project an adaptive interface will be developed for a more complex system, possibly an office workstation from the ICL range.

The project assumes that an application program and its human interface or 'front end' may be designed as two separate but communicating entities. The interface can then change freely, without any change in the application program. However, the interface will know about the application. And crucially, it will also accumulate knowledge about the person or persons using it. Within the interface software there will be two expert system-like modules called the application expert and the user modeller.

The other components will handle the main business of interpreting and formulating the messages which are exchanged with the user on the one hand, and the application program on the other. A kernel of common software will form the dialogue controller. Specific interface designs, such as that for Telecom Gold, will be embodied in a knowledge base called the dialogue description. The dialogue description will serve two purposes. As an executable program it will drive the dialogue controller as it handles the user's commands and the machine's responses. The dialogue description will also serve as a store of knowledge *about* the dialogue, which can be analysed and used by other parts of the interface software.

The overall design emphasizes the symmetry of the situation. User and application face each other. Each is, to some extent, a mystery to the other. The adaptive interface, with knowledge of both parties, can act as an intelligent go-between. With most existing software it is the user who does all the adapting. Adaptive interfaces could mean that the machine at last takes its share of the burden.

Adaptive interfaces have much in common with intelligent tutoring systems like Logica's, which may in future be embedded in many software packages. A user model and a student model differ only in name. Adaptation changes the system's behaviour; tutoring is likely to change the behaviour of the user. The two are not incompatible. But the purpose of the STL-led project is to see what can be done with adaptation alone.

The user model will be the computer's own picture of an individual's knowledge, skills and preferences. As far as possible, the model will operate at the 'task' level, looking at the things the user might wish to do (send a message, read a mailbox . . .) rather than the actual keys that are pressed.

A user with complete knowledge of the application is assumed to know all the concepts or procedures on a checklist. Less knowledgeable users will know only a subset of the items on the list. This model recognizes that people with apparently similar skill levels may actually know quite different things.

The computer can never be quite sure what the user knows. It only knows what the user has done. From this, the user modeller forms a model of what the user knows. But it is only a model, and some guesswork is inevitably involved. The intention is that the model should accommodate uncertainty, and should look actively for evidence to resolve alternative hypotheses. The user should also be able to state explicitly a preference for, say, a high level of help or prompting. An adaptive interface can combine automatic adaptation with the more familiar user-driven variety.

Two individuals might need, or want, quite different interfaces to the same application. Someone experienced with Unixmail might want to make Telecom Gold respond to Unixmail commands. A user profile could describe this and many other dimensions of an individual's preferred style of dialogue, according to STL's Ian Clowes. One dimension might be the level of prompting, which could range from no prompting at all, to a complete list of all the options open to the user at a given moment. Another is the level of on-line help: some users might need longer explanations than others.

One time-saving feature of an intelligent interface might be the freedom to omit redundant commands. To read a mailbox, for example, you might just type 'read 3' without explicitly entering the mail program first. Your user profile could arrange for this even if 'read 3' were also a valid command in some other context.

According to Paul Cooper, STL's coordinator for the project, certain commands might be blocked for certain users. While some novices might be glad to be denied some of the more 'dangerous' commands, other users want access to all the facilities from day one. Other dimensions which could appear in a user profile are the degree of system initiative, and the style of presentation: command-driven, menu-driven or mouse and icon-driven.

The application expert module will be an intriguing object: a program containing expert knowledge about another program. It will not be a mirror image of the application program. It will not be able to take over the application program's job. But it may contain explicit knowledge about the application which is nowhere stated explicitly in the application code itself – the kind of knowledge that a programmer might express in commenting the code.

According to Robin Pyburn of Data Logic, the original idea was that the application expert would merely interpret the responses which came back from the application program. Pyburn now believes that the application expert should be able to predict the outcome of the user's actions. He suggests that at a later phase of the project the user might be able to ask the application expert, 'What would happen if I did this?'

Knowledge of the workings of Telecom Gold is being culled partly from published manuals and partly from experimentation with the electronic mail system itself. The team is also working with Telecom Gold to learn more about the electronic mail system.

One source of reliable knowledge about an application would be a formal specification in a machine-interpretable language. But as yet, very little software is written by fully formal methods.

The Telecom Gold interface will be largely hand-crafted, but a major aim of the project is to produce general tools which could be used to develop adaptive interfaces for many applications. Tools will be developed to look 'inside' the interface, preferably while someone is actually using it. The researchers want to be able to watch how the user modeller reacts when a real user is out there hitting the keys. They would also like to be able to reach inside, change the user model, and see what happens.

The planned tools may help software developers to get prototypes up and running quickly. When the application exists already, Paul Rautenbach, a member of the STL project team, suggests that one might begin the design of an adaptive interface by casting a human being in the role of intelligent interface. The person chosen would be an expert, already familiar with the application program.

A less experienced user would sit somewhere else at another terminal. For the user, the expert would just be part of the machine. The strategies used by the expert to establish communication between the user and the program could guide the design of an intelligent front end.

Like a window system, or natural language input, an adaptive front end is the kind of feature that many programmers would like to use if the necessary tools were available. Windows are big business, natural language (or a fair imitation) is ready for lift-off. Perhaps the next thing will be software that learns to do things your way without being told.

The first phase of the AID project was completed in February 1986. As planned, the team had constructed an adaptive front-end for Telecom Gold, built around a dialogue controller, a user model and an application expert. By the end of 1985 the researchers had begun evaluation trials to see how well the 'phase one exemplar' fulfilled its purpose.

Work on the practice and principles of adaptive interfaces continues in phases two and three, to be completed in 1988. Phase two of the research was intended to produce several further small exemplars in the area of office automation. Having gained some experience of hand-crafting adaptive interfaces, the team intended, during phases two and three, to produce software tools which would help them and others with similar developments in future.

8

Magic window on the fourth dimension

And now, a quick journey into hyperspace as a reminder of the ever-surprising things that can happen when computers mesh with the human imagination.

12 April 1984

Thomas Banchoff has been fascinated by the fourth dimension ever since he was ten years old. It was, he says, a story in a *Captain Marvel* comic that aroused his interest. For him as for many others, the fourth dimension symbolized everything transcendent, everything that lay tantalizingly beyond the reach of the human mind.

As a mathematics student he envied his colleagues studying biology and astronomy. Like him, they studied invisible things. But they had microscopes and telescopes to make the invisible visible.

Not even Captain Marvel foresaw that mathematicians were about to acquire a powerful instrument which can transform mysterious mathematical objects such as hypercubes into vivid visual images. The magical window into the fourth dimension was provided by computer graphics.

Banchoff is now chairman of the mathematics department at Brown University in Providence, Rhode Island. For years he and his colleagues have been making films such as *The Hypercube: Projections and Slicing* which regularly draw capacity audiences at mathematics conferences.

Mathematical discoveries have been made with the help of their computer images. Researchers in other subjects such as oceanography and meteorology are beginning to use their techniques to visualize data too complicated to be plotted on paper.

A new generation of students is rediscovering mathematics as an observational science. Interactive computer displays transform the obscure formulae of differential geometry and complex functions into living shape, movement and colour. The students actually see things that few mathematicians are able to imagine.

Brown University's computing department has a teaching laboratory with 60 Apollo DN300 graphics workstations lined up on the desks. The scene resembles Houston Mission Control.

Banchoff visited London last month and showed a selection of his films at the Polytechnic of the South Bank. He told how his work has also attracted attention in the world of art. He has had several meetings with Salvador Dali, and says that the 79-year old surrealist painter has developed an interest in catastrophe theory. (Catastrophe theory describes the sudden discontinuities of behaviour that can occur in systems controlled by two or more variables. Up to six dimensions are required to plot the graphs which arise.)

An early film of a rotating hypercube was produced at Bell Laboratories in the 1960s. But the first dedicated and systematic producers of four-dimensional movies were Banchoff and his colleague Charles Strauss. Strauss left Brown University five years ago to pursue a successful career writing commercial software.

David Salesin joined the team and introduced algorithms for displaying four-dimensional surfaces, complete with shading, highlights and true colour on the computer screen. The earlier work had been done with 'wire-frame' images, with colour introduced by filming through filters. After three years Salesin left – for a job at Lucasfilm, the company which produced *Star Wars.*

Living in a universe with only three space dimensions, we can never hope to see four-dimensional objects as four-dimensional beings would see them. But more than 100 years ago, the Victorian cleric Edwin A. Abbott saw how we might grasp the structure of higher-dimensional objects. Understanding might come, if we could see a number of different views of the object in succession.

Banchoff has unearthed a great deal of information about Abbott, and on 6 June he will deliver a lecture at the City of London School where Abbott was headmaster. The lecture marks the centenary of the publication of Abbott's book *Flatland.*

Flatland is a two-dimensional world, and in the book one of its inhabitants ('A Square') describes the experience of being visited by a three-dimensional being. The Square sees only a circle which grows, shrinks and finally vanishes. But the visitor explains that his true shape is spherical. The Square eventually begins to understand that the circles he sees are merely two-dimensional slices of a three-dimensional object.

The extraordinary films made at Brown University use precisely the same method to arouse an intuition of a fourth dimension, in an audience of three-dimensional beings.

Four-dimensional objects are depicted in one of two ways. One option is to imagine that the object actually juts through our world exactly as the sphere passed through Flatland; in this case we see a three-dimensional form which is a single slice of the four-dimensional object. The shape of the visible slice may mutate strangely as the object shifts or rotates.

Alternatively one can imagine that the four-dimensional object casts a shadow on our three-dimensional world. The shadow, like a slice, is itself a three-dimensional object. And like a slice, it changes shape if the object moves. You know that your four-dimensional intuition has begun to develop when you can believe that these sometimes drastic transformations are merely changing views of an unchanging object.

A computer screen is only two-dimensional, of course. Banchoff and his colleagues take advantage of the human brain's readiness to see a scene as three-dimensional if simple cues such as shading and perspective are provided. Movement helps greatly. Some objects are baffling when seen as a stationary image, but leap into solidity the moment they begin to rotate.

The first moving images had to be recorded frame by frame on film, because of the time required for computation. But faster hardware made it possible to control and manipulate the display in real time, using dials or a joystick.

With the muscles involved as well as the eyes, people acquire a much more powerful intuition of the four-dimensional world. You not only see it, they say, you feel it.

As a research tool in mathematics, the technique has led to discoveries in the geometry of surfaces in four-dimensional space. For example, one surface, though known already, revealed an unexpected five-petalled pattern when viewed from a particular angle in four-dimensional space. This led to the discovery of a new symmetry in the surface, which had not been apparent from the formulae. The computer supplies new observations, but the mathematicians still go back to the formulae for proof.

Banchoff believes that researchers in many disciplines could benefit by examining their data from, quite literally, a new angle. In physics, even the apparently simple problem of two coupled pendulums is four-dimensional. Even when time is excluded, the problem has four variables since the state of the system depends on each pendulum's position and momentum. To represent the motion of the pendulums one must plot a twisting, circling curve in four-dimensional space.

The Office of Naval Research, which supports Banchoff's work, is using his techniques to analyse data from atmospheric and oceanographic studies. Here the phenomena depend on a large number of variables such as temperature, pressure, humidity and wind velocity. These can be represented as dimensions of a multi-dimensional space.

The eye, assisted by computer graphics, can sometimes spot trends and patterns that would be hard to detect by statistical number-crunching.

'Standard programs in regression analysis may not be very useful when you have a large-dimensional dataset,' says Banchoff. Medicine, ecology, economics – there are many other subjects where the problem space is commonly multidimensional.

Linear programming is used in industry to optimize the use of constrained resources, and the standard algorithm seeks a path across a many-faceted multi-dimensional surface. Certain codes used in military communications are connected mathematically with the arcane problem of packing spheres into spaces of as many as 24 dimensions.

But no coding theorists or linear programming specialists have been beating down Banchoff's door. Perhaps those who have scaled these intellectual heights without visual aids see no need to resort to computer graphics now. For the younger generation, however, the college students reared on video games, Banchoff has no doubt that the natural approach to the fourth dimension is through the computer screen.

Banchoff is a professor of mathematics, and has not been primarily concerned with the psychology of these computer-aided explorations of worlds where there are more ways to move. But at the very least his work can surely tell us something about the possible scope of interaction and cooperation between people and computers. It is very striking that people say they begin to 'feel' what is going on. Not 'see', but 'feel'. There is surely support here for Alan Kay's stress on the gestural and kinaesthetic component of our interaction with computers.

The experiments also raise some fascinating general questions about human vision and mental imagery. Can people learn to see four-dimensional objects? Can they learn to imagine them? Different people, asking these questions, would probably mean different things. Indeed, to a behaviourist the question about imagining would be meaningless.

But it is just the kind of question that might be addressed by the new school of investigators who call themselves cognitive scientists. In contrast to behaviourism, cognitive science concerns itself with the internal representations and information processes that we use in our mental activity, and believes they are open to scientific investigation. It explicitly draws analogies between these representations and processes, and those embodied in computer programs.

First, perhaps, we should decide what it means to perceive or imagine an ordinary three-dimensional object. If I visualize a cube, I form a mental image of a cube, seen from a definite viewpoint. There is a sense of depth. But, as when I look at a real cube, the dimension of depth has a different quality from the other two dimensions. No matter how I try, I cannot imagine the cube itself. I can only imagine how a cube would look from whatever viewpoint I have chosen.

I can imagine what a cube would feel like. It helps if I fit my fingers to the imaginary cube. But as I do this, I cannot prevent a visual image also forming. I do not think the visual image is the only representation of a cube that exists in my mind, but it seems to be the dominant one. It elbows all others aside to thrust itself on my conscious attention.

My own mental imagery is predominantly visual. I am sure that other people have very different imagery. Those mathematicians who do not see the point of Banchoff's graphics are probably abstract, symbolic thinkers, for whom formulae come alive in the same way as pictures do for me.

We are beginning to learn something about our internal representations of two- and three-dimensional objects. It may seem premature to ask how people mentally represent higher-dimensional objects. But it could be that by studying the more general case, we can gain insight into the special case of three dimensions. This is a common experience in other fields of science. The study of Mars and Venus has enormously advanced our understanding of our own planet Earth. And hyperspace travel is a lot cheaper than space travel.

In November 1985 Banchoff reported that he was at work, with colleagues Hüseyin Koçak, David Laidlaw and David Margolis, on a new film concerning surfaces on a hypersphere. He also mentioned that he is no longer chairman of his department.

Basil Blackwell of Oxford, Abbott's publishers, sadly decided not to issue a new edition of *Flatland* for the centenary, but they say that the third edition is still in print. My own copy, treasured but not valuable, dates from the 1932 reprinting of the 1884 second edition.

Further reading

Abbott, E.A. (1884). *Flatland: A Square.* Oxford: Basil Blackwell.

Cooper, L.A. and Shepard, R.N. (1984). 'Turning something over in the mind' *Scientific American*, December, 114–120.

Dewdney, A.K. (1986). 'Computer recreations' *Scientific American*, April, 8–13. (With instructions for writing a simple program to generate views of a hypercube.)

Finke, A. (1986). 'Mental imagery and the visual system' *Scientific American*, March, 76–83.

O'Shea, T. and Eisenstadt, M. (1984). Eds. *Artificial Intelligence: Tools, Techniques and Applications*. New York: Harper and Row. (Chapter 6, 'Cognitive science research', by Jon M. Slack, includes a discussion of Stephen Kosslyn's theory of visual imagery.)

Rucker, R. (1986). *The Fourth Dimension and How to Get There.* Harmondsworth: Penguin.

PART 2

Mindware

9

Expert systems are not the grave of human skills

This part of the book is, broadly speaking, about artificial intelligence. There is nothing comprehensive or even balanced about it. Whole areas like natural language processing go unmentioned. Expert systems, on the other hand, are given far more space than readers might expect. The achievements – and the shortcomings – of expert systems raise interesting issues. What cannot be defended is the ridiculous hype that has surrounded them.

It would make a pretty picture if the sole purpose of artificial intelligence (AI) research had been to help people and machines to work together better. That may have been an important motive for some AI researchers, but AI has been driven by many other forces. The fact remains that it is to this heterogeneous area of research that we must turn, to find the techniques and knowledge which could help to bring about 'computing as if people mattered'.

Artificial intelligence research has two aspects. As science, it explores theories of the human mind or Mind in general, using the computer as a laboratory. As technology, artificial intelligence gives the machine useful new abilities: to reason, to speak, to listen, to see, to understand and translate human languages, to plan, to solve problems, to move in the world and to manipulate objects.

Most of these abilities are still rudimentary, but often the computer's precision and thoroughness can complement human insight and wisdom. Specialized knowledge, rather than abstract reasoning power, has been the key to many AI successes. Expert systems can provide high-quality advice or assistance with well-defined problems of many kinds. Companies are finding that expert systems can save them large amounts of money. Expensive and powerful hardware and software are used in developing expert systems, but the most difficult part of the process is to extract and codify an expert's knowledge. Also, many expert systems have only a superficial knowledge of a problem, and lack deep understanding.

Intelligent tutoring and language translation are other areas where AI techniques are being put to commercial use. Major theorems in mathematics have been proved by human–machine cooperation, with humans providing the deep insights and the machine developing the detailed arguments.

Computer vision systems attempt to guess what combination of objects and lighting gave rise to a particular pattern of light and shade. Research labs are developing general-purpose vision techniques, but industrial vision systems can generally take a short cut since they know what kinds of object they are looking for.

Whether it is trying to perceive the objects behind an image, or the rules behind an expert's judgement, an AI system must be able to distil an abstract description from a mass of unorganized data. Arguably this skill is the essence of learning and creativity. 'Machine learning' is already a powerful aid to expert system development, but is this true learning? Computer scientists do not yet agree on this.

David Levitt argues that if computers are to help us to synthesize music they must also be able to analyse it. Humans seem to have no trouble perceiving structure in a mass of notes. Surprisingly similar AI problems arise when cancer researchers analyse DNA, and when machines are programmed to read handwriting, Douglas Hofstadter (author of *Gödel, Escher, Bach*) believes that the 'simple' task of recognizing and designing letters in stylized typefaces captures the essence of intelligence and creativity.

A key task for AI research is to find more powerful and flexible ways of representing knowledge. Past computer systems, in which essential knowledge has been represented poorly or not at all, have exhibited the phenomenon of artificial stupidity. The last chapter in this part of the book investigates this sinister problem, and may help to explain why we have looked at artificial intelligence before moving on to what many would regard as the mainstream of software engineering.

Expert systems have not entirely shed the awful burden of artificial stupidity, but they have strained nobly against it. For those who are tired of the same old expert systems story, some of the interviews which follow may suggest some new angles. Probably the best way to think of an expert system is as an unusually rich and dynamic form of communication between one human being and another. It is usually neither realistic nor desirable to regard an expert system as a replacement for a human being.

Another misconception is the one which says that expert systems are a nice little earner, but a dead end in research terms. Researchers are trying to improve on the somewhat limited capabilities of the current generation of expert systems. In doing so, they have had to confront genuine, difficult AI problems. Machine learning is one such problem. Even people whose primary interest is machine learning *per se* have turned to expert systems as the area in which they can test and apply their theories.

Bob Muller provides an excellent overview of the field of expert and knowledge-based systems, and though most of the circumstantial details are by now out of date, most of the issues and ideas are still very much alive.

3 May 1984

Rapid developments in the field of knowledge-based systems have themselves created a hunger for knowledge. Abingdon-based systems house SPL International saw the opportunity, and organized Europe's first conference on fifth generation computing, in July 1982.

Well attended and widely reported, that conference prepared the way for Bob Muller's launch of SPL-Insight, a £7,000-a-year club for organizations determined to keep abreast of advanced information technology.

Muller counts the study visits to Japan and the US among the high points of Insight's first year. He believes that Insight's closed meetings, with no press admitted, encourage members to report their failures as well as their successes. 'You can learn more by failures than by successes in many cases,' he says.

He is now canvassing for new members, at £7,800 each, as Insight prepares to enter its second year with an expanded programme of meetings and visits, and with new stars (including Japan's Hideo Aiso) on Insight's advisory panel.

Whether or not you accept the claim that 'Insight is now recognized as *the* European organization that gives members the opportunity to monitor developments in this field', Muller's own observations on current trends and issues in knowledge based systems are certainly worth listening to.

During his career in the data processing industry Muller has seen a number of fads come and go, but this time he feels that 'the excitement has returned' to computing.

'I think artificial intelligence could have the same kind of impact as the car or the plane, over the next twenty years.' he says. He quotes a forecast from the Arthur D. Little organization, that US spending on artificial intelligence will rise from $256 million in 1985, to $11.8 billion in 1990 and $67.6 billion in 1995.

Muller expects expert or knowledge based systems to spread gradually into many aspects of life. He concurs with the view that much of this new-found 'intelligence' will be directed into making machines and information systems easier to use. And he predicts a radical reassessment of our concepts of human skill.

Organizations developing expert systems still face the problem of knowledge acquisition. The techniques for extracting knowledge from skilled humans and transplanting it into machines are still primitive.

Muller points out that even the dimensions of this problem are still uncertain. 'Is the obstacle of knowledge acquisition so major that that must be the area where perhaps 50 per cent of the effort should go?' he asks.

The alternative, he suggests, is that people should get started with the limited tools available today. We would have to accept that 'Whatever is produced now will obviously look very crude in five to ten years' time.'

One school of thought, with Donald Michie as a prominent exponent, seeks to automate the process of knowledge acquisition to a high degree. The machine would take the initiative by 'inducing' new rules and actively testing them against a human expert's knowledge. Induction can be regarded as the beginning of true machine learning.

Muller believes that we should also explore methods which leave the initiative in human hands. 'We need what are called "deeper expert systems", some tools for knowledge acquisition,' he says. 'I think induction is just one technique. I think other techniques will develop.'

Among these techniques might be highly structured interviewing methods. The 'knowledge engineers', who interview experts today, rely heavily on their own intelligence and intuition. But as this new profession finds its identity and expands its numbers, there may well be a move to formal training and formal methods based on psychological research.

Muller also anticipates that expert systems will move from an advisory role into applications where they help to monitor changing and developing situations. These would include the control of complex industrial plants, and more contentiously, various forms of crisis management.

Could a knowledge-based system handle an accident at a nuclear power station better than human beings can? Muller believes the question poses the wrong alternatives.

Could technicians handle the crisis better with the support of a knowledge based system than they can with an old-fashioned control panel? If that is the question, Muller's answer is a confident 'Yes'.

SPL itself is investigating the 'blackboard' type of expert system, where a number of sub-systems or knowledge sources feed suggestions and hypotheses into a shared database. SPL is working on a set of tools which will formulate suggested courses of action, using the information on the 'blackboard' and in the underlying knowledge base.

Muller also sees knowledge-based systems moving rapidly into defence applications such as the monitoring of enemy communications and the identification of aircraft.

Questions of data integrity and confidentiality take on a new dimension in the context of knowledge based systems. 'A lot of companies are successful and make their money because they have expertise in a particular area,' Muller points out. Once that expertise is made explicit in a knowledge base, the company will want to protect it like the family jewels.

'It's a strength of expert systems that they are open, they are unencrypted,' says Muller. But he foresees situations where the owners of an expert system may want to keep something back. A company might wish to let its clients consult an expert system on specific questions, while at the same time building in safeguards to prevent the client gaining direct access to the precious knowledge base.

One could easily become persuaded that no application is too big or too small for expert systems. Muller had just returned from a conference in Zurich where a speaker from Siemens had described two consumer-oriented expert systems. One was a system for designing kitchens. The other system helps amateur photographers to select appropriate equipment.

Already our perception of human skills is changing, as one by one those skills are captured by machines. The first surprise, of course, was that the skills of highly trained professionals were easier to capture than the 'simple' human skills that all of us exercise almost unthinkingly every day.

But the future that Muller foresees for expert systems, in business, in the service sector and in leisure, is not one where machines are doing all the interesting jobs.

'I like music. I can't play an instrument. But I can imagine getting more fulfilment, either by using an expert system to teach me, or by using an expert system to cull the components of what I'd need to create something.'

It is an enticing prospect: even if you have never acquired any formal skills in art, in music, or in management for that matter, you can call upon an expert system which makes good your deficiencies and allows you to turn your ideas into realities. Of course, they may still be mediocre ideas.

The cry is always for more engineers, but there may be opportunities for those who leave the education system with qualifications in less fashionable subjects. The best knowledge engineers, Muller believes, may be people trained in the arts or in psychology. People with a data processing background may not be so suitable.

Expert systems can all too easily appear to be a kind of black hole, sucking in human skill which is never seen again. Bob Muller sees no reason why the human–machine relationship should be so one-sided. One can learn from expert systems, too.

'Expert systems actually help to grow experts within the company,' explains Muller. 'Apprenticeship using expert systems could be very valuable.' Far from being the grave of human skills, expert systems could become the vehicle by which they are passed on from one human being to another.

Not long after this article appeared, SPL merged with another leading software house, Systems Designers. Late in 1985 Bob Muller reported that the former SPL-Insight was still alive and well, though its full designation now is 'Insight, sponsored by Systems Designers'. Meetings are now almost invariably members-only, which may help to explain why Insight has not been much in the news lately.

Subsequent *Over the Horizon* articles explored many of the issues raised here, notably the subject of knowledge acquisition and machine learning, which has important implications not only for expert systems but for artificial intelligence in general.

10

Expert systems: practical experience

Experience with expert systems is more widespread, and advice easier to come by, than was the case when this article was written. Many discussions revolve around the relative merits of frames and production rules for representing knowledge, or Lisp and Prolog as programming languages. Each make of AI workstation has its fans; each expert system shell or programming toolkit has its devotees.

Important as these choices are, they leave enormous questions untouched. Where in our organization could expert systems help? How would they affect our way of working? How do we set about developing them and introducing them into the organization? How do we specify what we are trying to achieve? How do we measure how well we have achieved it?

Here, Annie Brooking concentrates on just one of these questions – how one sets about developing an expert system. Surely technology will be the star of this drama? Far from it. Like Fortinbras in *Hamlet*, the computer only makes its entrance when the main action is already over.

13 December 1984

The speaker had proudly described an expert system which plans the loading of military equipment onto aircraft. It had taken five years and untold dollars to develop it, but it worked. The big problem now was to move it to run on another computer system.

Annie Brooking was unimpressed, and at this Californian gathering she rose to ask a couple of pointed questions. She describes how the audience warmed as she winkled out the facts that no feasibility study had been performed before the project began, and there was no functional specification of what the system could do.

'They can't move it, there's no specification, and they didn't do a feasibility study. And that's regarded as a success,' she comments witheringly.

It is the kind of success she is keen not to repeat as her group at the Polytechnic of the South Bank works to establish a methodology for the design of knowledge based systems. She is an enthusiast for the Yourdon method of structured systems analysis, and her aim is to develop a comparable method, for expert systems and other systems based on explicitly codified human knowledge.

The Knowledge Based Systems Centre (KBSC) was set up in August 1982 and now has a staff of 15. It has completed a pilot study with the University of Amsterdam, as part of the European Community's Esprit research programme.

Financially, KBSC has survived on Esprit money – half from Brussels, half from the Polytechnic's coffers – and by selling research and training services to industry.

The two centres of learning hope that in the next few weeks Esprit will approve a full-scale study, with two industrial companies participating. But approval of the project will not end the academics' problems, since their part of the project, like the industrial part, only attracts 50 per cent funding from Esprit. 'The academic institutions are finding it very hard,' observes Brooking.

Her team is drawn from a number of disciplines. Besides the computer scientists there are a couple of psychologists, a philosopher, a statistician, a physicist, an engineer and an educationist. Their approach is centred round people rather than machines. No matter how much mathematics and computer science goes into any methodology, the goal will always be the successful management of a human enterprise.

The Centre's current work is not, of course, guided by a fully developed methodology. But a number of principles have already been established.

At KBSC a typical expert system is developed in three chronologically overlapping stages. The first stage corresponds to systems analysis in conventional software development. This stage would often consist of a painstaking investigation of the way one person solves problems.

Ace is an as yet unfinished expert system which suggests what kind of air conditioning should be used in each part of a building. Alan Dunn, a heating and ventilation expert on the polytechnic's staff, had approximately 25 three-hour taped sessions with an interviewer and an assistant. The assistant usually said nothing, but suggested fresh questions when the interviewer's line of inquiry dried up. After each session, the interviewer and assistant took a week or so to sort out what they had learned, to draw up glossaries of the subject, and to fill in with background reading.

Systems analysis is followed by system design, where the outlines of a workable expert system are drawn. Brooking accepts that the two processes may sometimes merge together. But she insists on an absolute firewall between design and implementation.

'The system designer is not permitted to code.' she says. 'I just forbade him to go anywhere near a machine.'

There are several reasons for this. First, it is a way to ensure that the knowledge base is portable. 'The approach is machine-independent and tool-independent,' Brooking says. 'It could be,' she adds, 'that "Mr Industry" decides to use this knowledge base in a form other than that of an expert system. It may be in the form of a manual.'

At KBSC the specification for an expert system is written in structured English. 'If you're doing an analysis with an expert you have to give them something they understand,' Brooking reasons. Structured English uses ordinary English syntax and can be read as English, but it attempts to maintain a clear logical structure. Words like 'if', 'then', 'and' and 'or' are used much as they would be in a programming language.

The Centre uses a variety of languages and programming environments, including Carnegie-Mellon University's OPS-5 and Sussex University's Poplog on a Digital Equipment VAX multi-user system, and Loops (an extension of Lisp) on a Xerox 1108 workstation.

Brooking has found that it does not take long to turn the structured English specification into a working program. In the case of Ace, she reports, 'The specification was given to four programmers. One did it in Prolog. One did it in Lisp. One did it in Loops. The other did it in a Poplog environment. None of those took longer than three weeks.'

Brooking describes how 'truisms' emerge as the interviews with the expert continue. 'These invariably turn out to be in the form of some kind of rule,' she says – though this does not mean they will necessarily be programmed as IF-THEN production rules. The Ace knowledge base, for example, is partly in the form of production rules, and partly in the form of 'frames.'

When 30 or 40 rules have been formulated, in English, the system designer produces an initial design for an expert system, and the programmer codes it.

The resulting program is then demonstrated to the expert, who says what is wrong with it and what needs to be added. 'By implementing what I call the first functional specification you speed up the knowledge elicitation process,' comments Brooking. 'But you haven't got an expert system.'

KBSC people resist calling this process 'rapid prototyping', on the grounds that a great deal of analysis has already taken place before the first implementation begins.

The interviewer and assistant carry on talking to the expert and bashing out rules until maybe 100 rules exist. At that point, says

Brooking, they might perceive some more powerful and sophisticated rules and thereby squash the knowledge base down to 50 or 60 rules. In the light of this, she says, to measure an expert system's size by number of rules is 'a daft thing to do'. It all depends how simple or complex the rules are.

One thing that is missing from the first specification is a user interface. Before the interface is designed, Brooking believes it is important to go to industry and ask how the system could best be used. Some expert systems actually take over the expert's role and offer clear decisions. Others are used as advisers or consultants. Yet others are used to teach people. Each of these requires a different interface. A tutoring system will probably have to give fuller explanations than an advisory system.

Nearly all programming at the Centre is done in bare Lisp or Prolog. Brooking feels that the use of a commercial expert system 'shell' can force a system into a pre-determined structure which is not necessarily the best for the purpose.

Even a powerful tool like Loops has been used mainly as an ideas organizer, and not for implementing working software. Brooking and her colleagues do not want to produce systems which are locked into the Xerox or any other machine.

The main Esprit project, if it goes ahead, will investigate the entire process of developing a knowledge based system, from feasibility study through analysis, interface design, system design and testing, to the final tuning of the system and education of the end user. Practical experience will be gained through the design of two separate expert systems.

As part of the work on the human interface, the South Bank Polytechnic group will investigate hardware, languages and software tools, and how to choose them. They will also study machine learning techniques.

Machine learning can automate the process of guessing rules from examples, or refining a knowledge base down to a few simple, powerful rules. Brooking believes machine learning methods could be used to refine new knowledge from the combined expertise of many specialists. But she fears that machine learning could mean a loss of human control. 'What we want to ensure,' she says, 'is that the system has a lot of integrity. And that becomes a problem if you let the machine learn on its own.'

It is just one instance of a general rule that Brooking and her colleagues have learned to follow: keep the machine on a tight leash at all times.

We shall return to the attractions and dangers of machine learning.

Annie Brooking left the Knowledge Based Systems Centre to work as an independent consultant in London and in Cupertino, California. She then joined Symbolics, the leading manufacturer of AI workstations.

Frank Hickman took over as director, and has now managed to put the Centre on a more secure financial basis. The staff was reduced to seven and then cautiously increased again. By early 1987, eleven people were working in the Centre.

The main Esprit project on methodology went ahead, and was followed by a second contract (or third, if the pilot study is included) for further research on the same subject. Financially, the Centre is no longer so dependent on Esprit as it was. It earns roughly equal amounts from Esprit, from training courses, and from industrial research contracts. Its postgraduate diploma course in artificial intelligence and computing is popular. There were over 400 applicants for 30 places on the 1986–87 course. AI skills are now regarded as highly marketable, and graduates in many different disciplines are keen to acquire them.

11

Expert systems: commercial prospects

Where Annie Brooking placed the emphasis on methodology and human skills, Tim Johnson's report on the commercial application of expert systems paid special attention, naturally enough, to the specialist hardware and software that were on offer for the would-be developer of expert systems. But there is no real contradiction here, and Johnson stressed that amid the wealth of expert system shells and development kits, there was a shortage of the necessary knowledge engineering skills.

The report provided intelligent explanations and sober assessments, badly needed at a time when very few people understood what artificial intelligence was about. A few star performances by expert systems had led to claims that machines were now exhibiting human-type intelligence. It is no wonder that some people assumed the whole business must be run by charlatans.

Two years later, a few wild claims were still in evidence at the snake-oil end of the personal computer software market, but in general one could detect a more balanced and informed attitude to artificial intelligence and expert systems. Tim Johnson's report played its part in spreading that attitude.

4 October 1984

The US is surging ahead with the application of expert systems technology, according to market researcher Tim Johnson. Europe could be left behind. Even Japan, for all its ambitious fifth generation plans, could be a loser.

Johnson's report, *The Commercial Application of Expert Systems Technology*, portrays a well developed technology which can already make, or save, large sums of money for those who apply it.

The main constraint, the report suggests, is the shortage of people with knowledge engineering skills – expert systems experts. In addition, it takes a while for expert systems technology to bring concrete results since major projects take three years to implement. Thus only five major expert system projects were expected to begin routine use in the US during 1984 – and only one in the UK. But Johnson's economic model of the industry predicts steady growth, so that by 1987 one major expert system per week will be going live in the US.

Johnson is particularly critical of British efforts to build artificial intelligence programming tools round the logic programming language Prolog, instead of using Lisp-based programming systems from America.

'A lot of talent in the UK is being diverted into the whole Prolog business,' he says. 'Extremely powerful Lisp-based tools have been developed in America. We ought to be learning how to use them. I would like to see much more effort being made by the UK to really master the tools that are available from abroad.'

Japan's choice of Prolog as the kernel language of the fifth generation computing project was 'Probably a mistake, it put them further back,' says Johnson. 'It meant the project was less relevant commercially. In return for that they got a kind of aesthetic advantage. The appeal of Prolog is almost aesthetic. But it will take a good many years before beauty triumphs over brawn.'

A typical Lisp workstation has a special processor microcoded to run Lisp efficiently, 1 to 30 megabytes of main memory, 10 to 500 megabytes of hard disk backing store, a high-resolution bit-mapped display and a mouse pointing device.

Its software will include editors, debuggers and similar programming tools, and a multi-window operating system. The two main software contenders are Interlisp, originating from Stanford University, and Zetalisp developed at the Massachusetts Institute of Technology.

Higher-level software tools designed specifically for knowledge-based programming include Xerox's Loops, and Art from Inference Corporation.

No one has yet put together a Prolog package to match these Lisp-based workstations and software tools. But Johnson mentions several high-performance Prolog implementations which are under development in universities. (Edinburgh; Uppsala, Sweden and Imperial College, London) and by companies such as California-based Quintus.

The Symbolics 3600 is by far the biggest-selling Lisp workstation by dollar value, according to the report. Symbolics prices range from $84,500 to $108,000. The technically advanced and somewhat cheaper LMI Lambda – 'a very innovative product,' according to the report – has captured about 20 per cent of the market.

Johnson sees a clear division in the market between these high performance machines and the Xerox 1108, which is priced around $30,000 and 'emphasizes ease of use'. Xerox has sold approximately the same number of machines as Symbolics.

ICL is using 1108s in its Alvey project on applications of expert systems in the Department of Health and Social Security. 'I think that was a rational choice, obviously,' says Johnson.

Other firms including Texas Instruments are rumoured to be developing Lisp workstations. Racal-Norsk's multi-user system will run US-imported Zetalisp on European hardware.

Johnson believes that the experimental Prolog-based hardware emerging from Japan's fifth generation project must be compared with commercially available American Lisp workstations. 'The LMI machine for example, as far as I can see, is very similar in architecture to the Japanese Personal Sequential Inference machine,' he says. 'It has many of the same ideas, but you can buy it off the shelf.'

According to Johnson, the most efficient Prolog implementation running on 'stock' hardware is Edinburgh Prolog on the DECsystem 10. DEC's decision to discontinue the DECsystem 10 and 20 range was a severe blow to Prolog, and a setback for Japan's fifth generation work which was to have relied heavily on DEC 20 mainframes.

Companies cannot be expected to buy $100,000 workstations for all the scientists, technicians and managers who will be the actual users of expert systems. Johnson believes there will be a market, still largely unexplored, for target systems or 'delivery vehicles'. These will have megabyte memories and a suitable architecture (probably 32-bit) for fast running of expert systems. But they will be stripped of all the extra features which are required only by programmers.

Tektronix has announced a relatively cheap Lisp workstation based on the Motorola 68010 processor, priced around $15,000, and potentially useful as a delivery vehicle.

Xerox is developing an AI machine that will be at home in an ordinary business office rather than a specialist software house.

Apple had made no overt move into expert systems, but Johnson says Apple 'must be doing something. I suspect that Apple's policy must be to keep very quiet about true 32-bit personal computers, which they must be developing,' he says. 'The relevance of that to expert systems is pretty clear,' he adds.

The IBM PC has already been adopted as an expert system delivery vehicle by independent software houses, though it has no pretensions as a specialist AI machine.

Johnson rejects the view that since small systems running on microcomputers cannot possibly equal the performance of human experts, they should not be called expert systems. He is prepared to use the term 'expert system' for any program, however small, which is constructed in a particular way. The essence of it is that the system's knowledge base, which is a richer and more flexible structure than a conventional database, should be clearly separated from the inference engine which operates on the knowledge to make judgements or answer questions.

Small systems running on micros could give advice on personal finance, or help to set up complicated scientific instruments. Johnson foresees the development of a distinctive market for small expert systems, which he says could have more practical impact than the big ones, at least in the short term.

As a rule of thumb, 1 kilobyte of memory is needed for each rule in a true expert system. Many small systems, however, will be compiled into a form which occupies less memory (typically 250 bytes per rule). Compiled programs will no longer be true expert systems, in Johnson's view, because the knowledge base can no longer be augmented or edited. This will bring problems, especially in areas such as finance where the rules change frequently. 'But as far as the user is concerned,' the report points out, 'compiled systems will appear equivalent to true expert systems, and in fact this will probably be the form in which expert systems are most frequently used, at least for years to come.'

IBM itself has traditionally had a cool attitude to artificial intelligence research, but it is now believed to be one of the most active companies in the field. IBM's expert systems work was unveiled publicly for the first time in August at the annual conference of the American Association for Artificial Intelligence.

YES/MVS gives expert assistance to operators on an IBM mainframe at Yorktown Heights. It is believed to be the first expert system in routine use that advises in real time on a constantly changing situation. It can be seen as the forerunner of fast-responding expert systems for the money markets or the battlefield.

Tim Johnson, recently returned from the AAAI meeting in Austin, Texas, was impressed with YES/MVS. 'It's running in real time,' he said. 'They are doing real work on that machine, and people get pretty cross if it doesn't work.'

AI workstations, including the Symbolics range, have come down in price. Texas Instruments brought out a product, the Explorer. Racal-Norsk did not. The IBM PC AT, a true 16-bit microcomputer based on the Intel 80286 microprocessor, proved to be better equipped than the basic PC, as a delivery vehicle for expert systems. The first full 32-bit microcomputers appeared in 1986, but an Apple was not among them. Prolog still has its teeth into Lisp's leg, and will not let go. Quintus, in particular, has persuaded Americans to take the logic programming language seriously.

While his colleagues were writing two new and up-to-date volumes on expert systems, Tim Johnson was busy for much of 1986 on a report on parallel processing. As his co-author I enjoyed the opportunity to look into a subject rather more deeply than is usually possible when one is writing for a weekly newspaper.

Further reading

Hewett, J. and Sasson, R. (1986). *Expert Systems 1986: The USA and Canada.* London: Ovum.

Hewett, T. Timms, S. and d'Aumale, G. (1986). *Commercial Expert Systems in Europe.* London: Ovum.

Johnson T. (1984). *The Commercial Application of Expert Systems Technology.* London: Ovum.

12
Help the expert 'shells' don't offer

In the early 1980s, large organizations like British Telecom became aware of the potential value of expert systems. But those who looked into the matter learned that it took considerable time and effort to develop an expert system, and it might in any case be hard to find someone with the necessary skills. The software available at the time was useful for constructing an expert system that had already been designed, but it did not address the task of eliciting and organizing an expert's knowledge.

Experts are often better at judging the individual case than at formulating general rules of the kind required for an expert system. One very interesting approach to the problem was to employ software which automatically formulates rules from examples. This hands a large part of the job to the machine, and in simple cases may obviate the 'knowledge engineer' altogether.

A more conservative approach brings in the machine as an assistant to the knowledge engineer, speeding up the process but not changing its basic nature. This approach, requiring an intimate cooperation between human and computer, is the one we shall examine first.

30 May 1985

Marc Eisenstadt and his Open University (OU) colleagues are working with British Telecom on an Alvey-funded project to develop a 'knowledge engineer's assistant'. Their aim is a dramatic speed-up in the development of expert systems.

The 'assistant' software is intended to help with those parts of the process that commercial expert system shells cannot reach. Specifically, it will help knowledge engineers to impose some structure on the mass of information they collect while interviewing an expert. According to Eisenstadt, who is the director of the OU's Human Cognition Research

Laboratory, most 'shells' assume that you have obtained and organized your knowledge before you come to the computer.

British Telecom is interested because it could use expert systems by the dozen, to troubleshoot its many different items of telecommunications equipment. In 1983 George Pollard and Charles Church of BT wrote an expert system called Tracker to diagnose faults in telephone exchange power supplies. 'BT want to do this for everything they can get their hands on,' declares Eisenstadt. 'It would be nice to have expert systems to help them diagnose all their gear.'

The aim is to help the generalist technician to service a piece of equipment he may not even have seen before. 'He still has to know how to run his voltmeters,' Eisenstadt explains. 'But he doesn't know about Monarch power supplies type 153. It really helps him to focus his own diagnostic skills on this particular power supply without having to take the time off to study the thing.'

Experience with Tracker suggested that the computer on the work-bench could reduce the amount of conventional training that a technician requires. 'The people who have tried it have actually enjoyed it, and they can gain some expertise' says Eisenstadt. 'They can actually use the expert system as a training device, though it was not designed that way.'

With BT convinced of the value of expert systems, the next problem was to develop a way of producing them fast and in large numbers. This is the main aim of the BT–OU collaboration with its £300,000 Alvey funding.

Eisenstadt envisages that the process of building an expert system will begin conventionally, with long interviews with the 'domain expert'. These will be taped, transcribed, and entered into a computer. Then the knowledge engineer, using the 'assistant' program, will set to work. By stages the rambling transcript will metamorphose into a well-structured, working expert system.

The task is complicated by the fact that the expert technician has many different kinds of knowledge. 'He knows about part hierarchies, he knows about objects; he has different taxonomies of all the things he's dealing with,' explains Eisenstadt. 'He knows that if one thing happens it may cause another thing to happen. He has various algorithms in his head. He knows that when he walks in to the workbench with this faulty equipment he should first do A then B then C. He has various diagnostic rules, and so on.'

Repair-shop folklore may be important. Circuit boards from one factory may get a reputation for a particular kind of fault. 'The amount of folk wisdom that comes out is amazing,' says Eisenstadt. 'But it is actually very important. And it is possible to build that into the expert system.' He is blunt about the confused and rambling nature of the typical interview transcript. 'It's not the case,' he reports, 'that you get these beautiful expert system rules that you always hear about in all the well-hyped spiels about expert systems: if A then B, if B then C and so on. The expert doesn't just sit down and give you those rules.'

Others have tried to avoid this problem by using carefully prepared 'structured interviews'. Eisenstadt is unimpressed. 'It turns out,' he says, 'that they do have a secret pre-structured interview phase, where they actually interview the guy and see what he knows, and it's very unstructured.'

Despite the rambling nature of the initial interviews, Eisenstadt suspects that the expert's private and inaccessible store of knowledge is well organized. 'Deep inside his head,' he says, 'if we had privileged access to what he really knew, and how his knowledge is represented, I believe with my artificial intelligence hat on that it is highly structured.' But experts also often tell him that building an expert system has helped them to think more clearly about problems.

Knowledge engineers can spend months trying to impose some structure on what an expert has told them. 'One of the things we are trying to do is to provide a toolkit to make this job a bit easier,' Eisenstadt explains. 'We are trying to cut down the expert system building time from a man-year for a typical expert system, to a couple of weeks.' This, he adds, is a very optimistic target.

There comes a point in the development of an expert system when the accumulated scraps of paper spill off the knowledge engineer's desk, spread across the carpet, and crawl up the walls. This is in fact the point when structure is beginning to emerge in the previously undifferentiated mass of knowledge. To recreate this phenomenon in a paperless environment, Eisenstadt and his colleagues have developed a software tool called CREF (cross referenced text editing facility) which uses the windowing and browsing facilities of an advanced graphics environment. Initially implemented on a Symbolics 3600 Lisp machine, this and the rest of the project's software will be transferred to a Racal-Norsk KPS-5 multi-user system. For the 'delivery systems' on the technician's workbench, 16- or 32-bit microcomputers may be used.

Eisenstadt explains how CREF works, with a 'paper' metaphor: 'Bits and pieces of the interview are actually spread out on index cards, and you can thread different pieces of string through these index cards in different ways. Essentially you can yank on a piece of string and get only those bits of the interview that are relevant to a particular concept. It is more than a keyword search,' he adds, 'because you are actually reorganizing the interview in different ways, according to the different concepts that are being discussed.'

The links – the pieces of string – are of several kinds. Some show that A influences B causally; some indicate that C is part of D. Several other possible relations between concepts can be represented. A further type of link allows comments to be attached to nodes of the network.

Most expert systems are able to explain which rules they have used to reach a conclusion. But they cannot usually explain where the rules came from. CREF provides 'justification links' which attach an explanatory comment to a rule. 'Our rules have not only "if A then B" but then in brackets after it, "justification: C",' Eisenstadt explains. 'If there is a bug in your expert system, you want to say: now why on earth did I put in this crazy rule? What is the justification for it?' The justification links may refer back to specific paragraphs of the original interview. They should help the knowledge engineer to resolve any conflicts when, for example, the system detects that two rules are contradictory.

Using CREF, one can introduce structure into an unstructured text, and progressively distil the text into an appropriate and consistent set of rules. These can then be coded up into Lisp or Prolog. At the moment, prototype systems are being written in Lisp, but BT has a commitment to Prolog and that is the language in which the expert systems will finally be delivered.

OU research fellow Enrico Motta is developing frame-like 'intermediate representations' for knowledge – 'intermediate' because they come halfway between the unstructured transcript and the finished expert system code that can be run on a computer.

Charles Church, who acted as knowledge engineer on BT's original Tracker expert system, finds it useful to summarize an expert's knowledge on standard A4-sized forms. There might be 100 or 200 of these, each for a different type of equipment fault. Each sheet would have spaces for the name of an item, the preconditions which make this item suspect, a diagnosis strategy, possible actions and outcomes, and so on. At present, Church passes these paper forms to a micro-Prolog programmer, who then spends some time writing code. 'I think it is possible to eliminate that last phase entirely,' comments Eisenstadt, 'and actually give the knowledge engineer these templates on the screen – which he could just fill out, and that's it, he has finished.' He hopes to link the templates inside the system to vivid graphical displays. The expert and the knowledge engineer could sit together at the screen, using the graphics in a final interactive debugging session.

The 'templates' resemble the 'frames' which are used in other knowledge programming systems to organize knowledge in concept-sized modules. Frames or templates capture the regularity of knowledge while allowing local variations from the general pattern. One has certain expectations about *any* electrical fault, but each fault also has its own unique characteristics.

In a project which will lead not to one but to many expert systems, Eisenstadt hopes to discover other, deeper regularities which extend across many different domains of knowledge. 'Typically one goes off and builds dozens and dozens of expert systems,' he says. 'If you are lucky, you catch the generalizations. But we'd like to take it out of the arena of luck, and try to really encapsulate the relevant pearls of wisdom from all these different rules, and make them a lot more domain-independent.'

'That,' he admits 'is a really wild-eyed ambition.' But just supposing? 'Once you have achieved that generalization,' Eisenstadt continues, 'you gain all sorts of marvellous capabilities. You can not only build in that rule in the new expert system you are trying to build – you could build it in advance if it seemed to be relevant – but you can also prompt the knowledge engineer to ask a sensible question. Immediately, one does much more structured interviews.'

So the knowledge engineer's assistant may eventually assist with that part of the process which up till now has been most resistant to automation – the interview itself.

The two-year project was due to end in October 1986. By April the laboratory version KEA-0 was complete. As planned, it was now possible to generate code automatically from a freehand sketch of the expert's knowledge, created on the screen by the knowledge engineer. Work was beginning on a further prototype, KEA-1, which is intended to be suitable for use by industrial knowledge engineers.

Following the failure of the Racal–Norsk joint venture, Eisenstadt's group continued their research on the Symbolics 3670 workstation. They still planned to transfer the software, now known as Keats, to a lower-cost machine more suitable for the industrial environment.

13

Can a computer be more like a tutor?

Here is an example of a project which uses AI techniques, not to make a computer walk on its hind legs before the applauding crowd, but to provide inconspicuous and sensitive help to a human being undertaking an important task: learning. With a few honourable exceptions, the whole field of computer-assisted learning has suffered badly from the malaise of artificial stupidity. People took the most flexible and adaptive machine in existence, the computer, and turned it into an instruction medium far more restrictive than the traditional book. Mercifully this situation is changing, thanks to such projects as Logica's TUTOR.

---

20 June 1985

If you had to answer an examination question on 'why computers are useful,' you would probably expect to gain marks by including 'because they can help people learn' in your answer. Yet even among the younger generation there must be many who can truthfully say they have never learned anything important from a computer.

'Traditional methods of providing instruction using computers have actually failed to deliver the goods,' says Lindsey Ford of Logica. Under contract to the Ministry of Defence, Ford is developing an 'intelligent' tutoring system which abandons, once and for all, the idea that the machine leads the student on a programmed, branching path through the subject. Perhaps at this point one should state that the word 'intelligent' is used in its usual computer-industry sense of 'cleverer than what we had before.' This is a knowledge-based system, not an attempt to create human-level intelligence.

Nigel Davies, Simon Dickens and Rod Rivers complete the team at Logica. Consultants to the project are Bran Boguraev of Cambridge

University, Rod Johnson of the University of Manchester Institute of Science and Technology, Tim O'Shea of the Open University, and John Self of Lancaster University.

'Intelligent' computer aided instruction differs from its conventional counterpart in the same way as an expert system differs from a conventional computer program. Nobody has flowcharted the system, deciding that only B or C can happen after A. There is just a body of facts, or knowledge base, and a strategy for applying those facts to whatever situation comes along. Of course you could, in principle, draw a flowchart of everything an intelligent tutoring system or an expert system could ever do, but it would probably look like a plate of spaghetti and it would convey very little of how the system really works.

Ford uses the phrase 'open process invocation' to describe the way you can move from anywhere in the program to anywhere else within reason. This can give the student a bigger share of the initiative, resulting in a so-called 'mixed initiative dialogue' which more closely resembles the dialogue between a student and a human tutor. 'This is one of the things missing from conventional computer aided instruction,' comments Ford.

The only exception to the do-as-you-please rule comes when the student selects 'exam' mode. If you ask to be given an 'exam' you must stick it out. You cannot slip back into a tutoring mode to brush up your knowledge before tackling a difficult exam question.

The system uses a rule-based teaching strategy to decide what it will do next. But it can cope if the student decides to study road signs instead of motorway driving, or to take a test instead of a lesson. It keeps track of the student's performance and knowledge, and will return later for more work on weak points. A database called the 'student model' records how well the student appears to have grasped each of the concepts that the system is trying to teach. It also notes any evidence that the student is applying a correct concept in incorrect situations. Ford says this is a common type of error. His system will provide remedial teaching to correct mistakes of this kind.

Derek Sleeman, formerly at Leeds University and now at Stanford University, has developed tutoring systems which actually try to identify any incorrect concepts or 'mal-rules' that the student has picked up. While this is clearly a desirable approach it is also a difficult one: it requires a computer program to exhibit skills not far short of mind-reading.

Logica's student model does not include mal-rules, but it is more advanced than anything Ford has seen in commercial computer based training packages. 'As far as I am aware,' he says, 'they model the student in terms of how far he has got. I do not believe there are any commercial packages around which attempt to have some qualitative measure of how well he understands a concept.'

The teaching strategy is both simple and general. 'It is a set of rules,' explains Ford, 'and they are general rules for teaching, which we hope are applicable to a variety of subjects.' The rules steer the teaching towards a particular topic if the student has not spent much time on it yet, or has poor scores in tests on the topic, or if the student has grasped the concept but tends to misapply it.

Two subject areas have been chosen for the initial research: a subset of the Highway Code; and the flight safety regulations which air traffic controllers are meant to observe. The main framework of the system will consist of reusable code, which Ford says could be used to teach any subject. This is a familiar idea in the world of expert systems, where often one knowledge base is removed to leave a 'shell' in which knowledge of other subjects can be inserted.

The process can work the other way round, too: same knowledge, different shell. One of the precedents for Logica's project was the tutoring system (Guidon) that Stanford University built round the knowledge base of its well-known medical expert system Mycin.

A look inside the Logica intelligent tutor reveals a typical expert system architecture. Driven by the teaching strategy rules, the main administrative module has access to four separate databases. One is a historical record of everything the student has done. Another is a history of everything the tutor program has done with that student. Then there is the student model, constructed by inference from the student history. And finally there is a knowledge base containing facts about the subject being taught.

Ford argues that to teach effectively, a system must have some understanding of the subject. 'It should be able to solve the tests that it is going to give the student,' he says. It does not merely regurgitate answers from memory, but generates them by a process of logical inference. At the start of the project, the system was equipped with a natural language interface, and there was always the possibility that a student would fling a fresh problem at the system with the challenge: 'OK, how do you solve this one?'

Students often extract knowledge from their human teachers in this way. Sadly, users of the Logica system no longer have this option, since the natural language front-end was abandoned. Ford admits that the current system, which is menu-driven, could probably make do with canned answers though in fact it does not. What has gone is the student's freedom to pose problems to the tutor, not the tutor's ability to solve them. Natural language went on the back burner because it turned out to be a tougher problem than expected, and threatened to divert the research effort from the main issue of intelligent tutoring.

More and more people are using computers in their work, and everyone who uses a computer will have to learn to use at least one application program. Ford believes there are a number of advantages in embedding a training program in the application itself. When this is done, he points out, 'The responses of the user are in the language that he is using for the application, so there is no natural language problem.'

If the application program itself has an expert-system type of architecture, the training system can be integrated particularly closely. This avoids one of the snares of conventional training. 'Because the training system and the operational system are using the same knowledge base,' Ford explains, 'the training must indeed reflect current operational practices.'

Many of the ideas now being applied to online training have their counterparts in current research on advanced human–machine interfaces, such as Alvey's £2.7 million, multi-centre Adaptive Intelligent Dialogues project. User-friendly interfaces are now being designed like expert systems, containing a knowledge base about the application, and a sophisticated model of the user. In an adaptive interface, the emphasis is on the system learning about the user; embedded tutoring aims to teach the user about the system. But the two approaches may prove to be complementary, not contradictory. Certainly they have very similar requirements in terms of system architecture.

But while concepts like these are still at the research stage, it is best to try out one bright idea at a time. Then, if your project fails, you do not throw out sound ideas with the bad ones.

Ford is suitably cautious when asked about the benefits of intelligent tutoring. He broadly accepts the claim that conventional computer based training can reduce costs and break training bottlenecks, and sees no reason why 'intelligent' methods should not do the same. But for him the big issue is not cost but effectiveness. He hopes that evaluation trials, due to begin later this year, will demonstrate that with 'intelligent' tutoring, students are able to acquire more knowledge in less time. 'I suspect it will be better,' he says 'but I cannot make any claims of that sort at the moment.'

Helen Tang's name must be added to those at Logica who made important contributions to TUTOR. The second subject domain, Flight Safety Regulations, was never tackled. A military instructor was needed to supply expert knowledge of the subject, and none was available. But this did not rule out the possibility that TUTOR would be used at a later stage to train air traffic controllers.

A simple speech input facility was added for demonstration purposes. One day, perhaps, the student will be able to talk freely to the system, with a good chance of getting an appropriate response. But without a natural language processing capability, this remains a distant goal.

TUTOR has been picked for a role in one of the Alvey programme's large demonstrator projects. There are four such projects, each intended to show off a selection of Alvey technologies working together to do something useful. TUTOR will be used in the £6,750,000 effort to apply knowledge based systems to the operations of the Department of Health and Social Security.

Lindsey Ford has taken up a lecturing post at the University of Exeter and is active in another Alvey project which grows directly out of TUTOR. The new and potentially exciting ingredient is the videodisk, which means that the student's sessions can be enlivened with still or moving colour pictures and sound. Since pictures can be retrieved swiftly from any part of the disk, it should be possible to retain the do-as-you-please, anything-next quality that is one of TUTOR's virtues. Exeter's partners in the Knowledge-Based Engineering Training project are Logica, the Engineering Industry Training Board, and Imperial College.

Rod Rivers has in his spare time produced an interesting software package called Expert 4. It is an expert system shell with a strong injection of statistics.

Derek Sleeman returned to Britain in 1986 to take up a chair at Aberdeen University.

14 Improving proof

Bob Boyer and J. Moore were back in Scotland, where one of the longest running and most successful partnerships in artificial intelligence research began. They gave a demonstration of their theorem prover, the unique program that they have raised from birth to its teenage years, and that has yet to reach the height of its powers.

As Boyer points out, 'most of the people in the world simply balk when they see an algebraic formula.' But the theorem prover, he says, spews out algebraic formulae like its mother tongue. This is, if anything, an understatement. Hard-boiled computer scientists stopped and gawped as line after line of algebra scrolled up the screen of a Symbolics 3600, to an accompaniment of Bach fugues from the Lisp workstation's built-in speaker.

The Bach was actually played by a separate program, and had nothing to do with the mathematical fluency displayed on the screen. But onlookers at the Turing Institute's Machine Intelligence 11 workshop, held on the shores of Loch Lomond in March 1985, found it an appropriate and moving accompaniment to one of the wonders of the computer world.

What is theorem-proving and why does it matter? Every branch of mathematics is based on a set of axioms, which are unproven but reasonable-looking assertions – for example, it is an axiom of Euclidean geometry that parallel lines never meet. (The qualification 'Euclidean' has been needed since the early nineteenth century, when other geometries were discovered in which parallel lines do meet.) A theorem is any statement that can be deduced from the axioms by the rules of inference that have been declared to apply in this particular mathematical system.

Mathematicians spend their lives tracking down the important theorems which seem to encapsulate a lot of knowledge. They ignore the infinite number of trivial and inconsequential theorems which say nothing of importance. Between these two extremes there are certain theorems which are of practical importance but hardly qualify as eternal truths – for example, a theorem asserting that a particular microprocessor design faithfully implements its specification.

Warren Hunt, a graduate student at the University of Texas, Austin, used the Boyer-Moore theorem prover for just such a proof for a small microprocessor design.

Proofs which help to guarantee the reliability of hardware and software could be very valuable, indeed they may help to prevent disasters. But there is something more here than another worthy piece of utilitarian research. Boyer and Moore are not pompous people and its sounds pompous to say they have enlarged our understanding of reason itself. Super-hackers or philosopher-engineers? Let the reader decide.

---

16 May 1985

The question 'what has artificial intelligence achieved?' prompts a number of stock answers. One of them is that AI programs have proved important theorems in mathematics. But just what does it mean to say that a program has 'proved' a theorem? How much human help did it need? Had the theorem already been proved by mathematicians? And can a machine proof be trusted?

Robert S. Boyer and J. Strother Moore, associate professors at the University of Texas, have spent 13 years developing and improving a program which has now proved many important results in mathematics. Under their supervision a graduate student, Natarajan Shankar, produced a machine proof of the Church-Rosser theorem, one of the fundamental results of computer science.

Now Shankar is close to recreating, by computer, Kurt Gödel's famous incompleteness proof. Gödel's proof, published in 1931, established that there are true statements in mathematics which cannot be proved. It is regarded as one of the great achievements of twentieth-century mathematical logic.

Ironically, Gödel's theorem has itself been invoked as an argument against artificial intelligence, since it sets limits to what a computer program can prove. Actually those limits apply equally to human beings, unless humans are allowed to work to a looser definition of 'proof'.

The concept of proof remained vague from the days of Euclid until the nineteenth century. For 2000 years it was perfectly natural to think that proof required the mysterious operation of human reason. But the idea that certain truths were self-evident to the human mind took a severe blow with the discovery of non-Euclidean geometry. Then, following Gottlob Frege's pioneering work in symbolic logic, mathematicians turned towards the stricter view that a proof should be achieved entirely by the formal manipulation of symbols.

This did not only impose stricter standards on human proofs. It prepared the way for proofs by machine. As Boyer explains: 'Frege, and Russell and Whitehead and others made this breakthrough in which they applied mathematics to mathematics, and established the idea that one could present proofs exactly. When the computer became available, it was possible to get the machine to do a lot of the work in the checking of proofs.'

One of the first practical steps towards mechanical theorem-proving was Alan Robinson's invention of an algorithm for the method known as resolution. This method begins by assuming the theorem is false, and attempts to show that this leads to a contradiction. Resolution is used in the logic programming language Prolog.

The Boyer-Moore theorem-prover uses a different approach. 'Our theorem-prover is unusual,' claims Boyer, 'in that it implements the principle of mathematical induction.' This principle is often used by mathematicians, but has rarely if ever been used in the resolution-based school of mechanical theorem-proving. A proof by induction is recursive. Effectively it invokes itself repeatedly until some base case is reached. It then only remains to prove the base case.

The theorem-prover has a collection of rules for rewriting formulae, and applies them repeatedly until the desired result is reached. Sometimes it fails. But according to Boyer, 'it is constantly being improved, and it is checking the proofs of more and more interesting mathematical theorems.' By 1979 it had reached high-school level and proved that any number can be factorized into primes in only one way. 'We have gone on to what are really serious mathematical theorems,' says Boyer, citing Gauss's law of quadratic reciprocity as an example. This theorem, about the remainders obtained when squares are divided by prime numbers, was described by Karl Friedrich Gauss (1777–1855) as 'the gem of higher arithmetic'.

The machine proof was carried out by another of Boyer and Moore's students, David Russinoff, who already had a PhD in number theory. Boyer tells how Russinoff 'Sat down and painstakingly, over a period of a couple of weeks, gave to our theorem prover a collection of statements which were each in turn carefully checked, and when all chained together gave this theorem.'

Another milestone was the machine proof of the theorem in number theory which underlies the Rivest–Shamir–Adleman public key encryption algorithm. Public key ciphers use separate keys for encrypting and decrypting messages. Their advantage over other ciphers is that the information needed to decipher messages need never be transmitted. There is therefore less risk of the decryption key falling into the hands of an enemy.

Is Boyer being over-modest when he talks of the theorem prover merely 'checking' proofs? 'It depends upon your perspective,' he says.

'From the point of view of a serious mathematician the theorem prover is not contributing much at all. From the point of view of someone who is really relatively ignorant of mathematics, the theorem prover is probably much better than he'll ever be.'

Boyer is unwilling to admit that the theorem-prover does anything creative. To most people, he agrees, it looks as though it is doing mathematics. 'But from the point of view of the mathematician,' he maintains, 'there is nothing like real mathematical creativity going on.'

Proofs in mathematics textbooks often leave out the fine details, the little steps in the argument which are considered too obvious to mention. The Boyer-Moore theorem-prover, which does not suffer from boredom or information overload, goes through all these little steps. However, it usually has to be signposted to the major steps in a proof. Boyer estimates that about three pages of information had to be typed in before the system verified the RSA algorithm. About 20 pages were required for the Church-Rosser theorem. 'In all of these cases,' he says, 'I would say that the amount the user had to type in was proportional to an undergraduate text exposition.'

Boyer and Moore began work on their theorem-prover during the vintage years of the early 1970s at the University of Edinburgh. 'When I came to Edinburgh in 1971, Edinburgh was by any conceivable measure the world centre for automatic theorem proving,' Boyer recounts. 'There was Bernard Meltzer, and Bob Kowalski, and Pat Hayes, and Alan Bundy . . . just so many people who had great things to contribute to automatic theorem proving.'

'I came over and just had three utterly marvellous years working on the grand scheme of trying to get computers to prove hard theorems,' Boyer relates. 'More or less, Moore and I are still working along that general line. We're proving grand theorems but we are having to do lots of manual assistance to guide the theorem-prover along. So in a certain sense the vision is very far from having been achieved. On the other hand we are definitely getting the theorem-prover to check theorems of really enormous difficulty.

Has the enterprise proved harder than Boyer expected? 'It's an absurdly difficult thing,' he replies, 'the whole idea of trying to prove theorems mechanically, since we know that the whole enterprise is theoretically impossible in a certain sense. We have the famous theorems of Church and Gödel which say that you just cannot write a computer program with the ability to find the solution to any mathematical problem. It is known to be impossible, provenly impossible. 'The real challenge,' he adds, 'is trying to see why human beings are in some cases fairly good at doing it anyway.'

Boyer stresses that he and Moore have only automated the fine detail work of theorem proving. 'Mathematics is not that grinding process,' he says. 'Mathematics is the big steps, the leaps, the new concepts. But I claim that ordinary good working mathematicians, before they present their work to the public, actually do mentally go through these fine detailed steps.' Here, Boyer takes an unconventional view of the way mathematicians' minds work. Many would say that they fill in the fine details of their proofs unconsciously if at all. Boyer believes that good mathematicians do it consciously, even though they may not write down every step in their published papers.

One researcher who has tried to mechanize the 'big leaps' in mathematical thinking is now based, like Boyer and Moore, in Austin, Texas. Douglas Lenat, author of the programs AM and Eurisko, is on leave from Stanford University and working at the Microelectronics and Computer Technology Corporation.

Lenat's programs explored mathematics and looked for interesting conjectures to prove. Boyer regards this work as 'extremely interesting' and regrets that Lenat seems, for the time being, to have abandoned it. Boyer himself felt compelled to approach mathematics from the opposite direction. 'I guess that my own background in mathematics and logic is such that I feel almost irresponsible if I write a program that just makes conjectures instead of actually checking,' he explains. 'We've always developed our theorem-prover with absolute rigour as the principal goal.'

This is why the theorem-prover has not added any interesting new theorems to mathematics. It cannot make conjectures itself, and mathematicians have shown little interest in using it to check their own new conjectures. It has been put to practical use, however, in verifying the properties of computer programs. Boyer believes that machine verification of programs may help to prevent real disasters occurring as a result of software errors. This practical consideration has also weighed with the US Department of Defense (DOD) in its support of Boyer and Moore's research.

But Boyer believes that the DOD's 'A1 certification' scheme for military computer systems does not tackle the real problems of system reliability. 'This A1 certification that is now becoming popular worries me to death,' he says, 'because what you have is people sprinkling holy water over the correctness of the specifications of the system, when the specifications may bear no relation whatsoever to what is actually implemented. Actually looking at the details of the implementation is such a hard problem that the Defense Department does not require that the manufacturers do that.'

Boyer seems confident of the theorem-prover's own reliability. 'But it is nothing like an absolute confidence,' he admits. 'On the other hand,' he says 'we have had lots and lots of people use it, and we haven't had more than one or two really bright people find bugs.'

He and Moore had at one stage talked of jumping off the Golden Gate bridge if anyone found a bug. Then a friend at Digital Equipment Corporation sent in a bug report. 'In the end all we did was send him a certificate with a picture of us jumping off the Golden Gate bridge,' relates Boyer. 'We now have a very low bridge in Austin that we think of ourselves as being willing to jump off.'

Shankar successfully completed the Gödel proof. It occupies about two-thirds of his 1500-page doctoral thesis.

Boyer and Moore have both become full professors. With Donald Good, chief designer of the Gypsy program verification system, they have set up a company in Austin called Computational Logic. Neither has jumped off the bridge.

15

Seeing is deceiving

What we see dominates our consciousness, but vision is perhaps our least conscious skill. We are unlikely to learn how we do it, from introspection. Indeed we are largely unaware of the enormity of the task that eye and brain undertake so effortlessly. The complexity of that task was underlined when artificial intelligence researchers began trying to make machines emulate the human visual system. The early workers did not get very far. Many of those working in the field today believe that the necessary first step is to examine what computations any system - natural or artificial - must accomplish in the process of seeing. Only then, they argue, should one begin to implement a vision system.

Computer vision research at GEC and in the UK in general has been through major changes since this article appeared. Few of those mentioned are still where they were and doing what they were doing. It would require a complete new article - or several - to bring the story up to date.

Though much of this article is out of date, it does present a number of ideas which are still influential in vision research. Through research that GEC was doing at the time, it gives a flavour, but no more, of the approach pioneered by the late David Marr at the Massachusetts Institute of Technology. This can hardly be called an introduction to his theories, but it may encourage readers to delve into Marr's writings for themselves.

Is intelligence a single thing, or merely a name for a mass of unconnected abilities? Are there principles, insights or techniques which are equally applicable to expert systems, to theorem proving, and to vision? These are questions which inevitably arise as one surveys the rich variety of artificial intelligence research. The answers matter. In science it matters not only what people do, but what they believe themselves to be doing.

22 March 1984

GEC's research on computer vision combines work on theories, algorithms and hardware. Expertise in all three is gathered at the company's Hirst Research Centre. With its links to university groups working in the field, GEC is therefore as well placed as anyone in the UK to develop 'fifth generation' type systems which can, to a certain extent, understand the content of visual images.

Sound theory should ensure that the methods developed have power and generality. Algorithms are (or should be) the implementations of theories. They define the information processing operations that will be performed. And special hardware offers the hope that vision algorithms can be made to run faster than the plodding pace at which they perform on a conventional minicomputer. The GRID parallel-processing chip, designed by GEC's very high performance integrated circuit laboratory, shows promise here.

It would be silly, however, to suggest that GEC is about to produce a computer which can comment intelligently on a Cézanne landscape. In the nature of industrial research, the first results are likely to be modest improvements.

The influence of David Marr (a neurophysiologist who worked at the Massachusetts Institute of Technology) grows apace in spite of his untimely death in 1980. Marr's work at MIT pioneered a computational approach to the study of human vision. Marr maintained that research on visual mechanisms should be guided by rigorous analysis of the computational problems involved in vision. His theories have helped psychologists and neurophysiologists to ask the right questions in their experiments. They have also inspired a new, more formal approach to machine vision. This is a field where 'quick and dirty' solutions have often held sway in the past.

Marr called for an end to the conceptual confusion between theories and algorithms, algorithms and hardware. In computer vision especially, 'hack' algorithms which happen to work have often been misrepresented as advances in theory. And the virtues claimed for certain hardware designs often sprang, in reality, from the algorithms they implemented.

The purpose of the GEC vision project, as distinct from a number of other image processing projects within the company, is to develop general methods for interpreting real-world scenes. Almost by definition this means three-dimensional vision. 'If you want to understand the world you have to understand it in three dimensions,' says Margaret McCabe, leader of the Hirst Centre's theoretical methods group. Hardware and system development goes on in another division of the laboratory, led by Peter Collins.

Information about the third dimension is available even in a static, two-dimensional image such as a photograph. Most of this information, however, is suggestive rather than conclusive. One has to make reasonable assumptions. The brain is easily tricked when, for example, one eye peers through a hole into a trick room with sloping floor and ceiling.

Normally, of course, the brain uses additional sources of depth information to remove such ambiguities. The GEC vision project is investigating two of these sources: stereoscopy and optic flow. Of these two, optic flow is the less familiar. It is the apparent movement of image points which occurs when there is relative motion between an object and the eye or camera. This could be a useful source of depth information when the relative motion is known. The work on optic flow is being pursued in HRC's long range laboratory.

Stereoscopy is so well known that there seems to be little mystery about it. In fact it is remarkably difficult to program a machine to make correct deductions about depth, given two views from cameras separated by a short distance. The different viewpoints give rise to disparities between the two images. To extract depth information, it is necessary to pair features of one image with matching features in the other. This is called the correspondence problem.

The GEC stereo vision project is making use of David Marr and Ellen Hildreth's theory of the 'primal sketch', and an edge-matching algorithm developed at the University of Sheffield. A key idea is that the images must be processed before there is any attempt to match them up. Attempts to match small 'windows' of raw, grey-level image have not been very successful. The very differences between the two images, which make stereoscopy possible, also defeat simple-minded matching schemes.

Following Marr, the GEC group searches the image for edges or, more precisely, for steps in light intensity. Edges can be found by relatively low-level procedures, using data-driven image processing techniques. (Artificial intelligence techniques come into play at the higher levels of the vision problem.) Some edges in an image may correspond to physical edges. Some arise from other causes such as shadows.

A key process in all image processing is convolution. This is a kind of weighted averaging of the intensities within a neighbourhood. The use of negative weights means that convolution can sharpen up detail instead of simply blurring it. There are many convolution functions which detect edges, but the simplest ones suffer from various faults and tend either to miss genuine edges or to throw up erroneous ghost edges.

Marr and Hildreth proved that the best compromise is provided by a smooth function which gives a positive weight to points in a central spot, and negative weight to points in a surrounding circular halo. More picturesquely, the function appears as a Mexican hat if it is plotted as a three-dimensional surface.

The ideal function, for the technically minded, is a second derivative of a Gaussian. A simpler function which is almost as good is the difference of Gaussians or DOG function. The GEC group's edge-finding method is based on convolution with a DOG function. The human eye is thought to use a very similar function to find edges.

Next, edges must be matched between the left-eye and right-eye images. Matching edges will usually have similar contrast; the change in brightness as the edge is crossed will be similar in both images. Matching edges also usually have similar orientations. But contrast and orientation alone cannot guarantee a correct match. In a repeating wallpaper pattern, for example, there are any number of edges which match for contrast and orientation.

This is where the algorithms have to get a little more intelligent. 'Two edges are most likely to match,' says McCabe, 'if they both have neighbours that match.' So every correct match, like a correctly solved crossword clue, helps to confirm others. 'Cooperativity' is the buzzword for it, borrowed from thermodynamics. Cooperative methods are inherently suited to parallel processing. John Frisby and his colleagues at Sheffield University have come up with a refinement of this technique called disparity gradient filtering, which prevents the cooperative process running away with itself. Essentially it halts the process wherever there are abrupt changes in depth. Such a change may be a sign that you are no longer looking at the same object. Frisby says that on office scenes and similar pictures, his method matches more than 99 per cent of edges correctly. It would run into trouble, he admits, 'If you were looking at a swarm of gnats.'

The next step is easy. Simple triangulation locates all the matched edges in the third dimension. But most of the picture points still have no depth indication attached to them, because they lie on surfaces rather than edges. Now things get tough. The next, and still problematic stage in Marr's model of stereo vision is the so-called 2½D sketch. This is the stage where essentially every visible point is assigned a position in the depth dimension.

Nor will it end there. Like many vision researchers around the world, McCabe and her group would like to transform the sketch into a full three-dimensional representation, which would include inferred information about invisible surfaces. This would not be a mere three-dimensional bit map (which is neither useful nor an economic use of computer memory) but a hierarchical description of the scene, the objects, and their geometrical structures. This is just the kind of description that is used in computer aided design systems. For example, the constructive solid geometry approach, developed at the University of Rochester, models three-dimensional bodies by adding and subtracting blocks, cylinders and other shapes.

If computer vision research could slash through the algorithmic jungles to the point where vision systems can describe objects in the same language as CAD systems, it would be the technological equivalent of Stanley's meeting with Livingstone: a significant event for robotics, artificial intelligence, and computer-integrated manufacturing.

Further reading

Marr, D. (1982). *Vision*. San Francisco, Calif.: W.H. Freeman.

Mayhew, J. and Frisby, J. (1984). 'Computer vision.' In O'Shea, T. and Eisenstadt, M. (Eds). *Artificial Intelligence: Tools, Techniques and Applications*. New York: Harper and Row.

16

Model-driven vision

Vision research strikingly illustrates the dual identity of artificial intelligence, as science on the one hand and as engineering on the other. For some researchers, the goal is to understand human and animal vision. For them, artificial vision is valuable only to the extent that it faithfully models natural vision.

By contrast, psychological authenticity is largely irrelevant for an engineer building a system to inspect castings, pick fasteners from a bin, or guide a missile to its target. A thriving machine vision industry has grown up, selling systems which ignore the third dimension, frequently ignore colour and the finer distinctions of brightness, and generally require good light and a well-controlled viewing situation. These systems do not attempt to mimic the human eye and brain. Instead they generally rely on easily measured attributes of two-dimensional shapes, such as diameter, area, perimeter and number of 'holes'. They work fine on their specialized tasks.

A whole spectrum of possibilities exists between the two theoretical extremes. I had hoped that the previous article (about research at GEC) and this one (about research at Plymouth Polytechnic) would respectively illustrate the scientific and engineering approaches. But it turned out that the two projects lay close together on the spectrum, and the similarities were more striking than the differences.

7 June 1984

'Industrial research problems are now very much in line with academic research problems. Now every company is using micros, and they're trying to solve really difficult problems.'

Keith Baker speaks from experience. His interdisciplinary team at Plymouth Polytechnic has been successful in attracting industrial research contracts. He and his colleagues have often been asked to solve problems which called for artificial intelligence techniques.

With British Robotic Systems Ltd they came up with a vision system for the Greater London Council that can recognize (though not yet in real time) a double-decker London bus. Machine vision equipment, with cameras at major road junctions, could help London Transport to keep its buses running on time. The next step might be to give passengers at the bus stop some kind of indication of when the next bus is likely to come along.

It is significant that the AI approach was seen as potentially less costly than a traditional electronic solution with sensors buried in the road and a transmitter or a transponder on every bus. Which is fine for London Transport; but just how far does the development of a bus-recognizer advance research in machine vision, in artificial intelligence, or in information technology in general?

The same objection is often thrown at expert systems. OK, it can diagnose blood diseases, but why can't it play chess? OK, it can play chess, but why can't it write poetry?

It is in the nature of knowledge-based systems that each such system appears only to have solved one very small problem. In fact it is impossible to do much research in knowledge-based systems without at some point narrowing down to some real, specialized problem. But the knack of designing knowledge-based systems is to keep all the specialized knowledge in one place. Replace it with new knowledge and you get a new system. There is more to it than that, of course, but the Plymouth group hopes to extend its vision techniques from buses to other objects of industrial or military interest. With industrial and Government partners it is bidding for £2.5 million of Alvey Directorate money for a project on object identification from two-dimensional images.

There have been attempts to develop a so-called 'knowledge-free' approach to vision, using only universal facts about geometry and optics. But this only postpones the moment when the system compares what it 'sees' with an internally held representation of some object to be recognized.

Baker was converted to the knowledge-based approach during the 11 years he spent on the engineering and applied science faculty at Sussex University. Last year he decamped to Plymouth, with most of his research group.

Members of the group have wide-ranging interests, from chip design and computer architectures to expert systems. Plymouth Polytechnic is a sub-contractor to Plessey in a major five-nation programme of research on expert systems, which is supported by the European Community's Esprit programme. Geoff Sullivan, formerly an experimental psychologist, concentrates on image understanding. Other members, including Phil

Culverhouse and Jonathan Brumfitt, are designing and building special hardware for vision systems.

'Model-driven vision' is the name they give to their chosen approach. 'We are establishing a model of the objects that we expect to find in a scene,' Baker explains, 'and we are using that model to direct the pixel-based image processing activities.'

'Knowledge-free' methods are still used for the initial processing of the image, which in the bus example is a London street scene as seen by a black-and-white video camera. This processing employs the Sobel edge detector function, which knows nothing about buses and assumes nothing about the image beyond the fact that it is likely to contain edges.

In future work the group intends to use a more reliable edge-detecting function, the difference of Gaussians (DOG). The theoretical justification for using the DOG function comes from the work of David Marr at the Massachusetts Institute of Technology. Though his name has been linked with the 'knowledge-free' approach, Marr believed that the human visual system holds a catalogue of three-dimensional models. The general model for 'human', for example, might be a stick-figure built of cylinders and resembling the Tin Man in *The Wizard of Oz*. This, Marr suggested, is compared with a '2.5D sketch' of the scene, in which the viewer has already filled in some information about the third dimension.

The Plymouth work departs from Marr's theory of human vision by using a purely two-dimensional sketch. The system performs only a bare minimum of image processing before it calls on its specialized knowledge.

The bus-recognizing program was educated by showing it pictures of a bus approaching a junction at the Elephant and Castle. Coordinates of six points on the bus were supplied to the program. The remaining features such as windows were added by hand. The resulting wire-frame, three-dimensional model of the bus was then juggled around to generate a number of possible two-dimensional views. These views showed buses in various plausible positions as they might approach the chosen junction.

A few dozen views were sufficient. The system simply stores them and checks to see if any of them matches the pattern of edges it has found in an incoming picture. The match does not have to be perfect. Its quality is measured by an evaluation function or score, with points added for each matching edge. Partially obscured buses can still notch up enough points to be recognized.

Points are subtracted for any edges which are found where a bus should not have edges. Until this feature was introduced, the system was giving a 'bus' verdict on a test picture of a Portakabin on the back of a lorry. The cabin happened to have windows in the same places as a bus. It also had gable ends and other oddities, but these were being ignored.

The system gets by with so few sample instances because the camera is fixed, the position of the road surface is known, and buses behave rather predictably. 'We don't expect to find buses up on the pavement, or in the air, or coming side on,' Baker points out. 'That has reduced the number of instances that we have to generate.'

The bus-recognizer could probably be reprogrammed with a new model or knowledge base for recognizing, say, car transporters. But it could not learn to recognize the pigeons in the same street, since they appear in many orientations, at almost any point in three-dimensional space. The number of instances to be generated and stored would be astronomical. Further difficulties would arise because a pigeon has few straight edges and does not correspond visually to any wire-frame model. And it changes shape as it flaps its wings.

Surprisingly enough, these seemingly serious problems may not present an insuperable obstacle for model-driven vision. Many of them have been dealt with already, in a program by David Hogg, which can recognize the shape of a walking man. Hogg has remained at Sussex University, but works closely with the group now established at Plymouth.

The program uses a 'human' model, similar to that proposed by Marr, and composed of 14 cylinders in three-dimensional space. The mechanical degrees of freedom of the joints are specified: for example the knees cannot bend in all directions. It would be difficult to store all the possible views of a walking man, so the program generates the instances it needs as it goes along. Typical AI strategies are used, to find an appropriate instance in a vast search space. Having found what looks like an upper arm, the program will look for a forearm attached to it. This is easier than looking for complete arms or complete people.

Hogg's program also makes sensible assumptions about the movement between successive frames of video. When the Tin Man figure of the model is superimposed on the original image of a real walking man in a landscape, it moves as if locked onto its human original. Momentarily a model arm may slip out of alignment with the arm of flesh, but it locks on again unerringly. All this is best seen in a video action replay. The actual computations cannot yet be done in real time. But as Geoff Sullivan remarks, the demonstration shows that 'you can use high-level information about the object, to interrogate a rather dirty image.' 'In order to interpret it,' he adds, 'you must have a very high level of understanding of what you are looking for.' Rather dirty images of well-understood objects are frequently encountered in the factory and on the battlefield.

Most industrial vision systems are in a broad sense model-driven or knowledge-based, though some use very elementary knowledge – for example that a particular kind of washer is ten millimetres wide and has one hole in it. The hope is, that more sophisticated models (beyond the

Tin Man) and more intelligent search strategies (to match the model to the image) will lead to steadily improving performance.

Taking his group with him, Keith Baker has moved again, to Reading University where in 1986 he took up a newly created chair in an expanding Computer Science Department. The group is involved in Alvey research projects on 'Object identification from two-dimensional images' and 'Model driven analysis of radiological images'. These are classified as image processing and therefore come under Alvey's man–machine interface programme.

Meanwhile GEC's long range research laboratory (no longer the computer systems laboratory where the work described in the last chapter took place) is also participating in major Alvey vision projects. One project continues the work on optical flow and the extraction of depth information from movement. Another is concerned with ways of representing depth information and three-dimensional shapes. The important link between vision, robotics and computer aided design is being strengthened. These projects come under Alvey's intelligent knowledge based systems (IKBS) programme.

Of course both approaches involve image processing, and both are based on knowledge. The crucial distinction seems to be that Baker and his colleagues are feeding knowledge down to the pixel-based level of representation, and identifying objects at that level; while the IKBS projects make the link between what is seen and what is known at a higher level, where the scene can be treated as a network of facts or logically linked hypotheses, rather than an array of dots.

The splitting of vision research between the MMI and IKBS programmes is an obvious absurdity. At least the Alvey Directorate and the vision community have made some effort to establish communication across the administrative divide. It remains to be seen whether such remedial measures are effective in the case of London, which now enjoys a similar mismatch between administrative structure and the structure of reality. The mention of the Greater London Council in the above article is now, of course, historical, as is the reference to another part of the city's old order, London Transport. The buses still do not run on time.

17

People, not machines, are the real black boxes

Theorem-proving and vision would seem to be very different things. To find a single description which could refer to either of these intelligent activities, we have to resort to some very vague and general form of words – perhaps something on the lines of 'finding a series of transformations which derive the unknown example from known prototypes'.

Aha! The essence of intelligence? Hardly. There must be a dozen such formulations which can, with goodwill and a bit of imagination, be seen as fair descriptions of the entire range of intelligent activity. Many AI researchers have their own private definitions of intelligence. Should we be surprised when someone who works on vision says 'everything is pattern recognition', or when someone who works in knowledge based systems says, 'intelligence is having the right facts and rules'?

All of them are right. But the pattern recognition approach which fits snugly to vision problems will have to stretch a little to accommodate theorem proving. A similar stretch would be needed to arrive at an 'IKBS' description of the early stages of vision, where having the right hardware and algorithms seems more important than any facts or rules.

This next article sets forth the view that intelligence has to do with guessing what goes on inside black boxes, and perceiving simple rules behind observed complexities. It contains references to a number of articles which had already appeared in *Computing*, but here I have used it as an introduction rather than a summing-up. These mysterious references will be resolved later in the book. The arguments are somewhat unsharp and impressionistic, but I shall not attempt any self-criticism until readers have had a chance to wield the red pencil for themselves.

19 April 1984

Computers are very good at synthesizing and constructing things. Speech? The chips for synthesizing it are cheap enough to be incorporated in toys. Coded messages? Again, mass-produced chips will synthesize what is required.

Pictures? Engineering designs? Imaginary mountains as a backdrop for a Panavision space epic; circuit layouts as complex as a Los Angeles street plan; you can have them. You instruct. The computer constructs.

Entire miniature universes can be constructed from almost ridiculously simple rules. Cellular automata – grids of very simple processors connected to their neighbours – provide a magnificent demonstration of this, none more so than John Conway's 'game of life'. Conway speculates that given sufficient space and time, intelligent beings would spontaneously evolve within this microcosm. More practically, researchers like John Barker of Warwick University are investigating cellular automata as fault-resistant parallel computers.

Expert systems, too, are in the construction business. Feed in the appropriate facts and rules, and the system will build a pyramid of logical deductions to reach the same conclusion as a real, live geologist, chemist or physician. And of course we take for granted the computer's ability to construct a program in its own machine code, when instructed in a high level language. By comparison, the ability of machines to formulate their own programs on the basis of experience is still rudimentary.

Les Valiant of Harvard University defines learning as 'acquiring a program by any means other than programming'. He risked offending those artificial intelligence researchers who have beavered away at machine learning for years, when he told a London meeting, 'if you disregard human learning there is no evidence that learning exists at all'.

Closely linked to machine learning is the problem of 'knowledge acquisition' for expert systems. The typical rule-based system requires explicitly stated rules of the form, 'if this then that'. But skilled cardiologists or oil prospectors may never have formulated their knowledge so explicitly. It takes long sessions with a 'knowledge engineer' to turn seat-of-the-pants expertise into clearly stated rules.

There are already products such as Expert-Ease which attempt to automate this process. But no one pretends the problem has been solved. Donald Michie, the designer of Expert-Ease, has for several years been stressing the need for more research on knowledge acquisition.

In their book *The Fifth Generation* Edward Feigenbaum and Pamela McCorduck wrote, 'Right now, the problem of knowledge acquisition is the critical bottleneck in artificial intelligence'. Feigenbaum is Professor of Computer Science at Stanford University, and one of the leading advocates of expert systems in the US.

In fact the expert systems bottleneck is just one instance of a general problem which faces artificial intelligence research. The problem is to discern order, structure or rules in a mass of chaotic-seeming data, and thereby to refine data into knowledge. Easy enough at an elementary level, this problem seems to become phenomenally harder as one attempts to push machine performance towards the human level. What is needed is a machine equivalent of the process of induction by which scientists form hypotheses about the physical world. Most existing computer applications including expert systems perform no induction at all. They are purely deductive.

Some programs have shown sparks of brilliance in inductive reasoning. AM, written by Doug Lenat at Stanford University, was able to discover the concept of prime numbers for itself. AM went on to formulate the famous and unproven Goldbach conjecture, that every even number greater than 2 is the sum of two primes.

What is this skill of inductive reasoning? Margaret Boden of Sussex University argues, in her book *Artificial Intelligence and Natural Man*, that learning, creativity and problem-solving have a great deal in common. Certainly part of the skill is the perception of similarity and analogy – what Arthur Koestler called the Aha! experience.

The power of analogical thinking can be seen in Thomas Banchoff's computer-generated films which help the viewer to understand four-dimensional space by analogy with the familiar three-dimensional world.

In a very different context, UK research on system design has stressed the analogies which exist between all systems, whether hardware or software. Agnes Kaposi's department at the Polytechnic of the South Bank has used this approach to produce general methods of controlling complexity. Inmos has used it to design the transputer chip and the Occam programming language.

Can machines detect analogies? At a very simple level the answer is yes. Simple pattern matching is performed by content-addressable memories and by ICL's CAFS-ISP. Effective as such systems are for searching a database, they cannot cope with those occasions where the data must be, in some sense, understood before a similarity can be observed.

Research on machine vision has run up against this problem. Image understanding, as envisaged in the Japanese fifth generation computer project, is not just an extension of simple pattern matching.

A true image understanding system would generate a high-level description of a scene, the objects in it, and the parts of those objects. For example, Margaret McCabe's vision group at the GEC Hirst Research Centre envisages that a vision system might generate a high level representation identical to that employed in a computer aided design system.

CAD systems routinely convert high-level descriptions of objects into visual images. The reverse transformation has proved to be much more difficult, though there are now some promising approaches.

One visual task of special importance is the reading of handwritten text. Commercial optical character recognition (OCR) systems can only read machine printing or a very formal and constrained variety of hand print. Julian Ullman of Sheffield University believes that the OCR problem has been consistently underestimated. He says that it may be a more difficult problem than speech recognition.

Speech is another area where it is much easier to construct than to analyse. Though digitally synthesized speech still leaves much to be desired, it has made the essential breakthrough to comprehensibility. But researchers are still waiting for the breakthrough which will take speech recognition systems beyond the limited (though commercially valuable) performance they achieve today. The target is a machine which can cope with a total stranger who speaks normally as if addressing another human being.

Cryptology provides an even more striking example. Computers can readily encrypt messages, and they can decrypt them with equal ease if the key is known. Both processes are purely deductive. But the cracking of an unknown code calls for an act of induction. Codebreaking is still a task for brilliant cryptanalysts and mathematicians. Computers provide little more, as yet, than brute-force assistance.

Les Valiant drew a parallel between machine learning and code-breaking. He based his analogy on a particularly powerful approach which real cryptanalysts can rarely use: the chosen-plaintext attack.

Suppose you have burgled your enemy's office, and found his encryption machine. You can now type in any message you like, study the output, and try to determine the coding program. 'The problem of deducing an encoding program from its input-output behaviour is very similar to learning,' said Valiant. To see the analogy you must think of the black box as the world, and the cryptanalyst as an intelligent robot trying to make sense of it.

Now give the analogy another twist, and see how it applies to the major Alvey programme research area of the man–machine interface. The obvious version of the analogy puts the computer system in the role of the black box, and the human user in the role of the cryptanalyst. Anything we can learn about the general problem of guessing what goes on inside black boxes will help us to understand how people learn to operate unfamiliar computer systems.

But now try swapping the roles. Put the computer in the role of the cryptanalyst. Think, if you can, of the user as a black box, because that is how the computer sees the user. It is also a view of the user that comes naturally to psychologists. Two university psychology departments (at Warwick and Surrey) are planning to develop adaptive man–machine interfaces which treat the user as a black box whose workings must be understood. The point of this is that the interface can be more helpful if it can figure out the strong and weak points in the user's knowledge.

Intelligent knowledge-based systems have become the new philosopher's stone. The IKBS approach has achieved fame through expert systems, but it is now being applied to virtually all the fifth generation problems.

The rewards come quickest when the grammar of the problem is reasonably well understood and can be expressed as a (possibly large) set of rules. Machine translation has come closer to the human performance level than, say, machine vision, because the grammar of language is better understood than the grammar of vision.

Humans are still the experts at induction, at learning, at absorbing knowledge from their environment and at guessing what goes on inside black boxes. But AI researchers may very well succeed in codifying these very skills into deductive knowledge-based systems.

There is no paradox in the idea of an inductive system that appears purely deductive when examined under a magnifying glass. You will not see words and numbers if you examine a microprocessor under the microscope, but this does not stop microcomputers doing arithmetic and word processing. The whole can do more than the parts.

Deductive reasoning is the basic mechanism available to programmers using logic programming languages such as Prolog. But Prolog is only one possible starting point for the construction of systems which can perform inductive reasoning.

Systems which have to be fed with pre-digested knowledge are surely only a preliminary to knowledge systems which know how to add to their own knowledge. Developments in this direction are now beginning. Their effect will be felt not only in expert systems but in machine vision, speech, language translation, the man–machine interface, and many other areas of information technology.

To sum up the argument: there are forward problems, which are easy; and inverse problems, which are hard. The task of artificial intelligence research is to apply computers to the hard, inverse problems.

So far, so good. But with hindsight it was a mistake to identify the forward problems with logical deduction, and the inverse problems with induction. Deduction is sometimes hard. Induction is sometimes easy. A better statement would be that the easy problems are those which can be solved by computing a function or running the data straight through some program, while the hard problems require search.

'Search' itself can mean two different things. Sometimes a program must search through a real database such as a customer list or a telephone directory. This may take a long time but there is nothing intrinsically difficult about it. In artificial intelligence work, however, the search is often of the 'generate and test' variety, where the objects examined do not exist in advance, but are constructed in the course of the search. What begins as a search may end with the designing of some wonderful and complex object which satisfies the search criterion.

A speech recognition program cannot be equipped with a database containing every grammatical English sentence. The number of such sentences is infinite. It may, however, be possible to give the program a dictionary of English words, and a set of grammatical rules, which together define what is and what is not an English sentence. In its attempts to understand an utterance, this program might have to construct arbitrarily complex sentences.

Problems are perceived as hard when a solution by search is intractably difficult, or even 'impossible'. People, and AI programs, regularly solve problems which are theoretically impossible. Usually the theory refers to some general and difficult problem, but the instances of the general problem that arise in practice just happen to be easily solved. We seem to have been given a universe where it pays to be intelligent. It need not have been so. Hard problems become easy when short-cut methods are found. Artificial intelligence research sets out to make hard problems easy.

The difficulty of deductive logic does not lie in the individual inference steps, but in steering the steps towards some desired goal. The Boyer-Moore theorem-prover can steer itself for short distances, but it still needs to be shown the major landmarks along the way to a proof.

Rules which steer a search process towards supposedly profitable areas of the search space are known as heuristics. Many heuristics are based on hunches and have no formal justification. But it is quite all right to use heuristics in a theorem prover. Bad heuristics will not result in false proofs. They will merely increase the number of occasions when the program generates no proof at all.

Reasoning is occurring on two distinct levels: the rigorous 'object-level' reasoning of the proof itself, and the informal 'meta-level' reasoning which controls the search for a proof. It does not matter if the meta-level reasoning is heuristic or ill-justified; the object-level chain of inference, if you establish one at all, will be correct.

Here we come to one of the differences between vision and theorem-proving. Theorem-proving takes place in a closed world. If a proof is correct, no further information can falsify it. There are no surprises. If alternative proofs of the same theorem exist, all are equally valid.

Vision is concerned with an open world, where knowledge is always incomplete, and interpretations may have to be revised in the light of further information. A single image – one frame from a videotape – may be consistent with a number of possible interpretations, of which only one can be right. The masked robber might be Smith, or Jones, both of whom are 180 cm high and of medium build. The vision system prints out its guess: 'Smith'.

In the next frame, the robber pulls off his mask and reveals himself as Jones. It would certainly seem that the vision system was wrong. But there is an important issue of semantics here. If 'Smith' is taken to mean 'it was Smith', the system's answer was clearly false. But now the system's designer explains that 'Smith' really means 'the data are consistent with the hypothesis that it was Smith'. Therefore, the system's output was correct.

It is just such a question of semantics that underlies many of the debates about induction. Induction is the process of reasoning from the particular to the general. You see some white swans. You propose the general law, 'all swans are white'. Philosophers from David Hume onwards have been unhappy about such statements. Clearly, one black swan could prove you wrong.

Nevertheless, inductive logic does seem to have its uses. People cannot resist formulating general laws and teaching them to others. Induction is probably an important part of the process of learning, and in AI the terms 'induction' and 'machine learning' are used almost interchangeably.

Most of our civilization's accumulated knowledge is founded on the soft sand of induction. And now we have computer programs which derive general laws from specific examples. Are these programs to be trusted? What the programs do is not really at issue. It is all a question of what we believe them to be doing. What semantic value do we attach to their output?

Given six examples of white swans and none of black ones, we can be sure that almost any induction program would come up with the general rule, 'swans are white'. That is a perfectly good answer, if we assume it to be prefaced with the qualification, 'the data are consistent with the hypothesis that . . .'

Alternatively, it is a correct answer if we invoke the closed-world assumption. Under the closed-world assumption, the output 'all swans are white' may be taken literally, but the input data 'Swan 1: white. Swan 2: white. Swan 3. . . . . .Swan 6: white' must be assumed to carry the unstated implication that these are all the swans that exist and there are no others.

In mathematics, the closed world assumption is often justified. 'These are all the positive integers less than ten, and there are no others.' In science or everyday life, the assumption may be convenient but it is not to be trusted. Of course, we can define a closed world by our use of words. As a nineteenth-century Oxford lampoon declared of the Master of Balliol,

> I am Master of this college:
> What I don't know isn't knowledge.

Most of us are not omniscient, and for most of us the only way to be always right is to say nothing at all.

Further reading

Gregory, R.L. (1984). *Mind in Science.* Harmondsworth: Penguin. (Gregory is known as an authority on human vision. He argues persuasively that perception is an active process of making and testing hypotheses. This superb book includes some cogent reflections on artificial intelligence, a discussion of the relation between logic and the world, and an extremely lucid treatment of the subject of induction.)

18

The logic of learning

The next few chapters examine learning and induction. As Les Valiant points out, learning need not involve any inductive extrapolation into the unknown. Simple models of learning may merely refine or reformulate existing knowledge. The refined knowledge will probably be expressed in a concise form which exploits any pattern, order, or redundancy which is present. Most important of all, what is learned must be stored in an appropriate form for future use.

Induction may be admixed with machine learning in a controlled manner. It gradually becomes an inseparable part of learning as one moves from closed and artificial worlds to open and realistic ones. Human learning is inevitably inductive. We never see the same river twice. Without induction we could never learn that rivers flow downhill, only that a particular river flowed downhill at a particular place and time – a fact that will never be useful again.

Machines that are to be regarded even as part-way intelligent must be able to learn. The essence of a computer is its programmability, and yet computers will not be really useful to us until we can forget about programming them.

Seeing, planning, understanding language, problem-solving and other intelligent activities all involve the formation, testing and acceptance or rejection of hypotheses. Learning is only distinguished from the rest by the fact that the knowledge gained is integrated with existing knowledge and stored for future use. Any light we can throw on learning will reflect onto other AI problems.

AI programs which give eyecatching performances do not always add much to our knowledge. All too often, the author is unable to state precisely what the problem was, or how the program solved it.

Les Valiant goes to the opposite extreme. He picks a humble problem which can be stated clearly, details his algorithm, and proves mathematical results about the time and effort required for the computation. Yet this simple example already throws up major issues which run right through machine learning research: the elusive distinction between learning and being programmed; the perilous convenience of closed-world assumptions; the need to select the significant features of a situation before learning can occur; the loss of certainty, and the saving grace of probability.

---

1 March 1984

You have packed your bags for a holiday in Bali and you are about to leave your domestic robot in charge of your home for the next month. Suddenly you remember that you have not yet told the robot to feed the dog. Worse, you have not even taught it how to recognize the dog when it sees it.

This is the light-hearted scenario that Les Valiant of Harvard University invokes to dramatize the difference between learning and programming. His point is that the imaginary domestic robot must be able to learn. With the taxi waiting outside, it is no time for a heavy programming session.

'Even if you have all the time in the world, you might not be able to write a program for recognizing a dog.' Valiant pointed out. He was speaking at a meeting on mathematical logic and programming languages organized by the Royal Society last month.

Learning has been a central theme since the early days of artificial intelligence research. AI researchers have usually tested their theories of learning empirically. You write a program or build a machine, and see whether it works. The subject has now acquired commercial importance. Probably the biggest obstacle to the development of expert systems is the difficulty of getting knowledge out of the expert and into the system.

Valiant is attacking the problem from another direction, using formal logic and proving theorems. His results are on paper, but he believes they are more meaningful than some of the laboratory work. He defines learning as 'a process of acquiring a program without being programmed'. This definition excludes such simple learning machines as the adaptive control systems used in industry. These merely adjust parameters in a fixed program. The definition implies that knowledge consists of programs rather than data. 'The knowledge of what a chair is, will be a program for recognizing a chair,' says Valiant.

He set out to consider programs which were able to represent general knowledge. Another condition he imposed was that the learning algorithm should be computationally feasible. That is, the time required for learning should be no more than a polynomial function of the size of the problem. Finally, he stipulated that 'You should be able to characterize the class of programs which can be learnt'. This is possible with the formal approach, he argues, but problematic with the suck-it-and-see approach used by many AI researchers.

Valiant chose to work with propositional calculus, the simplest form of symbolic logic. 'There is a lot of evidence,' he says, 'that the propositional calculus is more powerful than people claim.'

The imaginary robot works with an expandable set of, say 10,000 propositions which may or may not be true in a given situation. 'Dog' is not a proposition the robot can verify directly from its sensors. So when it learns to recognize a dog, it has to express the proposition 'dog' in terms of things it can verify already. For example, dog = (animal AND NOT cat AND has four legs). A string of propositions linked by ANDs in this way is called a monomial. It is one of the simplest possible ways to represent knowledge. There also happens to be a simple algorithm for forming such a monomial.

The method is to show the robot 100 examples of dogs. If a proposition is true for every dog in the sample, the robot includes that proposition in its dog-recognizing monomial. Otherwise the proposition is excluded. Thus if every dog in the sample is black, the robot will mistakenly think that a dog has to be black. This would appear to be a serious fault.

While this problem cannot be abolished, Valiant has proved that it can be controlled. What you have to do is to teach the robot on a representative and sufficiently large sample of the dog population. The chance that the robot will learn the wrong rule can then be made as close to zero as you desire. False negatives (a rare white dog not recognized as a dog) can be made vanishingly improbable. False positives (cats and other things mistaken for dogs) should not happen at all, says Valiant.

'My notion of learning is a very pedestrian one compared with what some people mean by learning,' Valiant told the meeting. He categorized it as deductive learning. The process plods towards an almost inevitable conclusion.

Humans have the additional capacity for inductive learning. By 'guessing with good taste', a person who has seen only one or two dogs can form a provisional concept of 'dog'. Somehow we know that colour, for example, is unlikely to be an important criterion of doghood. Valiant's propositional robot has no way of knowing this.

Inductive learning may be beyond it, but more sophisticated forms of deductive learning are within the imaginary robot's power. It need not confine itself to monomials as a representation of knowledge.

A more flexible representation, still within propositional calculus, is the so-called conjunctive normal form (CNF). This is an expression of the form (p OR q OR . . .) AND (s OR t OR . . .) AND . . .

Valiant has proved that this kind of rule, too, can be learned from positive examples. He has found an algorithm that learns a CNF in polynomial time. This is encouraging. It means there is some hope that computers could use the method in practice. The only stipulation is that some ceiling must be set for the number of terms in each bracket.

Humans seem to like a somewhat different kind of formula called the disjunctive normal form (DNF). Applicants for a programming job might be asked to have (knowledge of HAL2001 mainframes AND experience of programming in Drastic) OR (knowledge of Milliard Gargantubrain machines AND experience of Alsoran programming.)

The robot could arrive at this kind of formula by using a different algorithm. But Les Valiant has not yet found a way of developing DNF formulae from positive examples only. At present the robot needs some extra clues, which it gets by asking questions. Valiant invokes the idea of an oracle which will answer these questions.

There are two kinds of oracle. The one which is needed in this example is the N-oracle. The robot gives the oracle a test formula, for example (animal = 1, cat = 0). The N-oracle returns the value zero, because this is not a sufficient condition for doghood. The P-oracle is less exacting. It merely decides whether the formula is consistent with the object being a dog. So in this case it would have returned a value of one. A non-cat animal need not be a dog, but it could be.

The trouble with oracles is that if they are allowed to become too powerful, they may simply tell the robot the correct program. What takes place then is no longer learning, but programming. On the other hand, it may be hard to eliminate the role of the oracle entirely. An expert system, or rather an expert system generator, could learn very acceptably, with a human expert taking the role of the oracle.

Humans themselves acquire many of their programs with the help of oracles in the form of teachers. The fact that humans have to learn at all may be an accident of evolution, Les Valiant suggests. 'If we had evolved with keyboards on our heads,' he remarks drily, 'perhaps we would be programming each other.'

19

Machine learning and human windows

Donald Michie was involved with computing at its birth. During the Second World War he worked at the Bletchley Park centre which cracked the Enigma code. One of his colleagues was the mathematician Alan Turing.

Later he helped to establish Edinburgh as a world-renowned centre of research and teaching in machine intelligence. (Michie has never liked the implications of the phrase 'artificial intelligence'.) He campaigned for the subject while it lay under a cloud in the 1970s, and was vindicated when the expert systems boom began and the West was enthused with fifth generation fever.

Michie insists that machine reasoning should remain accessible and comprehensible to humans. But left to themselves, machine learning algorithms can produce unstructured programs which work in mysterious ways. Once again, it seems, the solution is human–machine cooperation, with the person (for the time being at least) setting out the broad strategy and the program filling in the detail.

The chess end games provide a good example of knowledge refinement without induction. The system was given a complete database for a closed world, which it reformulated in a more compact form. The helicopter example, however, called for inductive reasoning. The set of examples provided by the expert engineer did not cover every eventuality. The system had to extrapolate from the examples to create a plausible general rule.

14 June 1984

Within the quiet, quaint and cramped surroundings of Edinburgh's Hope Park Square, the University's Machine Intelligence Research Unit is metamorphosing into a new and glamorous creature called the Turing

Institute. The institute is a non-profit distributing company, formally registered as Machine Intelligence Research Affiliates. It is about to spread its wings and take flight to a new home at the University of Strathclyde. Meanwhile at Edinburgh, teaching and research will continue in Jim Howe's Department of Artificial Intelligence. The move coincides with Donald Michie's 'retirement' – actually nothing of the sort. Michie will be overseeing a unique attempt at industrial-academic cross-fertilization.

The Turing Institute will do research in its own right. It will provide postgraduate teaching to the University of Strathclyde. On the industrial side, a small club of companies pay subscriptions to the Institute. In return they get a range of free or cut-price services including computing facilities, software, technical reports, consultancy and seminars.

The affiliated companies can also second staff to the Institute. Mutual benefit is the aim: the companies learn about artificial intelligence techniques; the Institute gets industrial brains and exposure to real-world problems. Software developed at the Institute will be marketed to the wider world through another company, Intelligent Terminals Limited, which has Donald Michie and his wife Jean as directors.

All this revolves round a continuing programme of research which touches on expert systems, machine vision and robotics. Its chosen tools include the language Prolog, the Unix operating system, and a set of machine learning techniques which may prove to have wide-ranging uses.

The U.S. Army is supporting Edinburgh research on machine learning in two different contexts: chess end games, and the teaching of high school algebra.

Alen Shapiro has produced a chess program which learns by example. So far, it has been exercised on just one of the many classes of end-game position. 'From examples given to it by chess masters,' explains Donald Michie, 'it has produced a rule which will classify positions into two classes: won for white, and not won for white.'

The not-won positions have not yet been classified into draws and wins for black. But according to Michie, 'Alen has produced a theory which is not codified in chess books.'

End-game experts are apparently very good at judging the outcome of a game, even though they occasionally make mistakes when it comes to choosing actual moves. The outcomes of the example games were judged by Danny Kopek, a national master.

Now, another chess player, John Roycroft, is joining the project. Roycroft works for IBM UK, and according to Jean Michie he is 'Britain's leading scholar of the end game'.

Andy Paterson has written a program which puts O level students in the position of teacher. The student has to show the machine, by example, how to solve equations. The program forms a rule or procedure for solving equations. The student can then examine the rule and decide whether it was what he or she really intended.

The theory of this method, according to Jean Michie, is that 'if you want to instruct, you have to actually make your own ideas explicit, and then refine them.'

Paterson has also wrapped a machine-learning algorithm in a spreadsheet-style user shell to produce Expert-Ease, a do-it-yourself expert system builder which runs on the IBM XT personal computer and is marketed by Export Software International. Surprisingly enough, the central algorithm is one of a family of machine-learning or induction algorithms whose history goes back to the 1960s. The original program was the Concept Learning System (CLS) devised by the psychologist Earl Hunt. 'Because it was used by a psychologist and not a computer scientist it was overlooked,' recounts Jean Michie. But eventually Ross Quinlan of the University of Sydney took up Hunt's work and incorporated it in a new algorithm called ID3.

Donald Michie now regards Sydney as one of the three main centres of work on induction outside Edinburgh. The others are Ryszard Michalski's group at the University of Illinois, and the Yugoslav group led by Ivan Bratko in Ljubljana.

ID3 (and its commercial versions ACLS and Expert-Ease) deal with objects or situations which can be described by a number of attributes. A typical Expert-Ease application, said to have been created in 15 minutes, is a system which decides how many more hours a helicopter gearbox can be allowed to run before servicing.

It bases its decision on such factors as the kind of debris found (coarse or fine) and the degree of vibration, (low, medium or high). Its decision rule is based on a small number of examples originally supplied by someone who knew a lot about helicopter gearbox maintenance.

When you consult the system on a particular case, it asks questions such as 'are the debris particles found during examination: 1. coarse, 2. fine?' The next question depends on your answer to the first one. The various possible answers lead into different branches of a decision tree. At the end of any branch you find a relevant answer. You are told either that you should remove the gearbox right away, or that you can leave it for a certain number of hours before servicing.

The rule, or decision tree, is grown by the almost universal strategy of splitting a problem into subproblems. The algorithm starts with a large 'space' of possible conditions of the gearbox. At each node, the space is split into a number of smaller spaces, until at the end of a branch only one possibility remains.

The cleverness of the algorithm lies in the methods it uses to decide which question it will ask next. The aim is to keep the branches of the decision tree as short as possible. This means getting information out of the unorganized data provided by the expert, and into the tree as fast as possible. ID3 uses a quantitative measure, based on information theory, to see how it may annex as much information as possible with each bite it takes.

A further refinement helps the algorithm to run faster, particularly when a large number of examples is available. It takes a small number of examples, formulates a provisional rule. Then it takes some more examples, and if any of them breaks the rule it adjusts the rule accordingly.

The algorithm works fine. But as Donald Michie observes, 'The problem is that it produces a solution in the form of a classification rule that is opaque to humans.' This flies in the face of the principle that the user should understand how an expert system reaches its conclusion. Michie himself has been a strong advocate of the idea that software systems should have 'human windows'.

Michie and his colleagues have therefore been driven irresistibly towards a technique which they called 'structured induction'. The idea is to create a rule which is no longer a vast thicket of a tree with hundreds of nodes; instead, the rule should consist of a number of relatively simple procedures. If one procedure cannot reach a decision, it calls another procedure which may be able to feed it the information it needs. That procedure can call further procedures and so on.

The process of breaking the problem up into procedures cannot yet be performed automatically. It still takes a human expert to see how the problem might be subdivided. 'You have to have a great deal of knowledge about the way the world works,' observes Donald Michie. But the bodies of the procedures can still be generated automatically from examples. Experts such as chess players like to deal in broad stretegies, leaving the detail to the machine.

Induction can be seen as a form of automatic programming. Tim Niblett and Alen Shapiro have developed a programming language called Concept Design Language (CDL). 'If you do induction using this language, you can't help doing structured induction,' says Michie.

The language has been designed so as not to overtax the human brain. It is known, for example, that the brain can only hold about seven items in short-term memory. In CDL, according to Donald Michie, 'Every constraint in the syntax corresponds to a known brain constraint'.

Structured induction is nothing other than a form of structured programming. The advocates of formal methods see structured programming as an expression of underlying mathematical theories. It is remarkable that artificial intelligence researchers should have reached so similar a conclusion, working from quite different premises which concern the functioning of the brain.

The Turing Institute successfully completed the move to Glasgow. Meanwhile Edinburgh University, with its newly established Artificial Intelligence Applications Institute, is moving into fresh fields of research, often with industrial partners.

In March 1985 the Turing Institute held the eleventh in the long-running series of Machine Intelligence workshops. It was an intimate gathering of a few dozen computer scientists, some of them already at the top of the academic tree, and others young, sharp and combative, the intellectual leaders of tomorrow. The peaceful venue was Ross Priory, a country house owned by Strathclyde University. The theme was 'Machine construction and validation of models'. Many of the papers dealt with learning and induction. Interviews conducted at this workshop were the source of no less than six *Over the horizon* articles, all of which are reproduced in this book.

Further reading

Hayes-Michie, J.E., Michie, D. and Richards, J.M. (1987). Eds. *Machine Intelligence 11*. Oxford: Oxford University Press. (Technical papers from the MI/11 workshop.)

Michie, D. (1982). *Machine Intelligence and Related Topics*. New York: Gordon and Breach. (The uninspired title conceals a witty and perceptive collection of essays on the past, present and future of computing.)

Michie, D. and Johnson, R. (1984). *The Creative Computer*. Harmondsworth: Penguin.

20

Knowledge grows on trees

Decision trees are a little more complicated than Valiant's monomials. But they still belong within propositional logic, and computer scientists have been able to apply mathematical analysis to their behaviour, and that of the learning algorithms which construct them.

They may not be suitable for expressing sophisticated ideas, but they are very good for classifying things. In many practical contexts that is exactly what is needed. Westinghouse Electric's nuclear fuel division, for example, is reported to have saved more than ten million dollars per annum with a simple program which generates decision trees. Underneath the user-friendly exteriors of such programs, you will often find Ross Quinlan's ID3 algorithm or something very like it.

25 April 1985

Whatever learning is, it seems that the acquisition of concepts is an important part of it. And while one could argue for some time over what a concept is, much artificial intelligence research has focused on the idea of a concept as a classification rule.

In a rough and ready way, one can say that if a machine learns to classify things into chairs and non-chairs, it has learned the concept 'chair'. This, of course, ignores the fact that the machine's classification rule may be very bizarre, not at all resembling the way humans recognize chairs.

Perhaps the best-known algorithm for deriving classification rules is Ross Quinlan's ID3. The algorithm is in the public domain, and it has been used in a number of commercial software packages as an aid to the construction of expert systems. Quinlan, who is head of the School of Computing Sciences at the New South Wales Institute of Technology, developed the algorithm in 1979. He, in turn, was inspired by work done in the early 1960s by Earl Hunt, who is Professor of Psychology at the University of Washington.

Apart from its practical successes, the most eloquent tribute to ID3 comes from the substantial number of researchers who have tried to make it work better. These investigators have drawn attention to the algorithm's undoubted limitations, but they have also demonstrated their confidence in the underlying ideas propounded by Quinlan and Hunt. Quinlan himself rebuffs the suggestion that ID3 and its ilk are suitable only for a limited range of tasks. And he is convinced that machine learning has a lot to offer the world.

'I think that expert systems are going to be one of the dominant forces in this next five to ten years,' he says, 'I see machine learning as having a very powerful contribution to make to the feasibility of expert systems for a lot of tasks.'

To decide whether Quinlan's algorithm can discover concepts for itself, you have to make up your mind what you mean by 'concept'. The algorithm does not think up any new categories. But it can generate an original and efficient method for sorting things into already established categories. It learns from examples. But it has to be told what they are examples of. This need not be a disadvantage in expert system work. Here, the aim is not to create new knowledge but to extract existing knowledge from experts who may not be very good at stating explicitly what it is that they know. The task is one of transferring or refining knowledge.

Quinlan points out that with traditional interview-based 'knowledge engineering' methods, it can take months or even years to extract a set of rules that encapsulate an expert's knowledge. Machine learning, he argues, may save much of this time and money. Where large databases of examples already exist, as they do for some medical subjects and some chess end games, it may not even be necessary to involve an expert until the final polishing of the machine-generated classification rule.

ID3 and kindred algorithims generate a classification rule in the form of a decision tree. At each point where the tree branches, one attribute is tested. An arc leads away from the test node for each possible result of the test. Every possible path through the tree eventually stops at a 'leaf node'. Each leaf node is marked with one of the classes into which all possible cases are to be divided.

Superficially, classification by a decision tree resembles a game of Twenty Questions. However, Twenty Questions players surely do not hold in their minds a complete decision tree for the game, which could have over two million nodes. It is more reasonable to suppose that each game traces a fresh path through a network of concepts that is much more richly interconnected than a tree.

One of the criticisms voiced against decision trees is that they impose a single view of knowledge. Rich networks of relations are more readily represented by IF . . . THEN production rules or by clauses of predicate calculus. But, as Ryszard Michalski has pointed out, the richer the language used to represent knowledge, the more complicated any learning algorithm must be.

Decision trees can be generated by a simple, efficient algorithm. And Quinlan believes they provide an adequate representation for many problems of interest. 'Almost everything can be reduced to a classification problem in the long term,' he argues. 'For instance, a lot of expert systems write reports. And the reports that they write are essentially a number of decisions: shall I or shall I not incorporate this piece of report? And if you view each of those as just a series of classification problems, that is, decision problems, you can write reports using this technology.'

The decision tree approach assumes that a suitable list of attributes already exists. It will not help you to identify useful new attributes – though it may show that some of the features you thought were important, in fact are not. Quinlan agrees that much of the work involved in investigating a new problem area goes into defining suitable attributes, and that ID3 cannot help here. But he points out that in existing medical databases, for example, the attributes have already been determined. Nothing can be done now to alter them.

Sometimes it is possible to supply a learning algorithm with a complete set of all possible examples. For some chess end games, exhaustive computer-generated databases exist. The learning algorithm can then derive a rule which is guaranteed correct.

But more commonly the set of examples is merely a sample taken from an enormous space of possibilities. On these occasions a learning algorithm will produce a generalized rule which may be applied to all cases, including those which did not appear in the original set of examples. This rule will not necessarily be correct. Also, different algorithms may produce rules which are not formally equivalent, and actually lead to different predictions.

Even without this complication, many different decision trees may be derived from a single set of examples. ID3 and related algorithms search for trees which satisfy differing and possibly conflicting criteria. One common requirement is that the tree should be comprehensible to humans. On the other hand it may be very important to minimize the financial and other costs of the test procedure. In medical diagnosis, for example, certain tests are both expensive and risky for the patient. Clearly one should try to find a decision tree which relies as far as possible on cheaper, safer tests.

Computer time is the least important cost. Decision trees produce decisions almost instantly. 'You can do it on an 8-bit machine in fractions of a second, even for quite complex trees,' says Quinlan. However, the initial learning process requires a substantial amount of computation, especially with large sets of examples. The time spent searching for a good rule is an important consideration in the design of learning algorithms.

Unless the classification problem is a very simple one, it is impractical to search through the all the possible rules. As in chess or Go, the combinatorial explosion forbids. The answer is to grow a decision tree in stages from the root upwards – or rather, downwards, since that is how computer scientists usually draw trees.

Surprisingly, all you really need is a good method of selecting the first attribute to be tested. If you were classifying animals your method might lead you to look first at the number of legs. You could then start five subtrees, for animals with zero, two, four, six and over six legs respectively. Now you could apply your method recursively to each subtree.

At each stage the problem gets simpler, because the example set is chopped up into smaller subsets. In the first subtree, for example, you are only dealing with examples of legless creatures, which cannot be all that numerous. Also, at each stage, one attribute is eliminated. After a finite number of stages, which cannot be more than the number of attributes, the decision tree will be fully grown.

Hunt explicitly tried to minimize the cost of testing and the chance of errors. In building decision trees his methods looked several moves ahead before selecting an attribute to be tested.

Quinlan's innovation was to use an evaluation function based on information theory. 'I don't look ahead at all,' he explains. 'You look at each attribute in turn, and you compute a function of the properties of an attribute, and you pick the best.' At each stage of the tree-growing process, the method selects that attribute which is likely to yield the greatest amount of information about the unknown object being classified.

Intuitively this makes sense. The more information you have gained, the fewer additional tests will be needed, you hope, to complete the classification. Indirectly this keeps down the cost of testing, since fewer tests are performed. But ID3 takes no account of the fact that one test may be much more costly than another.

Quinlan and others have tried many tricks to make their decision trees satisfy various criteria of cost or comprehensibility. But Quinlan also stresses that a good decision tree, like any other knowledge acquired by inductive learning, should make correct predictions.

This might be an interesting area for further theoretical work. Einstein said, 'The most incomprehensible thing about the world is that it is comprehensible.' How do machine learning algorithms manage to make correct predictions about the world? This may look like a question about algorithms. But it is really a question about the world.

21

Learning is a dangerous thing

Rules in a richer language than that of the decision tree emerge from the learning programs developed at the University of Illinois. Ryszard Michalski's group pursues theory, experiment and application with equal vigour. Michalski places the research in context philosophically, economically (with the promise of a payoff down on the farm) and socially. His principle of comprehensibility recalls Michie's plea for 'human windows'. In explaining why he has taken a particular technical approach, he invokes social and ethical considerations. He proposes that machine intelligence must always go in harness with human wisdom.

18 April 1985

Ryszard Michalski's intelligent systems group, part of the artificial intelligence laboratory at the University of Illinois, is one of the world's leading centres of research on machine learning.

Michalski says that his group's research has three branches, which develop in parallel. There is the theoretical work, which seeks an improved understanding of the process of learning. Then there is the work on programs and algorithms which actually demonstrate learning. 'The third direction,' explains Michalski, 'is applying those programs to very specific tasks, to see whether those programs indeed do something useful.'

The applied work has been mainly in agriculture and medicine, with subsidiary projects on chess and other subjects. One result which has achieved almost mythical status in the expert systems world was a set of rules for diagnosing soybean diseases. The rules were formulated by Michalski's AQ11 learning program, using 290 training examples. Each example was a description of various features of a diseased plant, together with an expert diagnosis of the plant's disease.

The machine-generated rules gave the correct disease top ranking 97.6 per cent of the time. Another set of rules, developed by human 'knowledge engineers' interviewing an expert plant pathologist, put the correct disease first only 71.8 per cent of the time.

'Learning has a special place in artificial intelligence, in my opinion,' says Michalski. 'We probably all agree that learning is central to intelligent behaviour. It is hard to imagine an intelligent person or a truly intelligent system that could not learn, that could for example repeat the same error again and again, never able to improve no matter how many times the procedure is repeated. We are now discovering that after many years of trying AI without learning, further progress in almost all areas of artificial intelligence very much demands progress in machine learning.'

As in the soybean example, machine learning may help to solve the 'knowledge bottleneck' problem in building expert systems. Michalski extends this to other areas of AI: 'In order to improve our vision systems, we have to be able to teach them visual concepts by example, rather than define everything by hand in the form of a program,' he says. 'The same in natural language understanding, the same in intelligent tutoring systems, or in robotics. All the major areas of artificial intelligence are now at the stage where further progress would greatly benefit by having learning capabilities implanted in the systems.'

Humans, and machine learning programs, often form general hypotheses from specific examples. Michalski points out that this process of inductive inference introduces an element of uncertainty. 'It leads to hypotheses or theories which may not be true, though the initial starting set of facts was true,' he maintains. 'Learning is a very dangerous type of activity because it may introduce things which are uncertain. So therefore the results of learning processes have to be tested. Now in order to test those results we have to understand those results.'

Michalski calls this the principle of comprehensibility. He argues that machine learning methods should produce knowledge in a form which corresponds closely to the way the same knowledge would be modelled in the human mind.

'The reason for strongly insisting on the principle of comprehensibility is that since you generate knowledge which may not be true, you are introducing a potential danger,' argues Michalski. If the knowlege is used, without understanding, in some new situation, 'It may lead to really very dangerous situations.' Michalski is serious about this. If we use a knowledge based system to recognize intercontinental missiles, he points out, we'd better understand how it works.

The solution he proposes is a 'knowledge ratification process'. 'Knowledge is generated by machines,' he explains, 'but a panel of experts looks at the knowledge, and ratifies it, and says, "this is the kind of knowledge which we have tested on some real data, and we are sufficiently confident that the knowledge can now be accepted by human society".'

Michalski's learning systems are intended to be useful in their own right, and not merely as models of human learning. But he argues that learning research must stay close to the human model. If the aim is to protect the principle of comprehensibility, we must know what kinds of things people can comprehend. Michalski believes machine learning researchers should work hand in hand with cognitive psychologists, as he has recently done himself.

Of course, a machine might learn a rule which is comprehensible to humans, without necessarily learning the same rule as a human would. Nor need the machine learn its rule in the same way as a human does. 'They are separate issues,' Michalski agrees. 'But you need a good model of the human mental processes which are involved in understanding and evaluating the result. So the studies which we do concentrate on the evaluation by humans of those results.'

But there is another motive, too, for studying human learning. We also try to understand how people arrive at those results,' Michalski adds, 'because those studies may give us some clues to better machine algorithms.'

He believes that it may be possible to formulate a computational theory of what it is possible to learn. But he points out that in practice, knowledge may be required in different forms for different purposes. His group has tried to build algorithms which produce knowledge in relatively simple notations, including one called annotated predicate calculus, which can be translated directly into natural language. The idea is that it may then be simple to translate the knowledge into other forms for specific purposes.

There is usually a trade-off. Learning algorithms are easier to write and quicker to run, if they use a relatively restricted language to express the rules that they learn. For example, the decision trees that are generated by Expert-Ease and similar programs are efficient, but can only learn a limited class of concepts. At the opposite extreme, no one knows how to write a program capable of learning every concept that can be expressed in English.

'So therefore you have to narrow down your language,' says Michalski. 'But then if you narrow down too much, you would be learning very simple, trivial concepts which are not that interesting. For example by restricting your language only to decision trees, as is done in Expert-Ease, you get solutions that sometimes are very incomprehensible, because you have a very limited language. But you do it very efficiently. We have been working with a more general language. Therefore the knowlege which we generate by our algorithm is in many cases much more easy to comprehend, and simpler in many ways. But it takes more computation.'

But Michalski argues that the trade-off is not always linear. 'By cleverly choosing the operators of your language,' he claims, 'you may suddenly gain more mileage by doing that, than you lose by increasing the complexity of your algorithm.'

Most AI researchers choose to represent knowledge in a form which allows some deductive inference mechanism to operate efficiently. Michalski's work, however, focuses on knowledge representations which can be learned – representations which allow efficient inductive inference. 'I would not say there is a conflict,' replies Michalski. 'There are simply two different criteria.'

'Most of the work in expert systems, knowledge representation and inference systems went into building representations which are good for deduction. We are saying that's not enough, because you not only want to use knowledge, you also want to update it, and even replace it by better knowledge.' Therefore, Michalski argues, you should not only consider the power of the language for representing things, and how easy it is to use the knowledge for drawing conclusions. 'You should take one more criterion into consideration, namely how easy it is to modify knowledge, or construct new knowledge. And that is exactly what we are trying to do, to somehow balance and take into consideration all three criteria.'

In March Michalski presented a paper at the Turing Institute's Machine Intelligence 11 workshop, on what he calls 'incremental learning' – the step by step acquisition of knowledge. 'Incremental learning', he explains, 'is a form of learning that we humans perform all the time. When we talk about very large knowledge structures, large knowledge bases which we will be building in the future for expert systems, then we will be facing incremental learning, because we cannot assume that each time we get more facts we have to redesign completely our knowledge base.'

The Illinois research has thrown attention on an important and potentially useful difference between human and machine learning. You know that nettles sting, but do you recall all the occasions that helped you to learn this? 'People have a hard time remembering facts,' Michalski points out 'but they remember, relatively well, simple and powerful theories. Machines have a hard time deriving powerful and simple theories, but can remember facts very well. So why not take advantage of the machine's ability to store and retrieve very many facts?'

This led to the idea of 'full-memory incremental learning'. This is something machines can do and humans cannot. Michalski points out that humans 'store some facts but not all of them. They just store representative facts.' The danger here is that as humans extend their theories, these may become inconsistent with facts which were once known and now are forgotten. (Though scientists, Michalski points out, can be fairly sure of maintaining consistency because they have a vast body of facts recorded in books.)

Machines with their vast memories need not fall into the trap of inconsistency. 'We'll be able to build very complex structures, modify them, but still make them consistent with all known facts,' says Michalski.

Intriguingly, philosophers have had difficulty with the idea of inductive inference. 'Not only Popper, but also Russell, Polya, and many other philosophers over many centuries starting with Aristotle, had certain problems with induction.'

One mistake the philosophers made, according to Michalski, was to imagine that induction was meant to produce true theories. This, he says, is impossible. His answer is to separate theory generation from validation, as in the 'knowledge ratification' process which checks that knowledge is not dangerous to human society.

'We cannot possibly do complete verification by machines,' Michalski argues, 'because we cannot put on the machine a complete model of the human mind, the human body, human goals, human expectations about the future, human relations. It is simply impossible to build a perfect model of a human being on a machine.'

Further reading

Michalski, R.S., Carbonell, J.B. and Mitchell, T. (1983). Eds. *Machine Learning: An Artificial Intelligence Approach*. Palo Alto, Calif.: Tioga Press.

22

Music as engineering

Many computer scientists are interested in music, but not many get to do a research project on it. This is a pity, because music provides tough challenges of many kinds for computer science. Music is physical. Like robotics, it is concerned with events in real time. As with natural language, or speech, or automatic programming, there is a synthesis problem, and an analysis problem. How is music created? How is it understood? And must machines understand music if they are to give us serious help in creating it?

Machines may generate music either with or without human cooperation. The problem is more interesting (and the music is likely to be, too) if human and machine work together on it. The creation of music is very much a design task, like laying out a magazine page, or writing a paragraph of clear English. Every decision has a chain of consequences, affecting decisions already made and others yet to be made. You stop when any further change you can imagine makes things worse rather than better. You hope you end up with something good. That, informally stated, is the method of constraint propagation.

The idea of computer aided design is that you make the decisions, and the machine chases the chains of consequences. This could be a good approach to musical design, too.

People often describe music as a 'language', but it differs in important respects both from natural languages such as English, and from programming languages. To be sure, music has a syntax: within a given style of music, certain musical structures are 'legal' and others are not. But in the West, our musical styles have changed much faster than the way we speak. Musical syntax is much more fluid and mutable than English syntax.

A person educated in musical theory can describe the syntactic structure of a musical passage. This might involve identifying the key or tonality, remarking key changes or modulations, naming scales, chords and cadences, and identifying a hierarchy of rhythmic units with the bar as the basic repeating unit. Grammarians do something similar when they parse an English sentence. The experts do this consciously and explicitly, but there would not be much point in their efforts unless they believed that all of us possess, somewhere between our ears, some secret knowledge of both musical and linguistic syntax.

Alternative parsings seem to arise much more frequently in music than in natural language. Actually it is wrong to describe them as alternatives, since they are not mutually exclusive. You can choose to hear the opening of Bach's first cello suite as a single stream of notes rising and falling. Or you can hear it as polyphony – three or four voices, each marking out its own musical line. Quite possibly you will hear the piece both ways at the same time. Ambiguity is the very stuff of musical expression and understanding. Douglas Hofstadter, who has his own chapter in this book (Chapter 26), has elsewhere written about this much better than I can.

Music theorists know perfectly well that their theories capture only a part of musical syntax. The rest is locked up in their minds as securely as it is in everybody else's. Could musicians be persuaded to make more of this knowledge explicit, in the same way as geologists or physicians yield up their knowledge to builders of expert systems? Or would it be better to let a computer program learn for itself, from actual samples of music?

Perhaps the strangest thing about music as a language is that though it has a syntax, it has no universally agreed semantics. Of course, in *Peter and the Wolf* or the score of a *Tom and Jerry* cartoon, musical sounds can be identified almost one-to-one with characters, things and events. But what on earth does it mean to say that a symphony is full of forebodings of the Second World War? A composer simply does not write a whole symphony as a roundabout way of saying 'I think there's a war coming'. If the symphony has a meaning at all (and perhaps we are wrong to always look for meaning in music), it means a whole lot more than that.

David Levitt is one computer scientist who has not only done the obligatory syntactic stuff, but has thought about some questions of a more semantic nature: for instance, 'What is humour in music?'

---

8 November 1984

It will be some time before the style and structure of a piece of recorded music can be analysed automatically in any but the most elementary terms. An essential preliminary is to devise a language for compact, high-level descriptions of music.

To be useful, such descriptions should require very much less information than a digital representation of the original sound wave. And they should reflect the way we naturally understand music, including information which is not stated explicitly in a printed score.

Fully automated musical composition is one possiblity. But perhaps the most interesting prospects are for human–machine cooperation both in making music and in listening to it. The extent of the human partner's contribution would be limited only by his or her inclinations and abilities.

For professional musicians the system might beocme a creativity amplifier, a computer aided design system for musical compositions and performances.

Novel consumer products could also result. Some electronic organs now provide simple canned harmonies and rhythms to support the shaky performance of the one-finger pianist. Future home instruments may allow amateurs to plan and control music in more powerful ways, without actually playing an instrument in the usual sense of the word.

Personal stereo players may have controls, not only for tone, volume and balance but for rhythm, harmony, instrumentation and perhaps even the style and mood of the music. Record shops would sell software for such machines. Each program would be capable of generating a vast number of subtly different performances, unlike today's records which capture a single performance only.

David Levitt proposed a machine of this kind when he was employed as a consultant by Atari. While he was with Roger Schank's group at Yale University, Levitt had written a jazz improvisation program. The program used simple heuristics or rules of thumb to compose jazz solos, given a melody and chord progression as raw material. Now, at the Massachusetts Institute of Technology, Levitt is developing a 'music representation language', and front-end software for creating and manipulating its constructs.

The language is based on the theory of music that is taught to music students. Most musicians would accept that the standard theory of music is far from complete, and Levitt feels this particularly strongly. As an amateur jazz piano player with an engineering background, he finds that standard music theory lacks the rigour of an engineering discipline. And he feels that it is based on a narrow definition of music. It has no words for most of the things which happen when Fats Waller plays the piano.

Levitt regards music as a branch of engineering. Bridges and aeroplanes either work or they don't. In music too, according to Levitt, 'There's a sense in which a piece succeeds or it fails: you're creating an effect.' The difference, he says, is that engineers use explicit theories to justify their designs. Artists succeed without knowing how. 'With a good psychological model,' he claims, 'you could make much better music.'

Levitt's music language is designed to be used in both directions. 'You can generate the music from the description or vice versa,' he says. Transforming a description into music is the easier of the two tasks. To extract a description from a given piece of recorded music – or even from a score – is more difficult. This is a substantial problem in pattern recognition or machine perception. At the moment Levitt gets little help from his software and does this job mainly by hand and ear.

Once you have an abstract description of a piece of music you can do surprising things with it. You can combine the harmonic plan of a Bach motet with a rhythmic plan from Dixieland jazz. Such experiments do not necessarily produce good music. The results are likely to be less dramatic, but more reliable, when elements are combined from two pieces of music in broadly similar styles.

Levitt's music language is one of a class of declarative languages known as constraint languages. He investigated constraint languages because they generate models which can be run 'forwards' or 'backwards' with almost equal ease.

His choice was also guided by the experience of improvising at the piano. In jazz improvisation, and no doubt also in classical composition, the choice of pitch for a note is constrained both by the overall shape of the melody and by the underlying harmonic progressions. Often, more than one choice would be consistent with the constraints. Constraint languages readily model this kind of situation.

In most programming languages, the statement $X = Y \star Z$ means 'multiply Y by Z and store the result in the variable X.' This only handles the situation where Y and X are known and X is unknown.

What happens when Y is the unknown quantity instead? Anyone with a knowledge of elementary mathematics knows how to reshape the equation $X = Y \star Z$ into $Y = X / Z$ (with suitable caveats about dividing by zero). This is the kind of knowledge that is built into constraint languages. The symbol $\star$ no longer refers to a single procedure (multiplication) but to a constraint which applies to the three variables. A number of alternative procedures or algorithms may be attached to a constraint. In this example, a multiplication algorithm would take care of cases where Y and Z are both known. A division algorithm would be invoked when X and Z were known and Y unknown.

One of the best known constraint languages is TK!Solver, marketed as an 'equation processor' by Software Arts. Users can set up a system of equations, and enter values for some of the variables. The program then works through the equations, filling in values for the remaining variables. It asks for help if it is given too little data or if its limited mathematical knowledge is overtaxed.

Some computer models, including some expert systems, are essentially sausage-machines for data. You pile information in at one end and results come out at the other. For some applications this may well be the right approach. A model built with a constraint language is different. It can be run in any direction. Whatever information is supplied, it uses. Whatever is missing, it attempts to infer. Information propagates in all directions through the network of constraints. The result is a system which can equally well suggest a chord to harmonize a given note in a given key, or find a note to be played over a given chord, or guess at the key of the music if this is not known. All this from a single constraint called 'consonance'.

Levitt's music language will be extensible. Musicians using it will be able to develop their own personal vocabularies. Later, induction algorithms could be added, to create a system which learns by example. Levitt believes that musical styles could be analysed automatically. Supplied with two examples of Scott Joplin rags, the system would home in on the essential structural features of the Joplin style. Levitt admits that his programs cannot distinguish good ragtime from bad ragtime. But he believes that increasingly sophisticated analysis of musical structure will gradually lead into the areas we think of as aesthetic.

You might think that humour, for example, is an aesthetic property of music. But Levitt believes that one can formulate a structural definition of a 'musical joke'. Musical jokes arise when the music sets up two or more expectations in the listener and then takes the less expected alternative. Levitt demonstrates this at the keyboard by introducing a false cadence into the harmonies of 'Tea for two'.

He is committed to music as engineering, and believes that the engineering approach will produce better music – music that achieves the desired effect more reliably. An understanding of what makes music 'danceable' could lead to many possibilities, including carefully programmed disco hits.

Some music-lovers might see this approach as cold-blooded. But Levitt can see little harm in bringing understanding to areas, such as musical aesthetics, which are currently shrouded in mystery.

David Levitt completed his doctoral thesis, on the representation of musical styles, in the summer of 1985. After that he joined MIT's Center for Arts and Media Technology and worked on a pictorial or iconic programming language. Initially it was intended for music, but it grew into a general purpose programming language which Levitt says is easy for novices to use.

In the same brand-new building Alan Kay started a project in which children studied the behaviour of animals in a vivarium. One thing the children did was to create animal computer programs, in which they tried to model some of the behaviour they had seen in the vivarium. With Levitt's iconic language this was no longer a program-writing task – it was more like building, on the computer screen, an electrical circuit of the animal.

There are a few commercial computer games which give children a taste of iconic programming. A.K. Dewdney (Chapter 43) skilfully described one of them, Robot Odyssey, in his *Scientific American* column.

Incidentally, some people regard logic languages including Prolog as members of the class of constraint languages. Prolog (Chapter 41) handles some things by forward reasoning and others by backward reasoning. Also it can be said to search for solutions which satisfy a set of constraints, though there is no gradual optimization or 'hill-climbing': Prolog either succeeds or fails.

Frank Kriwaczek, of Imperial College, London, used Prolog to write a spreadsheet program which goes one step beyond TK!Solver. Not only does it calculate values and solve equations in arithmetic: it does similar tricks in the realm of logic. (Though it has to be said that Logicalc is not as clever with figures as the finely-honed product from Software Arts.) On the screen you see a two-dimensional grid of cells. The cells can contain numbers, lists, diagrams or pieces of text. As with any spreadsheet, you must define how the contents of the various cells are related. Then, if you fill some of the cells, Logicalc will try to fill the remaining cells with values that satisfy the relations (or constraints) that you have imposed. Income tax is the kind of thing that should be meat and drink to Logicalc: some fairly straightforward arithmetic embedded in a mass of rules of a more or less logical character.

Further reading

Dewdney, A. (1985). 'Computer recreations' *Scientific American*, July.

Hofstadter, D.R. (1985). 'Pattern, poetry and power in the music of Frédéric Chopin'. In *Metamagical Themas*. New York: Basic Books. (Originally appeared in *Scientific American*, April 1982.)

Levitt, D. (1984). 'Machine tongues X: constraint languages' *Computer Music Journal*, **8**, no. 1, Spring.

23

The heart has its reasons

Human memory is capacious, but it can retain only a minute fraction of the constant torrent of information reaching our eyes and ears. We therefore have to select significant observations, seek patterns, form general rules and, as Ryszard Michalski pointed out, forget facts.

A little deep knowledge is more valuable than much superficial knowledge. Deep knowledge implies an awareness of the inner workings of things, and an ability to answer the question 'Why?' Deep knowledge gives the right answer, even when the situation is grossly altered and unfamiliar. Physicists have some claim to a deep knowledge of the behaviour of matter, having found laws which remain valid in the core of a neutron star or during the early moments of the Big Bang.

By contrast, expert systems tend to fail embarrassingly when taken beyond their familiar territory. Many of them cannot explain their judgements in terms that would satisfy a human enquirer. It would seem to be a good idea, when possible, to equip expert systems with a knowledge of the inner workings of things.

Machines tend to be comprehensible because they consist of separate parts with separate purposes, assembled in ways which limit the types of interaction which can occur. Causes are easily distinguished: 'The motor is not running, because the fuse has blown'. People can have a deep knowledge of machines, because machines are designed by people.

No one designed the human heart, and we have no right to expect that it should be susceptible to such a mechanistic analysis. Remarkably, it is.

2 May 1985

The heart is a mechanical pump with an electrical control system. Doctors can monitor the heart's electrical system by recording voltages which appear on the surface of the body. For most of us, an electrocardiogram is just a wiggly line on a screen. For TV producers that glowing squiggle (accompanied by regular thuds or bleeps on the soundtrack) is a convenient way to signal that the programme which follows has something to do with medicine. For a trained expert, however, the heart writes its signature and reveals its secrets in the electrocardiogram.

Heart specialists and computer scientists in the Yugoslav city of Ljubljana have developed an expert system which can diagnose electrical disorders of the heart, using as its input a qualitative description of the electrocardiograph (ECG) recording. The expert system, known as Kardio-E, is a remarkable for three reasons.

First, it works. Its diagnoses may not be quite as accurate as those of heart specialists, but its designers believe it performs as well as, say, a consultant physician whose work regularly involves interpreting electrocardiograms.

The next thing to be said is that the system was built using 'deep' knowledge of the workings of the heart. It is not just a computerized collection of rules of thumb. Ultimately, all the knowledge in the system is derived from medical experts or from books. But the computer has been used to synthesize new knowledge which was implied in the textbooks but never made explicit.

A third significant feature is the type of model that was used to represent the heart. Even though pulse-rates and voltages have numerical values, the model contains no numbers. Instead, it is based on qualitative descriptions similar to those that doctors themselves use when talking about the heart. Far from being imprecise, these qualitative descriptions may actually give more relevant information than mere numbers.

The system was developed by Ivan Bratko, Nada Lavrac and Igor Mozetic of the Jozef Stefan Institute, with medical colleagues at Ljubljana's University Medical Centre, led by Matija Horvat. Bratko spoke about the project at the Machine Intelligence 11 workshop, held near Glasgow during March. An account also appeared in the January 1985 issue of the journal *Expert Systems*.

Bratko was trained as an electrical engineer. Most of his research has been in artificial intelligence and expert systems. He and his colleagues built their causal model by hand, using knowledge about the physiology of the heart, gathered from experts and from books. 'Medical descriptions of the heart are qualitative,' he points out, though he knew that the changing voltages and propagating impulses are physical processes which could be described, in principle, by differential equations.

Bratko believes that a numerical model of the heart would not have worked. For one thing, the necessary computations would have been too complicated. 'Also there would be problems,' he adds, 'because the knowledge that we were using was from the medical literature, from physiologists and cardiologists, and that was all qualitative. All the descriptions are linguistic.'

Doctors favour qualitative descriptions even when they are talking about measured quantities like an individual's heart rate. 'They would not say it is 98 beats per minute,' says Bratko. 'They would say it is normal, or it is tachycardia, or it is fibrillation. In some patients they would say, this is a normal rate. In another patient they would say, this is tachycardia.' Hearts vary in size and in their mechanical and electrical properties. So a rate which is normal for one person may be abnormally fast for another.

'The model can be pictured, and it would look like an electrical network,' says Bratko. 'But what travels in an electrical network would be voltages, real electrical signals. In our model what travels along these pathways are symbolic descriptions, or qualitative descriptions of these impulses.' The model contains logical rules which determine what will happen to the impulses in each part of the heart.

The model can represent about 30 different things which can go wrong with different parts of the heart. Several of these 'elementary disorders' may be present simultaneously. The most direct way to use the model is to run a simulation, with some chosen combination of elementary disorders present. The model will then produce a description – still qualitative – of the possible ECG patterns that could result.

The model is described in Prolog, and like any Prolog database it can be interrogated in many different ways. For diagnostic purposes it would be useful to run the model backwards, so as to find what disorders are consistent with a given ECG description. 'That turned out to be computationally rather expensive,' says Bratko, 'so what we did was, we generated ECG descriptions for all possible combinations of disorders. We made a complete knowledge base.'

Fortunately it was not necessary to catalogue millions of possible disorders. Constraints built into the model ruled out many combinations of disorders which simply could not exist together. That left just 587 possible cardiac arrhythmias. Some of them were quite complex, but none was composed of more than seven elementary disorders. The resulting knowledge base consisted of 587 rules, each of the form '*if* arrhythmia is A, *then* its ECG pattern is E.' E would normally be a complex expression describing a range of possible ECG patterns.

All the knowledge used in the model was already familiar to cardiologists or recorded in textbooks. But never before had anyone attempted such a thorough and systematic classification of cardiac arrhythmias. The first version of the knowledge base was evaluated by cardiologists, using 36 clinical cases. Some deficiencies were found and remedied. An improved version of the knowledge base consisted of 8314 rules, relating 2419 arrhythmias to 140,966 corresponding ECG patterns. Bratko believes it would have been impossible to compile this knowledge base by hand.

The resulting expert system does not contain any explicit representation of the 'deep' knowledge that was used to synthesize it.

Indeed, the system gets away with very little logical inference. It is almost, but not quite, a table look-up operation. Not quite, because the 140,966 ECG patterns are not stored explicitly. One cannot just look up a pattern and read off the corresponding diagnosis. Instead, the system tries to match the patient's ECG against each of the stored, abstract ECG descriptions in turn. It finds a diagnosis by eliminating other diagnoses which are inconsistent with the patient's ECG.

Even though the system's knowledge is in this sense superficial, the user can ask it for explanations. If the user favours a diagnosis that the system has rejected, the system will state which features of the patient's ECG it regarded as inconsistent with that diagnosis.

No deep knowledge is involved in that. But the system reveals deeper knowledge in explanations of another kind. Suppose the user picks on a diagnosis which is theoretically impossible – a diagnosis which flouts the physiological constraints built into the model. As far as the system is concerned, this diagnosis must be wrong, whatever the patient's ECG pattern. In this case the system will explain which constraints in the model have been violated.

Version two of Kardio-E is not necessarily the ultimate expert system on heart arrhythmias, but it satisfies practical requirements. 'You can describe the heart at different levels or detail,' Bratko points out. 'You don't want to put too much detail into it because you don't want to have it too complicated.'

The aim was to obtain diagnoses which were detailed enough to allow doctors to select a suitable treatment. 'The first version turned out to be not quite sufficient for that,' says Bratko. 'The second version is sufficient to correctly handle 95 per cent of patients who have an arrhythmia.' That is an estimate. More precise measures of the system's performance should emerge once it has been through an international evaluation study involving some of the world's leading cardiologists.

One of Bratko's earlier expert systems, developed with Igor Kononenko and designed to guess the site of the primary tumour from which cancer cells had spread through the body, actually outperformed the experts. This time, however, Bratko will be happy even if the computer's guesses are not quite as good as those of a top cardiologist. 'Our goal here,' he says, 'is that it should compare favourably to practitioners who do ECG interpretation routinely but who are not really specialists in cardiology.'

If the computer outperforms these second-rank experts it will not be through superior knowledge but through inhuman thoroughness. According to Bratko, doctors sometimes fail to consider all possible interpretations of the ECG.

On this occasion a knowledge base was derived deductively from an abstract model. But Bratko has a longstanding interest in inductive learning algorithms which reason in the opposite direction, from examples to a general rule. Learning algorithms such as those of Ryszard Michalski can distil large databases down to relatively small numbers of rules, sometimes revealing significant structure in the data.

Bratko's group fed their cardiology knowledge base into a number of learning systems, including Michalski's, to see what would happen. As an exercise in data compression this was a resounding success. The six-megabyte rule base shrank to 25 kilobytes.

Builders of expert systems sometimes look to machine learning algorithms to formulate theories and extract significant generalizations from their data. In this sense, Kardio-E had nothing to learn, since from the start it was based on a physiological theory. Nevertheless, Michalski's algorithm performed outstandingly in its humbler role of saving disk space.

The heart is comprehensible because it is not a black box. Quite literally, we can open it up and see what makes it tick. It is significant that modern medical science began to develop when Europe shed the taboo on dissection. It would be very hard to understand how the body works without knowing something of how it is constructed. In Western medical thinking, physiology without anatomy is inconceivable. Our deep knowledge was won with the knife.

It remains an extraordinary fact that human and animal bodies do (at least to a first approximation) consist of separate organs with separate functions. Science fiction writers delight in imagining lifeforms that consist of undifferentiated gup. Such creatures are frightening because they are so different from us, having more in common with inanimate objects like rivers and thunderclouds. But people are visibly built like machines, and the theory that the body is a machine has been astonishingly fruitful for medical science.

The idiocies and excesses of Western medicine are often attributed to its mechanistic attitude. This may well be a correct diagnosis. But perhaps there is nothing wrong with mechanistic explanations, and the mistake is to treat a complex machine as a simple one. Would you attempt to repair a robot by strapping it to a couch and passing a high voltage discharge through its computer circuitry?

Computer programming used to be all physiology and no anatomy. Software was unstructured and incomprehensible, like some pulp writer's vision of jellyfish from Mars. Now the software trade has begun to build programs which can be dissected, programs which have separable parts with defined functions, programs which at last are built the way people have always built machines.

Further reading

Gregory, R.L. (1984). *Mind in Science*. Harmondsworth: Penguin. (Chapter 3 contains an illuminating discussion of the questions 'What is a machine?' and 'What are mechanistic explanations?')

24

Gene research calls for intelligence

Molecular biology has exposed the living cell as a wonderful and immensely complex machine. Each kind of protein or nucleic acid seems to be fitted to a well-defined function in the cell. The whole system appears to have been designed, painstakingly though not always elegantly. The occasional lack of elegance is inevitable, since natural selection designs without the benefit of deep knowledge. It can perfect an eye, by millions of years of trial and error, without ever formulating the principles of optics.

Proteins themselves are built from a standard kit of parts, the twenty amino-acids. But whereas the smallest nut or bolt in a machine has a well-defined function, one can rarely say the same of an amino-acid residue in a protein. Most of them just help, collectively, to make the molecule the right shape. At this scale the atoms of carbon, hydrogen, nitrogen and oxygen, which existed before life and have not changed one jot for its sake, begin to assert their identity. They do strange things which only quantum theory can explain. They refuse to be treated as billiard balls. So the individual protein molecule is not particularly machine-like, and it is hard to predict its behaviour from a knowledge of its parts.

Since the heart contains astronomical numbers of protein molecules, it is possibly surprising that the arrhythmias of the heart should be more susceptible to mechanistic modelling than the configurations of a single protein molecule. This illustrates an important truth about scientific explanations, which scientists themselves have often failed to acknowledge. A scientific explanation of the heart need not, indeed should not reduce its behaviour to that of billions of protein molecules. The best explanation of the heart is one which, as far as possible, is independent of what happens down at the molecular level. Pacemakers, valves and chambers are the appropriate abstractions for a model of the heart. Cardiologists do not want to know about the implementation at the molecular level, any more than Prolog programmers want to know about the solder joints inside their computers.

Physicists often claim that physics explains everything. This is nonsense. What they really mean is that when (if) God created the Universe, the only laws he had to impose were those of physics. Chemistry, biology and the rest developed as the universe evolved.

But science is not about how you create a universe. It is about how you understand a universe, without God-like omniscience. It is all about finding usually valid abstractions and approximations, so that you can ignore the detail and comprehend the grand scheme. These approximate theories are the stuff of chemistry and biology, and indeed of much of physics. As a statement of faith, some physicists may claim that quantum mechanics or general relativity are different from other scientific theories because they correspond exactly to reality. They may be right. But the theories which are today known to be approximate include many, such as Newtonian mechanics, which were once believed to be exact.

Atomic physics does not help to explain protein structures. In fact it gets in the way. It would be much easier if we could model atoms as billiard balls and chemical bonds as sticks. But atoms are not like that, and they let us know it.

---

11 October 1984

Nucleic acid, the stuff of genes, is life's source code. It is translated or, in computer jargon, compiled to protein by the cell's protein synthesis machinery. Almost everything that happens in a living cell is performed or controlled by enzymes and other protein molecules.

Programs for the construction and maintenance of living organisms are written in a universal genetic code which varies hardly at all across the whole kingdom of life. Important discoveries in biology have been made by the exhaustive analysis of proteins and, more recently, by the 'sequencing' of genes. Biologists find themselves in the same position as an engineer confronted with an unfamiliar, undocumented mainframe computer and its software. This enormous intellectual problem is providing a testing ground for artificial intelligence techniques.

Cancer research made a rare leap forward when the sequence of an oncogene – a cancer gene carried in this case by a virus – was matched with the amino acid pattern of a growth factor found in normal cells. It appeared that some cancers may arise when perfectly normal genes are switched on in error.

That discovery was made by a brute force search of a database of nucleic acid and protein sequences held on magnetic tape. But more genes and proteins are being sequenced every month, the databases are growing, and biologists are feeling the need for subtler methods of identifying matching sequences.

Fast string search routines such as Xsearch are available when an exact match is sought. The trouble is that exact matches rarely occur in biology.

In fact biologists are often looking for tenuous relationships. When two proteins with quite different functions have evolved from a single ancestral protein, only faint traces of their common origin may remain. The problem then may be to match two strings in which some characters have been altered; or, trickier still, where characters have been deleted and the gap closed up, or where new characters have been inserted.

Simple statistical methods can be used to measure how good a possible match is, but these methods treat the sequence as a meaningless string of symbols. It is, of course, nothing of the sort. The sequence is loaded with biological meaning. Statistical methods tend to throw up spurious 'hits', and the number of these grows in step with the growth of the database. At the same time, the search task itself becomes lengthier. The computational effort increases, but the quality of results declines.

'We want to be able to describe the sequence in biological terms, so the scientist can then query the database in biological terms,' says John Fox, head of the biomedical computing unit at the Imperial Cancer Research Fund. This calls for a system which can handle biologically relevant concepts and make logical inferences about them.

Protein chains fold up spontaneously into characteristic three-dimensional shapes. In theory, a protein's three-dimensional structure could be deduced from its amino acid sequence and a full knowledge of the complicated forces between atoms. The molecule always seeks a stable configuration in which no energy can be released by any further rearrangement.

The ICRF computing unit is collaborating with crystallographers at Birkbeck College, London. With many years experience of computing, the Birkbeck group has developed computer programs which attempt to predict parts of the three-dimensional structure of a protein from its sequence. Such predictions are useful both in basic research and in more commercial activities such as the design of new drugs. Complete three-dimensional structures cannot be predicted with accuracy at present. Mike Sternberg and Willy Taylor and their colleagues at Birkbeck have developed elaborate techniques for predicting the ways in which local regions of a protein molecule will fold themselves into so-called secondary structures. These predictions have been roughly 80 per cent successful. Some other laboratories have only reached a 60 per cent success rate. Now the Birkbeck group hopes to boost its accuracy to 90 or 95 per cent.

Traditionally protein structures are given a hierarchical description. The raw data from X-ray crystallography is a set of coordinates giving the positions of atoms in three-dimensional space. But the simplest biologically meaningful description is the molecule's amino acid sequence or primary structure. Locally, parts of the amino acid chain will adopt characteristic 'secondary structures' such as the alpha helix or the beta strand. A change in secondary structure accounts for the shrinking of wool. Tertiary structure is the name given to the overall folding which gives the molecule its characteristic shape.

The Birkbeck work has made use of an intermediate level of description, in terms of 'super-secondary structure' or 'structural motifs'. A structural motif may be built up from several different secondary structures. The concept is useful because the same motifs crop up in many different protein molecules. They are given descriptive names such as 'hairpin' and 'Greek key'. Each structural motif was formally defined in terms of the spatial relations between its parts. These relations were given names such as 'contiguous' and 'neighbour'.

Descriptions of protein structures, translated into somewhat cryptic alphanumeric codes, were being handled by programs in FORTRAN, a language designed mainly for numerical problems. The ICRF team felt that another language would be more suitable. Chris Rawlings undertook to develop, in Prolog, a representation of protein structures that would include motifs.

Prolog is based on a form of logic, the predicate calculus, which naturally expresses relations between objects such as parts of a protein chain.

'In five minutes we wrote a definition of a hairpin,' says Rawlings. The definition took the form of a Prolog rule. The same definition in FORTRAN might have required three quarters of a page of code.

It was not hard to make the Prolog statements look quite like English, for example 'strand (A) is contiguous with strand (B)'. But the shift to an AI language was not without its own problems. The Prolog representation of the data may be more powerful, but it also eats up memory and processing power. 'One of the real problems is handling the data volume within the Prolog implementations that exist at the moment,' Rawlings comments.

Data compression can reduce search times. One method is Huffman coding, which replaces common sequences of characters by short codes. This technique is used to compress English text both in huge mainframe databases and in small systems like Psion's pocket computer.

The statistics of protein and DNA sequences have been less thoroughly studied than those of English text. But Martin Bishop of the Cambridge University Department of Zoology has extracted some common sequences and used them to compress biological data.

At the ICRF, the focus is on intelligent search strategies which may cut down the time spent constructing lengthy but unfruitful chains of logical inferences. Prolog has built-in mechanisms for searching a database and performing logical inferences. So the definition of, say, a 'Greek key' can be purely declarative. The definition simply states what a Greek key is. Prolog itself works out a procedure for finding one.

The trouble is that left to itself, Prolog may search in a very inefficient manner. The Prolog interpreter cannot know the most efficient search strategy for a particular problem. That requires extra knowledge. It is up to the programmer to inject that knowledge in one way or another. Like any programming language, Prolog works best for someone who knows a little about what goes on under the 'hood'.

'When you write code in other programming languages you use your knowledge of the problem and the algorithmic solution to make the program run faster,' explains Rawlings. 'When you write Prolog you do the same.' Failure to understand this has led to much misplaced criticism of Prolog.

There are two basic ways of tuning Prolog's performance for a specific problem domain such as protein sequence analysis. One approach is to use a cleverly constructed knowledge base. At its simplest, this could mean re-ordering the clauses (statements) in the program so that Prolog automatically picks the juiciest plums – the clauses most likely to lead to a solution – first.

But the knowledge representation that suits the machine best may not be the most natural for the biologist. Another defect of this approach is that someone else may not be able to see why the programmer constructed the knowledge base in this particular way. The specific knowledge which makes the search more efficient remains implicit.

Rawlings favours an alternative approach, in which the extra knowledge is injected into the Prolog interpreter, rather than the main knowledge base.

'You write a Prolog interpreter which knows something about the domain, and therefore executes an intelligent search algorithm instead of a blind one.' In practice, Rawlings explains, the Prolog interpreter would not be rewritten from scratch. It is simpler to write an extra layer of Prolog code, to sit on top of the standard interpreter. This means that the knowledge base could be constructed in a way that makes sense to biologists.

And the additional knowledge or 'meta-knowledge' built into the special purpose interpreter, would be expressed in explicit, declarative form. In theory at least, it should be easy for a newcomer to understand the strategies built into the interpreter, and modify them if necessary.

The powerful underlying idea is that a knowledge-based or expert system can contain a small 'meta-expert system' embodying all the knowledge which makes the main system run fast and efficiently. And in artificial intelligence, efficiency is not a matter of 10 or 20 per cent extra performance. It is the difference between failure and success.

Perhaps this article did not sufficiently emphasize the main purpose of using AI in protein structure prediction. The researchers are not so interested in a small increase of accuracy as they are in a big increase of speed. Their work would be transformed if tertiary structure predictions could be performed interactively, instead of taking an hour or two on a supercomputer. The argument for using AI, Chris Rawlings explains, is that 'By using appropriate representations and by introducing diverse knowledge sources we can keep the search space as small as possible'.

The collaboration between the ICRF and Birkbeck College has prospered since the appointment of Jane Nyakairu, who officially works for both institutions. Among her contributions is a FORTRAN program which automatically converts the original protein structure data into Prolog clauses.

The many kinds of knowledge involved, and the sheer size of the databases, make this a challenging domain for leading-edge research on intelligent databases and database machines. During 1985 the ICRF entered into two collaborative projects which will draw upon the research reported here. The first, with Hewlett Packard Laboratories, is all about using knowledge to reduce search spaces and speed up inference. The second is concerned with novel hardware, a 'content addressable relational database machine' (CARDS). It is supported by the Alvey Directorate. The other participants are GEC and Reading University.

American biologists have recently been campaigning for a vast research programme with the aim of sequencing the entire human complement of genes. Such a grand trawl for knowledge would be unthinkable without computers. If it goes ahead, AI techniques will probably be required to create and manage the vast database which results. I suggest that they will certainly be needed to extract useful scientific knowledge from this bewildering mass of data.

Further reading

Rawlings, C.J., Taylor, W.R., Nyakairu, J., Fox, J. and Sternberg, M.J.E. (1985). 'Reasoning about protein topology using the logic programming language Prolog' *Journal of Molecular Graphics,* **3**, December.

25

OCR: a problem tougher than speech?

For some reason, teaching computers to read is an unfashionable line of research. The commercial potential is obvious. The intellectual pay-off for cognitive science could be substantial: if Julian Ullmann does not convince you of this, perhaps Douglas Hofstadter (Chapter 26) will. Everyone agrees that it is a tough problem; but since when has that discouraged either the AI community or the agencies which provide its funding?

16 February 1984

The ability to read grubby, unfamiliar handwriting is among the least celebrated and most mysterious of human mental achievements. But it could be the key to a world market worth billions of pounds per annum, according to Julian Ullmann of Sheffield University.

Ullmann is the chairman of the Alvey programme's Pattern Analysis Committee. He personally believes that 'The commercial potential for low-cost input of information from documents is fantastic'. But he also says that the Alvey programme may be the wrong framework for such an open-ended research project. The Alvey Directorate has initially been set up for a five-year period.

'This is an area where you cannot buy results by pouring in money,' claims Ullmann. 'The whole thing is inspiration-dependent. The timescale is unpredictable. It won't necessarily take twenty years. It could be done in the next three weeks.'

Optical character recognition (OCR) is not mentioned in the recently completed strategy document for the man–machine interface area of the Alvey programme. Alvey's MMI Director, Chris Barrow, explained: 'We are dealing with the fundamental problems of pattern analysis and image processing, which could be applied to OCR. It is not specific to OCR.'

The capabilities of commercial OCR equipment reached a plateau some years ago. The main advance since then is attributable to large scale integration, which has made the equipment smaller and less expensive. There are desk-top units, and hand-held wands which can be brushed over passports and similar documents. The range of machine-readable fonts has grown. Long ago, the OCR-A alphabet (which appeared to suffer from swollen glands) was supplemented by the more comely OCR-B. For more than ten years it has been possible to read standard typewriter fonts by machine. But the market has remained small. To use OCR successfully, the organization which reads the documents may need to have control over their printing. OCR, as it exists today, cannot handle a company's general incoming paperwork.

The machines can be upset by the slight line broadening which occurs on multipart forms and on documents repeatedly photocopied. Dot matrix printer output is unsuitable unless the printer is designed and operated in such a way as to produce overlapping dots.

Some users have found OCR to be a cost-effective method of moving data from a keyboard into a computer. One small OCR machine, reading 300 characters per second, can process the output of dozens of typewriters.

OCR is widely used for 'turnaround documents' like gas and electricity bill counterfoils. A phrase like 'leave this space clear for office use' usually identifies the machine-readable part of the form.

Machines have appeared which can read 'handprint'. Some gas and electricity boards use them to process the slips filled in by meter readers. But a typical handprint machine can only recognize hand printed numerals 0 to 9 and letters C, S, T and X. The characters have to be formed to defined shapes, by trained personnel. The main reasons for using OCR here, rather than the less sophisticated technology of optical mark reading (OMR), are that OMR is more prone to human error and requires a physically larger form.

Some progress in the machine analysis of handwriting has been achieved with pressure-sensitive pads which record the movements of the pen. The time-sequence of movements gives important information about the writer's intentions. It is much harder to recover that information from the resulting scrawl, by optical methods.

In optical methods the most powerful injection of new technology has not come from the OCR manufacturers at all. It has come from thrusting new firms selling machine vision systems for robot vision and automatic inspection. Some of these manufacturers have made a feature of their machine's ability to recognize alphanumeric characters. In an automated factory, such machines can read the serial number on a vehicle chassis or a silicon wafer, where the characters may be blurred or low in contrast. The equipment copes well with smudged, damaged, rotated or misaligned characters.

Applied Intelligent Systems and Machine Vision International are two machine vision companies which offer character recognition capabilities. Based in Ann Arbor, Michigan, both companies are spin-offs from the Environmental Research Institute of Michigan, a defence contractor which is believed to have worked on pattern recognition for cruise missile guidance systems.

Cognex, of Needham, Massachusetts, claims to use 'high-level strategies drawn from research in human perception'. Machine vision consultant Don Braggins is impressed with the Cognex equipment's ability to read imperfect or partially obscured characters. 'I have seen it working where a line had been drawn right through the characters. It will still work,' he said. But the system has to be 'trained' to read a new font. It does not have the human ability to read characters in whatever typeface comes along.

In Britain, the Home Office is using machine vision techniques experimentally, to read the number plates of cars travelling on the M1 motorway. Rapid motion, and variable lighting and visibility conditions make this a challenging environment for a vision system. Fortunately for the Home Office, number plates are retro-reflective. They can therefore be highlighted by an infra-red source mounted close to the camera.

Ingenious as it is, this rather specialized technology seems to be more useful for surveillance and detection on the roads than for any general industrial or commercial application. Once extracted from the background and 'cleaned up', a number plate does not present a very severe character recognition problem.

OCR technology has run into a barrier very similar to that which now faces speech recognition technology. Machines can do a useful job in carefully controlled conditions, but a breakthrough is needed to make the next step towards a 'human' type of ability, either for reading or for understanding the spoken word. OCR has an added handicap: for some reason it has failed to become a 'trendy' research topic in the way that speech has. But according to Ullmann, 'Speech is almost certainly easier because of its limited dimensionality'.

The 'back end' of an advanced OCR system will probably have a lot in common with those other activities which require language analysis: speech recognition, natural language programming, and machine translation. The system will need to know what words exist, how they can be put together, and what they mean – so that ambiguous messages can be resolved by referring to the context. Limited schemes for using context information have already appeared in OCR patents filed by IBM and other companies.

But advanced OCR will also need a specialized 'front end'. 'Of course you need syntactic analysis, you need lexical analysis, you need the semantic level,' observes Ullmann. 'But you also need to get the geometrical level right.'

It is hard enough for a machine to recognize an object like a cogwheel or a missile, which retains its basic shape but may look different in different circumstances. The letter 'A' has no fixed shape. Somehow, a recognition system must reach for the concept which underlies all the different 'As' which can be written.

Ullmann believes there are big rewards for whoever cracks this problem. 'There is a big crock of gold there.' he says. 'I see it every time I walk into a building and see the amount of copy-typing that goes on. That's an indictment of the state of the art of OCR.'

But no one has tried to make OCR one of the major targets of the Alvey programme. The subject's chequered history suggests that there can be no guarantee of a quick payback. 'I have watched a lot of failures, big companies losing a lot of money over OCR,' Ullmann comments. 'Over and over again, people underestimate the difficulty of the problem'.

The breakthrough did not come in the next three weeks, or in the next three years. The idea that solutions could emerge from Alvey MMI research, or any other generic research on vision, seems increasingly implausible. In the Alvey vision projects, the matching of image descriptions to stored models is almost always done on the assumption that the object is either rigid or subject to some simple mechanical deformation. Whatever it is that transforms one 'A' into another, it is not a mere mechanical deformation.

My own theory is that the variation in written and printed characters is of two kinds, one associated with the hand and one with the eye. The hand must be considered, because much variation arises from the physical process of writing. The letterforms used by an individual or a culture evolve so that they flow more readily from the pen. Strokes are exaggerated, diminished, displaced or distorted by minor errors in the timing and amplitude of movements. Very similar modifications may be introduced deliberately, for expressive or decorative effect. All teachers of writing (and observant parents) know that strange-looking letters result when the penstrokes are made in the wrong order or the wrong direction. This is even more noticeable in Chinese. Chinese calligraphy may depart wildly from the copybook character-forms, but the characters can still be identified because the reader senses the expressive motion of the writer's hand.

The success of dynamic signature verification testifies to the importance of hand movements. There should be more research on the relationship between hand movements and the resulting marks on paper, with the ultimate objective of reconstructing a sequence of hand movements from a sample of cursive script. This research could also improve the recognition of printed letters, since they often contain elements which have survived from handwriting and which the eye can still interpret as the marks of a moving nib or brush. Experiments with a robot hand, or a mathematical model of one, could throw light on these matters.

Through experience of reading and writing, our visual apparatus is sensitized to this kinaesthetic quality of the written word. But we also bring other, more universal visual capabilities and peculiarities to the act of reading. Our eyes and brains repair broken curves, reconstruct partly hidden shapes, and generally construct hypotheses which often prove correct; they may also lead us astray, as the extensive literature on optical illusions confirms.

These propensities of the eye are exploited by writers and typographers. Some of the more abstract display typefaces are only legible because they create an overpowering optical illusion of a letter which intellect tells us is not there. Perhaps this is the area where vision research has most to offer to OCR. But it must be research on human vision or, at the very least, on machines which share our optical illusions.

One OCR manufacturer wrote to me after this article appeared, listing a number of recent technical improvements, and informing me that his company was doing very good business. I do not think this invalidates the conclusion that OCR techniques have a long way to go, particularly where handwriting is concerned. Nor does the existence of flourishing OCR companies disprove Ullmann's assertion that a market worth billions remains untapped.

One of the few people from the AI community who have taken OCR seriously is Ray Kurzweil. His company, Kurzweil Applied Intelligence, developed two of the most advanced OCR machines on the market, one of them a reading machine for the blind, and the other a commercial data entry machine. The company then began developing a voice-operated writing machine. Interestingly Ray Kurzweil, like Julian Ullmann, sees a strong analogy between the OCR problem and the problem of speech recognition.

26

Hunting the slippable

The intelligent sketchpad envisaged by Ernest Edmonds and his colleagues (Chapter 6) would be able to look at a picture generated from one high-level description, and come up with another quite different high-level description. David Levitt's work with music (Chapter 22) also stresses the way in which synthesis and analysis support each other. The same theme will recur in the context of computer programming, when we come to another MIT project, the Programmer's Apprentice (Chapter 47).

I was reminded of all these when I read something Douglas Hofstadter wrote in his book *Metamagical Themas*. He looked forward to a time when programs are able 'to look at what they've done and perceive it in ways that they never anticipated'.

'The element lacking in current computer art,' he wrote, 'is the interaction of perception with generation. Computers do not *watch* what they do. They simply *do* it.'

Anyone who attempts to establish serious cooperation between humans and computers in any creative endeavour, must surely be driven to a similar conclusion. Human beings will probably keep the edge in creativity, and in any case they should be allowed the privilege of doing the most interesting part of the job. But it would be ungrateful to suggest that the computer contributes nothing creative to such a partnership.

This brief article gives only the barest outline of Hofstadter's highly relevant thoughts on these matters. His own much fuller account (reference below) is recommended.

6 June 1985

One might expect surprises, from the master of paradox who wrote *Gödel, Escher, Bach.* Douglas R Hofstadter, author of the cult book on human and artificial intelligence, recently appointed Professor of Human Understanding at the University of Michigan, and (from 1981 to 1983) *Scientific American* columnist, is now concentrating much of his research effort on a program to recognize simple matchstick letters.

It sounds a far cry from the great mysteries of Mind. Not so, says Hofstadter. There is nothing simple about pattern recognition. 'It's the only thing,' he insists. 'That's what intelligence is. There is nothing else.'

Central to human intelligence, for Hofstadter, is the effortless ability to sort things into categories, to observe analogies, and to say, in a seemingly novel situation, 'This reminds me of something I have seen before.' Staying in a house in Sussex this May, he was reminded of the London house where he lived for a few months during 1965. Despite the superficial differences between the two houses, Hofstadter found himself saying things like 'Here's where we had the television.' Commonplace? No, marvellous! Just try to capture that 'slippability' of human concepts in a computer program!

A favourite Hofstadter example is the question, 'Who is the First Lady of Britain?' The Queen? Margaret Thatcher? Neither of these is really Nancy Reagan's British counterpart. Hofstadter finds Dennis Thatcher the hottest candidate. The slippable concept of 'First Lady' can easily survive a sex-change. This is the flexible, abstract way in which people think.

Searching for a 'toy universe' wherein some of this extraordinary human ability might be captured in a computer program, Hofstadter chose the lower case Roman alphabet. Nothing too open-ended, nothing too abstruse. 'I would rather investigate concepts that everybody knows, and everybody has an intuition for,' he says, 'than concepts that only a few specialists could appreciate.'

As the Letter-spirit project took shape, the true dimensions of the problem began to emerge. More constraints: to keep things simple, letters were to have no curves, lines were not to be thickened. Letters built from dots, like those seen on computer screens, were rejected because they depend on a degree of blurring for their legibility. The idea which won through was a 'grid' of 56 vertical, horizontal and diagonal line segments. Different letters would be formed by selecting different combinations of segments from the grid. Similar, but simpler, grids are used to display numbers and letters on pocket calculators.

Letter-spirit has not yet reached the serious programming stage. But Hofstadter has paced out the territory by composing some 300 complete alphabets or 'gridfonts'. The resulting letterforms are often angular, jagged, contorted and bizarre. This, Hofstadter stresses, was not an exercise in typographic design. But he believes that professional designers, creating new typefaces for the printing industry, must go through some of the same thought processes. In creating an 'h', for example, he became aware of other letters like 'b' and 'k' which set limits to the possible shapes of 'h'.

These territorial disputes between rival concepts help to define what Hofstadter calls 'the geography of the space of concepts'. Unexpected influences sometimes reveal themselves. 'You may be surprised,' he says, 'that an unusual "b" may start to infringe on "z" territory. You didn't know it in advance. You just draw your "b" and find to your horror that it looks like a "z".'

There are now dozens of grid versions of the letter 'a'. Among them there must be clues to the Platonic essence of the letter 'a'. Hoftstadter believes that the wilder and more bizarre versions are important because they help to define the outermost boundaries of the concept of 'a'. He is interested both in the essence of the *letter* 'a', and in the *spirit* which runs through a complete gridfont from 'a' to 'z'.

Far from being a simple exercise in pattern recognition, Letter-spirit touches on questions of style and creativity. Hofstadter points out that the spirit of a typeface can be pursued into other quite different contexts. There are alphabets that carry an art deco spirit, he says. There are also art deco locomotives, art deco skyscrapers, and art deco chairs.

All this lies well beyond the simplified world of the gridfonts. Hofstadter's faith is that even within that simple world the same processes are at work. Styles have slippability. They must have slippability if a style of painting, like impressionism, can be translated into a style of music. And in the gridfont world? Hofstadter tells how he devised a typeface with slanting hexagons as its dominant motif. He called it 'benzene'. (Benzene is a hydrocarbon with hexagonal molecules.) When he came to design the 'x' he found that the hexagon concept 'slipped' in a remarkable fashion. The 'x' contains no actual hexagon, but it is there implicitly. You have to imagine cutting the 'x' down the middle, swapping the two crescent-shaped fragments, and gluing them together again – result: a hexagon.

There is an echo here of the 'First Lady' problem. The problem is to find something which fills a familiar role in a new context. To succeed, you may have to redefine the role itself quite drastically, allowing a male, for example, to fill the role of 'First Lady'. Hofstadter believes that a good representation of the concept of the letter 'b' will include a number of roles. Two obvious roles are those of the upright 'post' and the rounded 'bowl' of the letter. In different versions of the letter 'b' these roles might be filled by a variety of different elements. Provided the roles are clear, the elements which fill them may be quite exotic. Victorian nursery alphabets sometimes used human or animal figures to fill the various roles in letterforms.

In line with his policy of investigating extreme cases, Hofstadter designed a 'minimalist' alphabet which he called Hint. Hint is on the borders of legibility. Most letters consist of a few disconnected dashes. It is much easier to read a message in Hint if you already know what it says.

Hofstadter then began adding lines to produce a series of increasingly solid, and increasingly legible alphabets. He then realized he was 'turning a knob' which could be turned further in the same direction. Now the alphabet began to accumulate surplus strokes and flourishes. The end point was a tangled and barely legible font which Hofstadter named 'Hunt' – because you have to hunt for the letters among all the irrelevant excrescences.

Hofstadter believes that we recognize letters by grouping their parts into larger wholes. 'We feel that what is going on is a sequence of chunking at different levels,' he says. He and his colleagues will try to recreate this process when they come to serious programming. The program will have a strong random component. Letter segments or 'quanta' that are chunked together may not stay chunked. Hofstadter describes the whole process with a biochemical metaphor, with enzymes forming and breaking bonds, and the products of one set of enzymes activating further enzymes.

Overlapping waves of enzymes will gradually assemble small, strongly bound 'molecules', and then larger, more weakly bound ones. Even strong bonds, however, will sometimes be broken at random. After a time the program may have grouped several quanta into a reasonably stable molecule. 'So it perhaps decides that this is a candidate for a role,' Hofstadter explains. 'Then some of its features are used to address roles and to activate certain concepts in a permanent memory, such as the concept of bowl, the concept of post.'

If parts of the letter are found to fit the role of 'bowl', and others are found to fit the role of 'post', another enzyme-like bit of program will be activated. It will try to decide whether the post-bowl combination looks like a letter 'b'. Not only that. It will also try to determine what style of 'b' it is looking at.

Beneath Hofstadter's unique imagery there are echoes of well-known artificial intelligence concepts. The progressive, partly-random 'chunking' process resembles a simulated annealing algorithm or the operation of a Boltzmann machine (Chapter 59). The key concept of a 'role' resembles the 'slots' used in frames and related methods of representing knowledge.

But Hofstadter argues that his idea of a role is more slippery than the usual idea of a slot. 'You have to have a description that will bend and flex and adapt itself to the circumstances,' he says. 'And the circumstances can be defined by how other roles are filled. That's what is going on with the letters of the alphabet. How one role is filled may define how another role is filled.' A frame description would just have a slot labelled 'First Lady', to be filled with a pointer to another frame (say, Nancy Reagan's frame.) In a role description, the label would itself be something complex and 'slippable' enough to be matched with seemingly different roles in other contexts.

Hofstadter does not claim to know how human memory works. But he

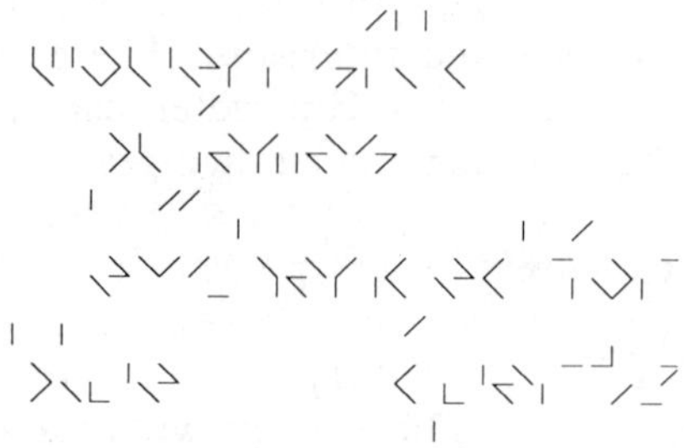

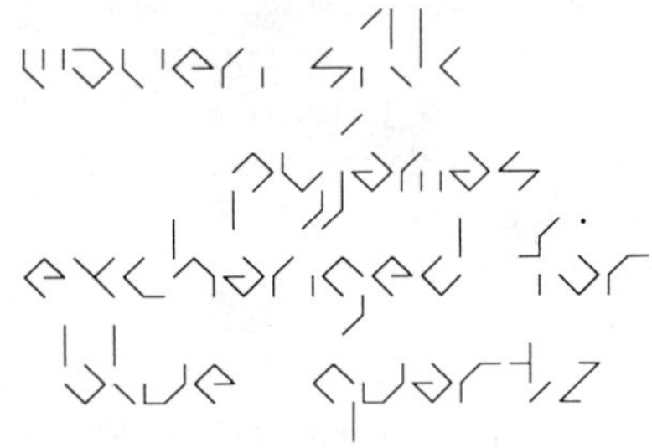

Douglas R. Hofstadter's *Hint–Hunt* series of gridfonts ranges from the minimalist *Hint* through (clockwise) *Hint 3, Hint–Hunt 5,* and *Hunt 3*, to the ornate *Hunt. Hint 2, Hint 4, Hunt 4* and *Hunt 2* are not shown.

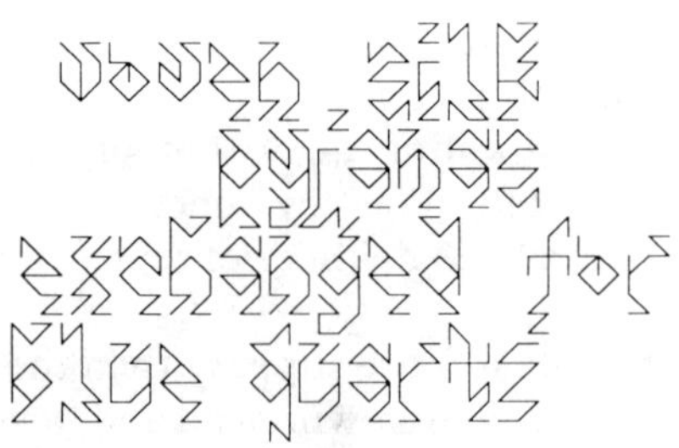

believes that something at least as clever as this must be involved, to explain our ability to recognize analogies between one situation and another. 'I think that abstract thinking is dominated by analogy,' he says. 'I think that recognizing the essence of a situation, deciding what a situation is, is really the crux of thought.'

The proposition that 'intelligence is pattern recognition' would make a good debating motion. Opponents of the motion might ask whether this concept of intelligence gives an adequate account of planned and purposeful action. Is action merely a part of the process of perception?

Most AI researchers seem to believe that perception can be separated from action. Programs for vision, for example, concentrate on perception. Planning and problem-solving programs are concerned with action. Robotics clearly involves both; but the usual assumption is that perception and action can be handled by separate program modules. Neuroanatomy supports this: the parts of the cortex involved in seeing appear to be distinct from those involved in controlling the muscles.

But the underlying philosophical assumptions are not universally shared. Zen Buddhism argues, from introspection, that perceptions and knowledge are fragile and misleading. But correct action may be accomplished by the person who achieves an unknowing, non-perceiving state of mind.

Behaviourism, by excluding all information obtained by introspection, arrives at a surprisingly similar conclusion. To separate what happens between 'stimulus' and 'response' into the two processes of perception and action implies some intervening mental state. Mental states have no place in the behaviourist account.

The neural-network model of computation is hostile to behaviourism (since it it very much concerned with what happens between input and output) but broadly compatible with Zen. A neural network has inputs or sensors, and outputs or effectors, and a seamless web of trainable units in between. It can learn to respond appropriately to its environment without formulating explicit descriptions or goals – by intuition, as it were.

One could try to assemble a very un-Zen neural network by joining two networks end to end, the first one trained for perception and the second for action. I suspect this would fail, but it would be interesting to see how and why it failed.

It may seem strange to crusade for computers which watch what they are doing. After all, one can very easily imagine a Zen master telling a pupil, 'Don't watch what you are doing! Just do it!' Is that not what computers have been doing all along?

This brings us back once again to the vital difference between learning and being programmed. A computer, once programmed, can 'just do' something without ever having had to 'watch what it was doing'. But people who are learning – even people who are learning Zen – have to watch what they are doing. Effortless skill is attained – if ever – when one can 'just do' something.

As Alfred North Whitehead put it:

> 'It is profoundly erroneous truism, repeated by all copy books and eminent people when they are making speeches, that we should cultivate the habit of thinking of what we are doing. The precise opposite is the case. Civilization advances by extending the number of important operations which we can perform without thinking about them.'

The point is, of course, that if you do not have to think about what you can do already, your mind is free to think about learning to do the next thing. The quotation from Whitehead has been used in an advertisement for Apple computers. As a statement of intention from a computer company this is admirable. As far as possible, we ought to be able to use our computers without thinking about them. This probably calls for computers which are able to think about us, and think about themselves.

Further reading

Hofstadter, D.R. (1982). 'Metamagical themas: variations on a theme as the essence of imagination' *Scientific American*, October, 14–21.

Hofstadter, D.R. (1985). *Metamagical Themas*. New York: Basic Books. (Chapters 12 and 13 are especially relevant. Chapter 12 is a reprinting of a magazine article, reference above.)

27

On artificial stupidity

My own experience of computers has had its moments of excitement, pleasure and triumph, but I have been much more permanently marked by all the times of pain, anger and disappointment. Foolishly, perhaps, I continue to believe that life with the computer can be better than this. I attribute my disappointments to the phenomenon of artificial stupidity.

21 March 1985

You would be rightly suspicious of a colleague who went round saying that computers are naturally intelligent, and that it is only pig-ignorant programming that makes them appear stupid. The proposition is so perverse and ridiculous that your colleague is most unlikely to influence your own rational and sensible views on the subject.

It can therefore do no harm if you look at computing from your insane colleague's point of view for, say, ten minutes. Right?

Computers act stupidly when they are kept in the dark. To behave intelligently they need the deepest possible knowledge of the problem in hand. All too often programmers hold back essential information that they would certainly have passed on if instructing a fellow human to do the same job. Consider one of the rudimentary principles of good programming: if you use something more than once, give it a name. This is how variables and procedures come to be used.

To refrain from using subroutines or procedures (or variables and constants, for that matter) is an act of wilful deceit. If you want to have the same operations done several times, but on different sets of data, the computer has a right to know this. If you treat the machine like a fool it will act like one.

Hence the broad injunction not to use 'magic numbers' in programming. If you find yourself frequently dividing by eight because eight bits is the word length of the machine, consider using a variable called *wordlength* instead of the number '8', and you may find the hardware more cooperative when you later port the software to a 16-bit processor.

There was a vogue for 'parametrized software', which could be adapted to the special needs of each customer by adjusting a few numbers. Introducing parameters allows the machine to develop just a little of its natural ability to adapt to its environment. Nowadays there are ways of making software a great deal 'softer' than that.

High level languages were an early, hesitant step towards the recognition that humans can address computers as intelligent entities. But we were still a long way from talking to machines in English.

People find it difficult to concentrate on more than one thing at a time. Timesharing and multitasking were 'invented' when programmers stopped assuming that computers shared this defect. Despite all the propaganda against von Neumann machines, such machines can in fact keep several jobs on the boil very effectively.

Multitasking is not a clever illusion. Nor does it require particularly fancy hardware. It is an intrinsic capacity of all computers. David Husband's implementation of multi-tasking Forth on the Sinclair ZX81, available from MicroProcessor Engineering Ltd, demonstrates this.

When ideas like virtual memory and memory management came along, the story was that clever programmers had made a computer pretend to be a more powerful 'virtual' machine. But no faking was involved. The power was real. It was the old way of doing things that had denied computers part of their true potential.

Once again, programmers had been less than honest with their machines. They had been telling their computers, 'Store this item at location 6AFF' as though the physical location really mattered. It would have been more honest to say from the start, 'Store it wherever you like, even on a disk, provided you can find it when I ask for it.' Virtual memory at last credited the machine with the ability to tie its own shoelaces.

Most virtual memory systems still retain the whole edifice of files and records for long-term storage of data, and force the programmer to move data laboriously in and out of files on the assumption that the machine is too stupid to do this for itself. The 'need' for this disappears when data is stored in structures called persistent objects, which have been the subject of a research project at Edinburgh and St Andrews universities.

Ron Morrison of St Andrews sees his job as 'identifying where the discontinuities are in programming languages, and eliminating them'. Last year he told *Computing*, 'after this one we'll hit the next'.

There are still plenty of discontinuities in languages – points where they fail to do what an intelligent computer would do and an intelligent user would expect. Some languages still do not support recursion, though there is nothing miraculous about a procedure calling itself.

Lisp is the kind of language where everything is legal unless it is expressly forbidden. Many of the familiar discontinuities, including the distinction between program and data, are absent. Computer scientists like Lisp because, for a variety of reasons, it does not actively obstruct their efforts to write flexible, intelligent programs. Or rather, Lisp does not actively obstruct a computer's efforts to behave intelligently.

Lisp provides dynamic data structures which grow and die (to be cleared up by the garbage collector routine) while the program runs. Yet in another context, the much less daring feature of variable length records attracts attention to the Pick operating system.

Mathematicians have gone to great lengths to eliminate discontinuities from their subject. A feeling that $3 - 5$ ought to be as meaningful as $5 - 3$ led to the invention of negative numbers. But the designers of early programming languages brought discontinuities back into mathematics. Thus $a = b$ no longer means the same as $b = a$. And $z = x \star y$ does not help the computer to calculate x, given y and z.

Functional languages like David Turner's Miranda have restored the equals sign from a device for updating memory locations to its original deeper meaning. Constraint languages like Software Arts' TK!Solver allow the computer to see a little more of what an O level maths student sees in $z = x \star y$ and in more complicated equations. Both languages merely give the computer the kind of knowledge we would expect any human being to use in handling equations.

Software Arts' Visicalc, the first of the microcomputer spreadsheets, knew rather less than TK!Solver. But it did introduce many users to the declarative style of programming. (Many did not think of it as programming at all.) In setting up a spreadsheet one merely states the contents of some cells and rules for working out the contents of the remaining cells. The machine pieces these facts and rules together to form chains of inference, until values have been entered in all the vacant cells.

Declarative programming recognizes the computer's ability to decide for itself how it will use knowledge to reach a result. This ability is given somewhat freer rein in expert systems, where a declarative knowledge base of facts and rules is kept separate from a procedural inference engine. Application generators and fourth generation languages tend to be declarative in style, as is the 'fifth generation' language Prolog.

A declarative knowledge base is still 'alive' in the sense that it can be used for many different purposes, some of which (publishing it as a book, for example) may not have been foreseen by the original builders of the system. Declarative knowledge is also readily edited, altered or extended. At the same time procedural knowledge (like the knowledge in an inference engine, or the knowledge that makes Visicalc tick) is more 'alive' and reusable by being untainted with any domain-specific declarative knowledge.

Organizing knowledge in these ways does not guarantee a brilliant performance. Facts and rules themselves may be rather superficial in their content. Many expert systems consist of hundreds of empirical rules with no underlying model. Asked to explain a decision, an expert system may reply 'because of Rule 55' and be quite unable to say why Rule 55 is true. This is less likely to happen in an expert system with a 'deep' knowledge of its domain. For example CASNET, developed at Rutgers University in the early and middle 1970s, is a medical diagnostic system with a built-in causal model of disease processes.

Deep knowledge of mathematics has been built into systems like Reduce, which will use an abstruse method based on modular algebra to factorize an easy expression like $X^6 - A^3$.

This may be using a sledgehammer to crack a nut, but the deep and powerful method comes in very handy for tougher factorization problems.

A final example is the way that screens have come 'alive' with the advent of bit-mapped graphics. In the WYSIWYG (what you see is what you get) style of word processing you are not really editing a document but an abstract data structure that can be used to generate a document. If a range of documents of different style and detail can be generated from one structure, you have what Theodor Nelson called hypertext. Nelson, one of the visionaries who always knew that computers are really intelligent underneath, invented hypertext in 1965.

The new Filevision database for the Apple Macintosh is typical of the many software products which now exploit the 'live' quality of a bit-mapped screen display. Point (using the mouse) to any part of the picture on the screen, and you get another picture, or perhaps some text, telling you more about the thing you pointed to. Bit-mapped graphics are the means, but it works because the computer also maintains a 'deep' model of what appears on the screen.

Artificial intelligence has not been mentioned, because there is no such thing. There is only artificial stupidity, which is what happens when you don't give computers the knowledge they need.

Despite all its protestations to the contrary, this impressionistic article was, of course, about the thing that is known as artificial intelligence. Its aim was to look at the subject afresh, as if the term 'artificial intelligence' had never been invented. One point I was trying to make was that so-called AI techniques should not be kept in a locked box for emergencies only. The tools which give leverage on the exceptionally hard problems of AI are also effective on more ordinary problems. They should simply be thought of as part of good software practice. Of course not everything that

AI researchers have done should be copied. Like most programmers, they often feel compelled to resort to quick and dirty programming methods. But the day of the hacker is coming to an end, as programming matures into a mathematically-based engineering discipline.

Artificial intelligence research can benefit information technology in two main ways. As science, it gives us insight into the abilities and needs of the human beings who will be designing and using computer systems. As technology, it provides us with some of the software components that will be needed to build those human-centred systems.

AI researchers should state clearly whether they are seeking psychological authenticity, or engineering elegance. They are not the same thing. Some people believe that the way the brain does a thing is the way machines should do it. There are excellent reasons (such as Donald Michie's 'human windows' argument) for paying attention to the way the brain does things. But a crude 'brain is best' argument does not stand up for a moment. This extreme position ignores the difference between building in crystalline silicon, and building in a mushy mixture of water and carbon compounds. Perhaps even more important, it ignores the difference between evolution by natural selection, and design by a purposive intellect.

Engineers should be aiming to build, not second rate human beings, but first class computer systems. If there are some things that computers cannot do as well as we can, we should be neither disappointed nor surprised. Nor should we be alarmed if they can do some things better than we can. They already outperform us in calculation and information retrieval. A big competition, them against us, will be counter-productive. We should look for ways in which human and computer capabilities can complement each other.

Further reading

McDermott, D.V. (1976). 'Artificial intelligence and natural stupidity' *SIGART Bulletin*, **57**, 4–9.

PART 3
Complexity

28

Von Neumann's other machine

Scientists believe that all the world's complexity derives ultimately from simple natural laws. Science attempts to crack nature's code and find the underlying simplicity. This is exactly what a computer vision program tries to do when it interprets a scene. It is what a computer user does when faced with a complicated new machine. It is what a cipher expert does when faced with a secret coded message. Sometimes the code is easily cracked, sometimes it seems impossible. Why?

Computer models allow us to watch exactly how complexity arises from simple laws. A computer graphics group at the University of Bremen has produced breathtaking colour images of 'fractal' objects which arise in mathematics and theoretical physics. Some of these objects are generated by very simple equations, but they contain a literally infinite wealth of pattern.

Cellular automata – large arrays of cells which respond to messages from their neighbours – may prove to be useful models of physical phenomena ranging from the forces between quarks to the formation of snow crystals. Edward Fredkin argues that the universe itself *is* a cellular automaton. The complex game of Go has very simple rules. Appropriately, Alan Scarff has written a Go-playing program on cellular automaton principles.

Stephen Wolfram believes that sometimes the only way to tell how a cellular automaton will evolve is to simulate it in detail. There is no short cut, no key to the code. He believes there may be parallels to this in biology. The fate of a living cell is written in its DNA, but there may be no way of predicting in advance what the cell will do. You just have to watch it develop.

Scientists trying to design new proteins by computer face similar problems. Computer simulations of protein molecules are improving rapidly, but to be sure of a new protein's properties, biochemists must synthesize and test it.

Computer systems are necessarily complex but they should also be comprehensible – both to those who design them and to those who use them. The control of complexity is the essence of good design. A well-designed interface makes the system appear simple to the user. Software engineering, the subject of Part 4, aims to keep things simple for the designers themselves.

On the other hand, powerful methods are now available for designers who wish to erect a wall of impenetrable complexity to protect programs and data from theft or tampering.

Cellular automata strikingly mimic the way things work in the universe around us – so much so, that one must take care to remember that the real world may differ from these microworlds in important respects.

It is best to observe them and experiment with them on a computer. You may not find a program for Conway's 'Life' in your local computer store, but various 'public domain' versions are in circulation. Writing your own program in BASIC is educational, but if you want your universe to evolve at reasonable speed you will have to use a compiled language such as Pascal. Or you can spend many long evenings crafting your program in assembly language.

Best of all is to watch Life or another cellular automaton running on a high speed image processor, or on the special machine built by Tommaso Toffoli at the Massachusetts Institute of Technology. Merely reading about it is not the same.

---

26 January 1984

Parallel processing enthusiasts who now sneer at the 'von Neumann machine' should remember that the man who gave his name to the standard sequential machine also created an archetypal parallel computer.

The machine was devised as an intellectual exercise, to prove that a rectangular array of simple cells, each connected to its neighbours, could function as what we would now call a computer. It was not meant as a practical design. It has, however, been simulated on a sequential computer. John Barker and his colleagues at Warwick University have done this as part of a broader study of the class of systems known as cellular automata.

The essence of this subject is that a lot of simple things connected together may exhibit complex behaviour. Cellular automata with their crystalline regularity appeal to physicists like Barker. Biologists have studied systems called associative networks which are broadly similar. But being modelled on the brain, they operate asynchronously and tend to be more haphazard in their wiring.

Each cell of von Neumann's machine has 29 possible states. It was later discovered that cellular automata with as few as two states can perform general computations. One which can is the game of Life, invented by John Conway of Cambridge University and first described in print in 1971.

Life unfolds on a rectangular grid like a Go board. A birth occurs in a cell when exactly three of the eight surrounding cells are occupied. Deaths are caused by overcrowding (four or more neighbours) or isolation (less than two neighbours).

Many home computer users have now watched the patterns of Life flare and fade on their screens like sparks on a fireback. Probably few of them know that in a big enough 'universe' the Life game can be set up in configurations which themselves act as computers.

By changing the rules for the individual cell, the behaviour of the whole system can be changed. Barker's group has investigated approximately 300 two-state cellular automata, with each cell connected to four, six or eight neighbours.

They are now beginning to study examples where each cell has three possible states. These, according to Barker, are interesting for several reasons. Some of them show marked self-organizing tendencies. A group of cells may form a polarized 'membrane'. 'You can have a large region with a boundary round it, which itself will act as a cell with respect to what is going on outside.' explains Barker.

Systems with three or more cell states also interest him for another reason. They can be made self-timing. The array can synchronize itself, without each cell being connected to an external clock.

Barker believes that a renewed assault on cellular automata is timely, and not only because they could be readily constructed with very large scale integration (VLSI) semiconductor technology. There have also been relevant advances in mathematics, particularly non-linear mathematics, and in physics. The Ising model used by physicists to describe magnetism in certain solids is to all intents and purposes a cellular automaton.

Research has shown that all cellular automata fall into four classes. Some evolve towards a limiting state and stop there. Others meander until they enter an endless loop or limit cycle. A third class exhibits seemingly random or chaotic behaviour. (All these behaviours, incidentally, also occur in physical systems of forces and particles.) The fourth class consists of cellular automata with more interesting behaviour. Some of these have been proved to be 'computationally universal'. In effect, these systems can be programmed to solve computational problems.

Barker believes that to be useful for computation, a cellular automaton should have the property of structural stability. It should be able to recover from the effects of noise and of small faults in its own hardware.

Conway's Life, for example, lacks this stability. Life depends on an interplay between the creation and the destruction of signals. According to Barker, 'The creation part is too strong. Just one point can blow the whole lot apart.'

Many cellular automata are non-linear. Their output is not, even in the most obscure way, the sum of their inputs. Non-linearity is usually essential for structural stability, and according to Barker the mathematics of non-linear systems are now understood much better than a few years ago. Linear systems can be seen as passive channels for information, unable to distinguish signal from noise. Non-linear systems have more of a mind of their own (figuratively of course) and behave more decisively.

One simple way of adapting to a hardware fault would be able to relocate the activity to another part of the system. Clearly this is possible in a cellular automaton since every part of it is the same. But Barker favours a more cryptic form of processing in which an item of information is not to be found at any specific location. As in a hologram, meaning is spread over the whole pattern.

John Hopfield of the California Institute of Technology has demonstrated this type of information storage in a simulated associative network. Unlike most earlier brain-like models, Hopfield's was strongly non-linear and exhibited the stable, decisive behaviour expected of non-linear systems.

Hidden information and concealed order are also encountered in cellular automata. Barker describes how sometimes the pattern appears completely random, then suddenly crystallizes into something that looks meaningful, and then instantly dissolves again into apparent chaos. The problem is to find meaning in this seeming chaos.

Stated more formally, the problem is to divide the vast numbers of possible patterns into equivalence classes. Patterns belonging to an equivalence class may look different but in some sense they are the same. Assuming the system has sufficient structural stability, they will evolve in similar ways and can be thought of as having the same meaning.

Barker believes that this problem must be attacked with the methods of topology, the branch of mathematics concerned with connectedness. But recent advances in topology (catastrophe theory is one of them) have mostly been concerned with a world in which things change continuously, with discontinuous change being the interesting exception. Topological techniques to suit the lumpy, jerky world of cellular automata are not so well developed.

This work is not as remote from practical application as it might seem. Barker is interested in developing very fast pattern recognition and image processing systems. He believes that cellular automata could recognize similar objects of different sizes, and identify a whole object when only part is visible. Both of these are difficult tasks with conventional methods.

The Warwick group already has one cellular automaton which, Barker says, 'will do all the standard image processing functions, but does them non-linearly'. Conventional image processing usually depends on linear operations such as deconvolution or the Fast Fourier Transform, at least for its initial stages. Barker also has a method which, he claims, extracts contours faster than the usual algorithm.

But perhaps the most challenging property of cellular automata is their self-organizing ability. In addition to grants from the Science and Engineering Research Council, Barker's group has a grant from the US Office of Naval Research to study self-organization and its possible application to VLSI (very large scale integration) design. The intention is to get predictable behaviour out of devices rooted in the uncertain micro-world of quantum mechanics. Probably not all semiconductor designers will see it like that. It may be some time before they can be persuaded that a self-organizing automaton does not necessarily have a rebellious will of its own.

When John von Neumann devised his 29-state cellular space, he was trying to discover a Turing machine (a computer) that could reproduce itself. It later emerged that a self-reproducing automaton need not also be a Turing machine as von Neumann's was. Edward Fredkin (Chapter 33) discovered a simple two-state cellular automaton rule which will reproduce multiple copies of any finite-sized starting pattern.

The research which distinguished four types of cellular automaton behaviour was Stephen Wolfram's. Wolfram's work is the subject of Chapter 31. The fact that a cellular automaton rule has been proved to be computationally universal does not mean that anyone has ever used that rule to construct a working computer. Generally the most anyone has done is to simulate the main components and describe how they might be put together into a computer.

When we look around us we are aware that we cannot see everything. We cannot see inside solid objects, nor can we see microscopic dusts and bacteria. When a cellular automaton simulation is running on a computer screen, everything is out in the open, before our eyes. Yet it is impossible to be aware of everything that is going on. Our eyes are sensitive to certain kinds of order and pattern. Other kinds of order may be present, but our senses are not attuned to them. I once asked John Conway whether he thought interesting developments would occur in a very large Life universe, say one million by one million cells. He thought the answer was 'Yes', but pointed out the difficulty of displaying or observing such a large universe in any way that would reveal the significant events.

John Barker is now Professor of Microelectronics at the University of Glasgow. His research interests include the physics and technology of 'nanoelectronic' devices at least an order of magnitude smaller than today's microelectronics. Under a contract with ITT, his group has studied cellular automaton architectures for optical computing.

Further reading

Berlekamp, E.R., Conway, J.H. and Guy, R.K. (1982). *Winning Ways.* London: Academic Press. 2 vols. (Required reading for the serious mathematical games addict. Volume 2 describes more of Life's wonders, and explains how one constructs a Life computer.)

Gardner, M. (1983). *Wheels, Life and Other Mathematical Amusements.* New York: W.H. Freeman. (Includes the best non-technical collection of Life lore.)

29

Capturing the images of chaos

Mathematics is one of the last remaining subjects in which an individual can make important additions to knowledge with no technical aids beyond an A4 pad and a supply of pencils. Understandably, mathematicians who rely heavily on computers to get their results are regarded with suspicion by some of their traditionally minded colleagues.

Eyebrows were raised in West Germany at the group of mathematicians and physicists who filled their laboratory at the University of Bremen with computer graphics equipment and began turning out spectacular colour pictures which were sought after by magazines and calendar publishers.

Bremen's reputation did not help. The University was set up in the 1960s with a radical administrative structure which greatly curtailed the traditional power of the German professor. Some of the more utopian features have been abandoned, but Bremen is still seen as a left-wing university where nobody does much real research.

In fact the creators of those superb computer graphics were deeply involved in the mathematics and physics behind them, and no more guilty of showmanship than astronomers who photograph the beauties of the heavens, or metallurgists who capture wondrous crystal forms with their electron microscopes.

Criticism should be reserved for those who have presented the Mandelbrot set as a pretty object (which it is) or an exercise in computer graphics (which it can be) without acknowledging its intellectual significance. I was keen that *Computing* should print these spectacular pictures in its newly established (and now, sadly defunct) colour magazine section. But I also wanted Heinz-Otto Peitgen, Peter Richter and their colleagues to explain what the images mean to the working scientist.

6 September 1984

Physicists and mathematicians at the University of Bremen in West Germany have taken to computer graphics in a big way. But sometimes they have trouble convincing colleagues that they are not just making pretty pictures. They believe that their images, by boosting the power of human intuition, may lead to a better understanding of such varied phenomena as magnetism, weather and ecology. But their pictures also show how mathematical models can disintegrate into chaos. The message is that some phenomena may for ever lie beyond the reach of computation.

Heinz-Otto Peitgen and Peter Richter, the two professors who set up the graphics laboratory last year, have notched up at least two discoveries which they claim they would not have made without help of computer graphics. They scorn the suggestion that the computer is a substitute for thinking. They show no sign of computer-induced intellectual paralysis. If anything, they have found the computer an enormous stimulus to thought. But since they moved into the glamorous world of computer graphics they have felt the pressures which threaten to turn scientists into showmen. They admit that a big slice of their time now goes on organizing exhibitions, and answering enquiries from art magazines, TV stations and fellow academics. 'This year we are planning to have six more exhibitions in Germany and one in France,' said Peitgen.

On an unseasonably grey and chilly Thursday in July, a visiting film unit was putting the finishing touches to a computer-animated movie planned by group member Hartmut Jürgens. For ten days, graphics equipment manufacturer Evans and Sutherland had loaned the group a high-performance colour terminal. During a break in filming, Jürgens dimmed the lights, switched on the stereo (playing a Jean-Michel Jarre track of the kind that tends to accompany underwater nature films on TV) and set the computer for a real-time runthrough of a two-minute sequence from the movie they were making.

The Lorenz equations, on which the film is based, are differential equations which describe the time behaviour of three variables. Treat the variables as the coordinates of a point in three-dimensional space, and the equations define a family of paths traced out by points in space. All the paths lead into a kind of double spiral which looks like a swirl of cream in coffee.

Pure mathematics is turned into cinematic experience by launching a small red pyramid along one of these spirals and letting an imaginary camera ride close behind it. The 'through the windscreen' view, the sense of speed and perspective, recall NASA's celebrated computer simulation of *Voyager 1* 's flight through Saturn's rings.

On an AED colour raster graphics terminal, bought for the group by the Volkswagen foundation, mathematician Dietmar Saupe summoned up a picture of a planet whose bizarrely patterned surface is the answer to a seemingly insoluble conundrum. Three empires share the planet. How should their boundaries be shaped to ensure that *all three* powers are present at every point on the border? The answer, which non-mathematicians may regard as a cheat, encrusts the border with an infinite number of enclaves, and enclaves within enclaves.

The pattern repeats itself endlessly at ever smaller scales. Many of the objects studied by the Bremen group exhibit this property of 'self-similarity'. Benoit Mandelbrot of IBM's Thomas J. Watson Research Center coined the adjective 'fractal' for such objects. Mandelbrot maintains that many natural structures, including coastlines, meandering rivers, and the moon's craters, are of a fractal character.

The Bremen graphics laboratory is the latest venture of the dynamical systems research group that was set up by Peitgen and Richter two years ago. The group's members share an interest in simple mathematical systems which show complex or choatic behaviour, and in the wide range of physical systems which seem to follow these mathematical models.

Chaotic behaviour, usually associated with such phenomena as turbulent fluid flow, can arise in systems as simple as a double pendulum – one pendulum hung on the end of another. For certain energy values the behaviour of the double pendulum becomes skittish and seemingly unpredictable. Computers are an important tool for modelling and understanding these phenomena, which often defeat both mathematical analysis and intuition.

Peitgen the mathematician, and Richter the physicist, were drawn together by a common interest in a particularly baffling mathematical equation connected with, among other things, the motion of the solar system. 'Very soon,' said Peitgen, 'we noticed that our intuition failed completely.' They decided to try to get a feel for the problem with some experiments in computer graphics. According to Peitgen, 'when we did this, our intuition really exploded.' Their reward was the discovery of a previously unobserved feature of the equation's behaviour. It was not an earth-shaking discovery, but it was enough to encourage them to continue.

In the winter of 1982–83, Peitgen had a sabbatical in that mecca of computer graphics, Salt Lake City, Utah. With Saupe and Jürgens he made a movie to illustrate a lecture to the American Mathematical Society. 'People liked it. Lots of things followed.'

A turning point was Peitgen's introduction to an almost forgotten corner of mathematics first explored 60 years ago by the French mathematician Gaston Julia.

Julia sets are intricate structures which appear when a mathematical function is repeatedly fed with its own output. Like the patterns seen when a video camera is fed its own output via a monitor screen, Julia sets contain miniature copies of themselves.

Physicists were beginning to suspect that Julia sets might be linked to such phenomena as the loss of magnetization when iron is heated, and the onset of superconductivity as certain metals are cooled close to absolute zero. These phenomena are examples of phase changes. The melting of ice and the boiling of water are also phase changes, but surprisingly they are far less well understood than their exotic relations.

A technique called renormalization was suggested by Leo Kadanoff and then used with great success by the 1982 Nobel Prize winner Kenneth Wilson, to elucidate phase changes. Renormalization allows blocks of atoms in a crystal lattice to be treated as if they were single atoms in a larger lattice. Again we meet the idea of equating the part to the whole, the large to the small. Kadanoff alerted Peitgen and his colleagues to work on Julia sets carried out in France by the leading thermodynamicist David Ruelle.

The Germans began to experiment with Julia sets, using the University of Utah's graphics equipment. The images were dramatic and seductive. A time of all-night computing sessions began. 'We didn't go skiing all winter,' remembers Peitgen. 'We just did pictures for about two months.'

Back in Bremen in the summer of 1983, Peitgen tried to probe beneath the glamorous exterior, into the underlying theory of Julia sets. Peter Richter found the subject fascinating, too. Then, towards the end of the year, they heard that three scientists in Paris, B. Derrida, L. Desseze and C. Itzykson, had managed to fit together the mathematical theory of Julia sets and the physical theory of phase transitions.

The latest crop of computer images from Bremen reflects this unification of the two subjects. The group's study of Julia sets has concentrated on functions which arise from simplified models of magnetism. (Unfortunately, fully realistic models of magnetism still defy computation.) The Julia set is interpreted as the boundary between regimes of magnetic and nonmagnetic behaviour. It is generated by running Wilson's renormalization process backwards.

Some of the images show how the magnetic behaviour changes with temperature. Others show how it alters as one dials different properties for the atoms of imaginary magnetic substances. The resulting pictures recall oriental carpets, Gothic rose windows, or sections through plant stems. They have an internal consistency and power that makes some so-called 'computer art' look shallow. Only the colouring is contrived. The forms themselves grow spontaneously from the equations.

The strange thing is that no one yet knows what these rich patterns really mean. The temperature charts plot not only real temperatures, which can be measured in degrees, but complex temperatures which require the odd concept of a degree multiplied by the square root of minus one. Physicists have argued that complex temperature does not make sense, so why waste time looking at it? Other images plot what happens when a parameter known as q varies through a continuous range of values – even though for real atoms q must be a whole number.

Peter Richter defended this use of computer power to explore 'unphysical' states. 'It's really helpful to look behind the curtain and see what's going on in the complex plane,' he said.

In some theories, too, phenomena in the ghost world of complex temperature seem to exert an influence on what happens in the real world. Richter points to the example of quantum mechanics, which is full of 'unphysical' quantities like complex angular momentum which nevertheless make themselves felt in the physical world.

As yet, the Bremen group's work on dynamical systems has thrown up more questions than answers. The project is unlikely to impress those mathematicians who measure achievement only in proofs and theorems.

Like a space probe or a high-energy physics experiment, a few months' work with the computer has brought in a mass of observational data which may take years to digest. As hunches harden into theories and theorems, it will become easier to judge the power of computer graphics as an aid to scientific intuition.

30

Infinite reflections

Because of the magazine's space limitations, the Bremen computer graphics and the accompanying text had to be published in two instalments. This, the second instalment, really consists of two articles on separate subjects.

The first of them attempts to make a connection between the Bremen research and the practical things that people do with computers every day.

The second is about a piece of pure mathematics which evidently has something to do with the physical world, though its exact significance is not yet clear. The thread which runs through all this is the now-fashionable subject of chaos.

13 September 1984

Chaos and numerical methods

Science and engineering rely heavily on numerical computations in which time, space and other continuous variables are treated as discrete. Engineering structures are broken down into finite elements for stress analysis. Time, in any computer simulation, progresses in tiny jerks. The justification usually given is that if the discrete intervals are small enough it does not make any difference.

But according to Heinz-Otto Peitgen of Bremen University this can be a dangerous assumption, especially when non-linear equations are involved. 'There is a deep gap between continuous time and discrete time thinking,' he argues. 'The trust that one can go from one to the other is not justified in non-linear equations.'

Non-linear equations are those in which variables are multiplied together or raised to powers. In linear equations, multiplication is by constants only.

Essentially the same method is used to run a computer model of any dynamical process, whether it is the world economy or the explosion of a hydrogen bomb. At each time step, the model is fed with the output it produced at the previous step.

The dynamical systems research group in Bremen has produced vivid visual evidence of a fact that was known to the French mathematician Gaston Julia 60 years ago. Even a very simple function, when fed with its own output, can exhibit wild and seemingly chaotic behaviour. 'Small deviations have a big influence in the long run,' explains Peitgen.

Some processes, of course, have a natural time period. A time step of one year might well be appropriate in a population model for animals which breed annually. Here, if the model behaves chaotically, one could reasonably expect a similar behaviour in real animal populations. 'People in biology know this very well, that many phenomena have to be modelled as discrete-time phenomena,' says Peitgen. But he points out that in physics almost all the laws and models are continuous-time equations.

Numerical analysts have developed ways of checking that their solutions are well-behaved, and controlling cumulative errors. One simple method is to recalculate, using a different time-step or spatial mesh, and see if you get the same result. This works well enough with linear models, where errors build up relatively slowly. But Peitgen argues that non-linear models are much more sensitive. Attempts to make a non-linear model well behaved may rapidly eat up all the available computer power.

'For a long time people have believed that if we put up enough weather stations and had fast enough computers, not only would we be able to do weather forecasts for the day, but we would be able to do long range weather forecasts,' says Peitgen. But he believes that realistic computer models of the weather may be intrinsically unstable. Quite literally, striking a match could start a hurricane.

'Then even the finest computer and the best network of weather stations does not help you,' Peitgen points out, 'because it is not computable in principle.'

An important issue, then, is to distinguish deep-rooted chaos from the almost accidental kind of chaos that can arise from an over-simple computer model. Simple, discrete models of magnetism exhibit chaotic behaviour. It is still not known whether chaos would persist in a more realistic model. Perhaps chaos is an intrinsic feature of magnetism. Perhaps it only reflects the inadequacy of our mathematical models.

But the Lorenz equations, subject of a computer-animated film made in Bremen, demonstrate that chaotic behaviour can arise even in completely continuous systems. All the signs are that chaos is not just a figment of our computers but an intrinsic feature of the physical world.

The Mandelbrot set

A recurring figure in the Bremen group's images is the 'little apple-man' with his bug-like appendages. This peculiar entity was discovered by Benoit Mandelbrot of IBM. From the central cluster of massive blobs extend frailer structures shaped like tree roots or forked lightning. On low-resolution pictures these filmsy structures disappear entirely, or appear as mere 'dust'. In fact they contain a wealth of structure, including tiny copies of the Mandelbrot set itself.

One of the most striking sequences of pictures taken at Bremen shows a small part of the Mandelbrot set under ever-increasing magnification. The final picture shows a region approximately one million times smaller than the first. During this colossal 'zoom' a rich variety of spirals, arabesques, and miniature 'apple-men' comes into view. Continued magnification would reveal an infinity of further detail. It is as if a camera in space were to picture the entire British Isles and then zoom in on a copy of *Computing* being read by a man in Soho Square.

In theory, one could go on for ever, bringing finer and finer details of the Mandelbrot set into view. In practice, the journey ends when the computer reaches the limit of its arithmetical precision.

Remarkably, this rococo structure of literally infinite complexity arises from a simple mathematical formula: $z \leftarrow z^2 + c$. The process of squaring a number z and adding a constant c, repeated indefinitely, will sometimes send z off to infinity. But for some values of c, this does not happen. Instead, z is attracted to some finite value, or hops around from one finite value to another.

The numbers z and c are allowed to be complex numbers. In this number system, -1 has a square root, denoted by the letter i. If $c = x + iy$, then the number c can be associated with a point in the plane which has coordinates (x, y). This provides a convenient graphical representation for complex numbers on the computer screen.

The Mandelbrot set is simply the set of all values of c, for which z does not shoot off to infinity if its initial value is 0. Mark a black point on the plane for every such value of c, and the mysterious apple-man takes shape.

The remaining points, those for which z goes to infinity, form the ocean which surrounds this dark continent. For some points z diverges faster than for others. The Bremen group has made these variations visible with gradations of colour. In open areas, these gradations resemble depth contours in a sea chart, but they twist into wild, Paisley-like patterns in the maze of creeks and lagoons around the Mandelbrot continent's fringes.

John Hubbard of Ithaca, New York, and Adrien Douady of Paris proved that these contours are identical to the contours of potential which would surround the Mandelbrot set if it were electrically charged. Since

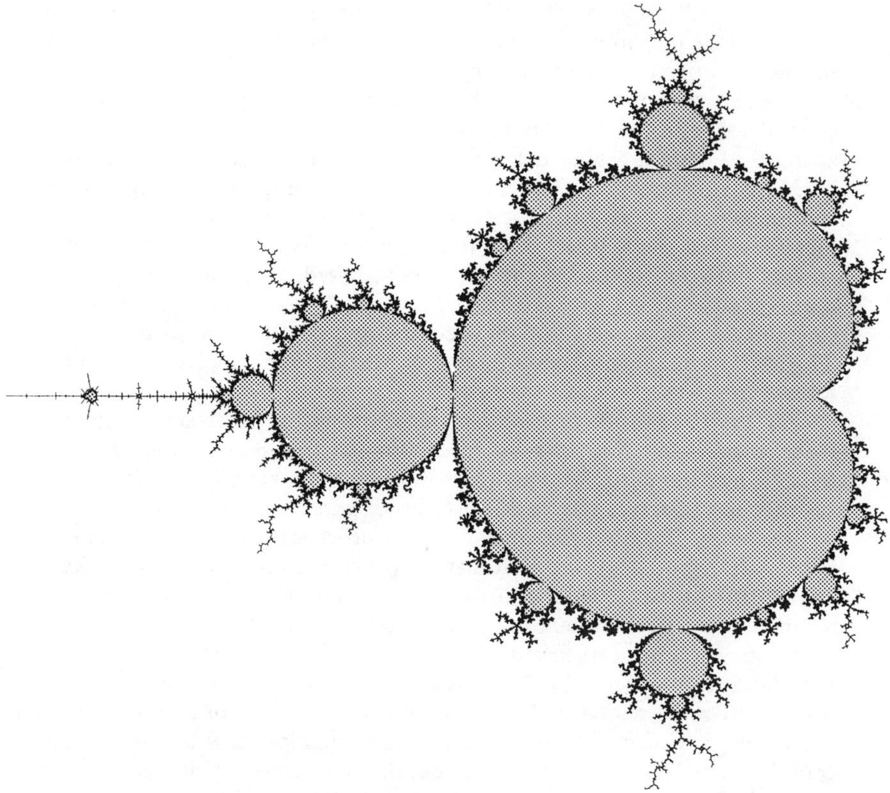

The Mandelbrot set

the set is a purely mathematical object, the physical significance of this, if any, remains a fascinating mystery.

But in quite a different way, the Bremen researchers have linked the Mandelbrot set to the physics of magnetism. They were studying a simplified model of the interacting atomic spins in a magnet. On a computer-generated plot which linked the overall magnetic properties to a parameter of the individual atoms, they spotted the silhouette of the 'apple-man'. 'The discovery, purely a computer-graphical discovery, was that something like the Mandelbrot set occurs as you change the parameters,' explains Heinz-Otto Peitgen.

The Mandelbrot set seemed to occur in regions where anomalous magnetic behaviour was predicted. 'Maybe,' Peitgen adds cautiously, 'the claim that the Mandelbrot set is a universal object in dynamical systems is true.'

It can be hard to believe that the Mandelbrot set arises from so simple a formula. It is not unusual to get something complex if you do something simple an infinite number of times, but the Mandelbrot set has a quite unexpected wealth of structure. Aesthetically the thing is a paradox. The general shape of the Mandelbrot set is graceless, warty, and cheekily anatomical. But at higher magnification, incredible beauties are disclosed.

Many mathematical objects (polyhedra and tilings, for example) have a sublime symmetry and regularity, and impress us because they are so inevitable and predictable. The Mandelbrot set is different. Here there is a tension between regularity and novelty, the predictable and the unpredictable. It is like a skilful work of art. Actually nothing quite like it exists in the visual arts. The most compelling parallels are with music. The appropriate metaphors are rhythm, texture, melody, harmony and form.

Parts of the Mandelbrot set consist of connected but visibly discrete blobs or particles. But the most interesting-looking parts of the set are those where the particle structure is too fine to be visible, and we see instead the collective effects of infinities of particles.

It is immediately apparent that higher-order structures are present: fronds and whorls, spirals within spirals. Each of these features has its own strong identity, yet one flows smoothly into the next. Any concepts we invent to describe them must have plenty of slippability.

In one sense it is surprising that we can make pictures of the Mandelbrot set at all. The object is known to contain infinite complexities. Remarkably, by sampling a mere million or so points we can make a very good picture of it. The reason for this is that almost all the complexity is concentrated on the boundary of the set, which can be thought of as a thin but very wiggly line. Turn up the magnification as you will; what you see will always consist almost entirely of non-boundary points.

The bottom of the creeks and inlets surrounding the Mandelbrot continent may be steep in places, but it is always smooth. We can therefore chart it to any required precision by making soundings at a finite number of points. That, at least, is what one feels intuitively. These are really matters for mathematical proof.

Peitgen warns of the dangers of modelling continuous change with discrete time steps. But there are also many cases where a discrete approximation is faithful to a continuous reality. The contours around the Mandelbrot set appear to be an example.

In physics, certain quantities including both time and space are usually treated as if they were continuous. Edward Fredkin (Chapter 33) suggests that this may not be so. It is a difficult assertion to test experimentally, since continuous and discrete systems mimic each other's behaviour so closely.

Further reading

Crutchfield, J.P., Farmer, J.D., Packard, N.H. and Shaw, R.S. (1986). 'Chaos' *Scientific American*, December, 38–49.

Dewdney, A.K. (1985). 'Computer recreations' *Scientific American*, August, 8–14. (How to explore the Mandelbrot set on a personal computer. Fine graphics by Peitgen and Richter on the front cover and in the article.)

Mandelbrot, B. (1982). *The Fractal Geometry of Nature.* New York: W.H. Freeman. (The main source book on fractals. Well illustrated but rather mathematical for the casual reader. It says very little about the Mandelbrot set itself.)

Peitgen, H.-O. and Richter, P. (1986). *The Beauty of Fractals.* New York: Springer-Verlag.

31

Exploring the cellular microworld

Stephen Wolfram believes that cellular automata provide simple but powerful computer models of the physical world, and his research has produced persuasive evidence that this is so. Wolfram's work, like that of Peitgen and Richter, has attracted additional attention because it appeals not only to the brain but to the eye.

Exciting things have been happening recently on the borderland between computer science and theoretical physics, and Wolfram has been in the forefront of the activity.

17 January 1985

Cellular automata have been known since John von Neumann investigated them in his search for self-reproducing systems. Most research in the subject has centred on two-dimensional cellular automata, where the cells are spaced regularly on a plane surface.

At each 'tick' of the clock every cell switches to a new state determined only by its former state and the states of its neighbours.

For the past few years Stephen Wolfram, an English theoretical physicist, has been investigating the behaviour of simpler arrays where the cells are lined up in a single row. With his colleagues at the Institute for Advanced Study in Princeton, New Jersey, Wolfram has shown that these one-dimensional cellular automata exhibit almost all the interesting behaviour seen in two dimensions.

If the row of cells runs across the width of the display screen, the vertical dimension of the screen can be used to show the history of the cells' past states. One can then see not only patterns in space, but patterns in time.

Wolfram still expresses amazement at the way simple rules, and simple beginnings, can lead to enormously complex events. 'I find it really remarkable that such simple things can make such complicated patterns,' he says.

Some rules give rise to fractal patterns, which reproduce themselves repeatedly on ever larger scales. On other occasions the evolution is chaotic, with no visible regularity either in space or in time. Yet other rules yield a harvest of static and moving 'objects' which might be used to construct a universal computer within the cellular automaton microworld.

Wolfram believes that cellular automata can provide useful models of natural systems. Persisting structures which either stay put or move through space at a constant speed invite comparison with physical particles. Ironically, the way physicists imagine a particle no longer has much to do with this commonsense picture. Quantum mechanics has disposed of the idea that a particle necessarily has a definite position.

The moving things which leave diagonal trails across the screen may be a poor model for physical particles, but Wolfram believes they might be linked with a peculiarly indestructible type of wave called a soliton.

Cellular automata often give rise to areas of single colour or uniform texture. Wolfram refers to these as 'phases', the word used by physicists for specific solid, liquid or gaseous forms of matter. Sometimes a 'seed' of a particular phase, injected into a cellular automaton, will grow and grow, like a seed crystal dropped in a crucible of molten metal.

The branching (dendritic) crystal growth seen in snowflakes has been modelled at Princeton by Norman Packard, using a two-dimensional cellular automaton. Wolfram says this is the best-yet cellular automaton model of a physical process.

When a small 'packet' of vapour or liquid crystallizes there is a release of latent heat, which is thought to inhibit the crystallization of neighbouring packets. Growth inhibition of this kind is easily built into a cellular automaton rule. In fact Wolfram argues that growth inhibition is present in virtually all cellular automata with interesting behaviour.

Fluid flow, electromagnetic fields and other physical systems are usually modelled with partial differential equations. Quantities change smoothly with space and time. Occasionally an exact solution can be found by manipulating the equations algebraically and plugging in numerical values at the end. More commonly, partial differential equations are solved approximately, by number-crunching techniques which would be very laborious without computers.

Smooth, continuous space and time are approximated by a closely spaced mesh of points. At each point, in a typical numerical solution, physical quantities such as temperature, pressure, or velocity are represented by 32-bit numbers.

A cellular automaton model would probably use the same fine mesh of points in space and time, or possibly a finer one. But the amount of information stored for each point would be drastically reduced, perhaps to only two or three bits.

The resulting model can be run much faster than a model based on partial differential equations and floating point variables. But it will be of little use if it no longer behaves like the physical world.

Wolfram believes that a cellular automaton can be 'a good first model' of a physical system. 'My belief is that in fact it will turn out that most of the qualitative and many of the quantitative aspects of partial differential equations are preserved even in the limit of extreme discretization,' he explains. 'It's certainly true that cellular automata have enough variety and enough complexity to be like physics,' he adds.

But he does not go as far as Edward Fredkin of the Massachusetts Institute of Technology, who hopes to reduce all of physics to discrete, exactly computable models. Fredkin actually believes that the universe is a gigantic cellular automaton. Wolfram sees the attraction of this idea, but says that no actual evidence for it exists.

Apparent randomness often arises even from the simplest 'seed' configuration: a single non-zero cell in a line of zeroes. Such a seed may set off an expanding pattern of activity which appears on the screen as a triangle with an ever-growing base. The vertical midline of the triangle records the subsequent history of the original non-zero cell. The sequence of cell values along this midline often appears completely random.

'If you run all kinds of statistical tests on it they just say it's random, which I find rather interesting because it clearly isn't random, in the sense that it was made by this extremely simple procedure,' says Wolfram. He believes that pseudo-random sequences from cellular automata might be useful in enciphering messages. Another kind of pseudo-random sequence generator, the linear feedback shift register, has gone out of favour with cryptographers because its behaviour can too easily be analysed and reduced to a formula.

There are some cellular automata whose behaviour can never be reduced to a formula. The only way to find out what they do is to simulate them step by step. No simpler computation provides a significant short cut. This property is known as computational irreducibility. Universal computers such as general Turing machines are among the systems which possess it.

Given any problem, a universal computer can always be programmed to solve it by the fastest possible algorithm. No other computer can then take a short cut which is not also available to the first computer. (The fact that one machine may have more powerful instructions than another does not materially affect this conclusion.)

At least two cellular automata are known to be universal computers. They can be programmed to solve any computer-soluble problem, by setting up an appropriate initial configuration of cells.

But a system need not be a universal computer, to be computationally irreducible. Though he cannot yet prove it, Wolfram believes that computational irreducibility is widespread among cellular automata and other systems with complicated behaviour. Turbulent fluid flow, weather, and other systems exhibiting 'chaotic' behaviour are obvious candidates. This means that certain questions about cellular automata – and about the physical world – may be intrinsically difficult or even impossible to answer.

Suppose you wanted to know whether a particular cellular automaton will ever halt. The obvious way to find out is to start the system and see what happens. With luck, it will either halt, or go into a loop (proving it never halts) within a fairly short time. But it may go on for a month without doing either of these things. It may go on for a million years. In fact, no finite computation can guarantee to answer the 'halting problem'.

If the system is computationally irreducible, there is no short cut to knowing its ultimate fate. The halting problem must then be one of the undecidable problems whose existence was first proved by the logician Kurt Gödel.

Wolfram expects that physics, like mathematics, may prove to be full of undecidable problems. 'It would be a very remarkable thing if the kind of mathematics that crops up in theoretical physics is just that special kind that happens to avoid the pieces where there are undecidable propositions,' he argues.

Physicists often ask what will happen to something after infinite time has elapsed. This is merely an idealization. It is a convenient way of talking about the state a system will reach when it has been left long enough to settle down. But Wolfram warns that some questions of this kind will be formally undecidable because they require an infinite amount of computation.

'What this is really trying to say is that some of those idealizations may just not be sensible,' he says, ' – that if you make the idealization you then can't work anything out.'

It is perhaps no surprise that we cannot always expect to know the infinite future. But even the next year, or the next hour, or the next microsecond in the life of a computationally irreducible system may be impossible to predict in practice.

Many problems appear to be intractable in the sense that the computer time or memory size needed to solve them grows explosively as 'bigger' versions of the problem are attempted. Wolfram argues that intractability, like undecidability, is likely to be common in the physical world. There are some experiments, he suggests, that theory simply can't handle. 'You just have to try it and see,' he says.

Wolfram thinks it unlikely that genetic engineers will ever be able to sit at a computer terminal and design new creatures to order. He points out that there may be no quick way to predict the effect of a particular modification to the creature's DNA.

'If this process of getting from the DNA to the finished creature is computationally irreducible,' he says, 'then you expect that effectively the only way to find out what the creature looks like overall is to let the thing grow and see what it looks like.'

Scientists have always sought to reduce the behaviour of the universe to simple laws. But cellular automata demonstrate graphically that simple laws can lead to extremely complex behaviour. This behaviour not only looks complex, it is complex in the absolute sense that a vast amount of computation is needed to predict or 'explain' it.

Before the arrival of the computer, science was more or less compelled to stay within those areas where not only the laws but the calculations were simple. The orbit of the Moon was easily calculated. The dynamics of Saturn's rings were not.

Wolfram believes that cellular automata will help scientists to explore the areas where the rules are simple but the calculations are not. This belief rests on two hunches.

One hunch is that much of the real world is computationally irreducible. That is to say, if we want to understand it we have no alternative to doing very large computations. The other hunch is that cellular automata have the power to handle these computations. At the moment, the constructions that have been used to make cellular automata function as universal computers are elaborate, contrived, and of no practical utility.

In practice a cellular automaton need not be a universal computer to provide a useful model of physics. But it will be a great boost to the morale of Wolfram and his colleagues, if some very simple cellular automaton can be proved, by natural, elegant methods, to be a universal computer.

Wolfram believes intuition and serendipity may be more productive than a carefully planned assault on this problem. The game of Life, a two-dimensional cellular automaton, sparked a craze among computer hackers in the 1970s.

Bill Gosper, then at MIT, managed to prove that Life is a universal computer. The only one-dimensional cellular automaton known to have universal powers has eighteen states per cell. Wolfram is sure that a much simpler candidate can be found, and he thinks that microcomputer users could join in the search. 'There are a lot of kids and hackers out there,' he points out.

Late in 1985 Stephen Wolfram reported that the application of cellular automata to cryptography had been worked out in some detail, and that work was in progress on the use of cellular automata for pattern recognition. He had also been studying the sources of randomness in physical systems.

One of the most interesting developments was a simulation of fluid flow, based on a two-dimensional cellular automaton. The simulation runs on a Connection Machine and faithfully reproduces such phenomena as the eddies which form behind an obstacle. Wolfram has been working with Thinking Machines Corporation, manufacturers of the Connection Machine. The machine is suitable for research on cellular automata since it has a large number (65,536 or more) of simple processors, each connected to a number of neighbours. The Connection Machine could itself be described as a cellular automaton, though it has rather richer connections, and rather more states per node, than the phrase usually implies.

Further reading

Dewdney, A.K. (1985). 'Computer recreations' *Scientific American*, May, 10–16.

Wolfram, S. (1984). 'Cellular automata as models of complexity' *Nature*, **311**, 4 October, 419–424.

Wolfram, S. (1984). 'Computer software in science and mathematics' *Scientific American*, September, 140–151.

32

Protein makers wait for simulation tools

It would be unimaginably difficult, as Stephen Wolfram suggests, to predict the form of a higher plant or animal from its genome. Even a single-celled organism is probably too complex ever to be simulated in the required detail. It is just conceivable that the shape of a virus could be predicted from a knowledge of its nucleic acid, since most virus particles consist only of a few types of protein and the nucleic acid itself. To predict the shape of a single protein molecule is difficult, as we saw in Chapter 24, but it is regarded as a feasible goal.

Press articles keep talking about 'designing drugs by computer' as though this were a comparable exercise to designing microchips or oil refineries by computer. In fact the complexities of biochemistry are far greater, and the designer of molecules has a much tougher task. Carbon, hydrogen, nitrogen and oxygen atoms were not designed for the designer, in the way that nuts and bolts and silicon gates were. They do not behave like engineering components or the statements of a good programming language. To a certain extent, everything in an organic molecule affects everything else. Molecules, and protein molecules especially, may be machine-like to the extent that their behaviour exhibits a few nice clean chains of cause and effect. But many other influences, less easily analysed, are at work. Complexity is inherent to the problem and cannot be designed away.

22 November 1984

Biotechnology is a curious business. On the one hand there are the dreams – spaceship hulls reinforced with synthetic spider silk, and 'magic bullet' cures for cancer. On the other hand the commercial realities: a fraction of a cent off the cost of a can of lemonade; a better mixture for clearing blocked drains.

Most of the industry's effort to date has been spent on reproducing natural products such as insulin and interferon. Recently the biotechnology business has become excited about 'protein engineering'. Protein engineering aims to improve on nature. Computer techniques are central to the plan.

The development of these techniques has been uneven. In interactive graphics, the protein engineers are using the most up-to-date technology. But they are still hampered by the lack of reliable simulation methods.

Genex is a Maryland company which has a major stake in protein engineering, and even claims to have originated the concept. The company's vice-president for advanced technology, Kevin Ulmer, believes the work being done in protein engineering today will prove as influential as that of the German chemists who laid the foundations of synthetic organic chemistry 100 years ago.

Genex has been losing $5 million a year, and is relying on America's sweet tooth and its blocked drains to pull it into short-term profit. Last year it began manufacturing phenylalanine, one of the raw materials of the artificial sweetener aspartame. Its latest product is an enzyme which clears bathroom drains by dissolving wads of hair.

Unable to afford a major effort in protein engineering by itself, Genex struck a deal with the engineering group Bendix. Bendix paid $1.5 million for computer and laboratory equipment, and committed $15 million over five years to support Genex's research. Bendix and Genex would share the right to exploit the resulting technology.

The joint venture was short-lived. Bendix was taken over by Allied Corporation (formerly Allied Chemical) in January 1983. The new management paid off Genex and wanted nothing more to do with the protein engineering venture. 'We walked away with all the rights and $12 million in cash,' said a delighted but still perplexed Ulmer. 'They gave us rights to all the technology, past, present and future, and left all the equipment.'

Natural proteins come in a bewildering variety. Some, the enzymes, are catalysts. Some are hormones. Some, like the antibodies or immunoglobulins, are highly selective binding reagents. Some, like hair and silk, are strong, lightweight structural materials.

'At present,' said Ulmer, 'even with the most high-falutin' genetic engineering we are still making natural products. Even if we make human insulin in bacteria it's still the natural human insulin that human beings once made. 'But we've also developed techniques that would allow us to change the insulin molecule or any other protein, to make a protein that didn't exist in nature before.'

Twenty amino acids provide the building blocks for all proteins. Each type of protein consists of amino acids chained together in a unique sequence. Attractions and repulsions between these amino acids persuade the chain to fold up in a shape that is characteristic for that protein. It is this three-dimensional, folded structure that determines the protein's physical, chemical and biological properties.

No one at this stage is attempting to design new proteins from scratch. Genex and other companies are taking natural proteins and attempting to modify them in simple ways, perhaps changing only one amino acid. One aim is to produce industrial enzymes that perform better and last longer. Enzyme technology has not yet fulfilled the rosy predictions of the 1970s.

'There are perhaps ten or fewer industrial enzymes of any significance in the world,' explains Ulmer. 'And those ten constitute 80 or 90 per cent of the total world market for enzymes.'

Genetic engineering has made enzymes cheap to manufacture. The gene for virtually any enzyme can be spliced into hard-working industrial micro-organisms which will then churn it out in bulk.

But a natural enzyme does not always have the right properties for its new role as an industrial catalyst or a household cleanser. Ulmer explained: 'Typically you want to work under non-physiological conditions, at extremes of concentration, extremes of temperature, extremes of pH, in the presence of solvents or ions that the enzyme doesn't encounter inside the cell where it's normally found.' (pH measures acidity and alkalinity.)

Genex has calculated that a typical factory making high fructose corn syrup could save $4 million a year if the enzyme glucose isomerase were toughened up by protein engineering. The enzyme turns glucose into the much sweeter fructose. The higher the process temperature, the more fructose is produced. But the enzyme needs alkaline conditions. At high temperatures and alkaline pH, some of the sugary mixture turns to caramel. So the syrup factories use additional processes: they use ion exchange to boost their product's fructose content, and they use activated carbon to filter out the caramel.

An ideal, re-engineered glucose isomerase would work happily for long periods in hot acid conditions. The factories would save millions, according to Ulmer, if they could make the desired 55 per cent fructose syrup directly. He 'would love to improve' phenylalanine ammonia lyase (PAL), the enzyme Genex uses to make phenylalanine. Compared with the aspartase used in another Genex process, PAL is unstable and inefficient. 'We'd like to make it more like aspartase,' Ulmer said.

Antibodies, too, are candidates for re-engineering. Antibodies engineered for toxicity could seek out and kill cancer cells in the body. Radioactive and other markers, carried by antibodies, could pick out specific tissues in medical imaging.

Toughened-up antibodies could be packed in columns to separate and purify biological products. Natural antibodies are used already to purify expensive products like interferon, but they are too frail and costly for use in mass production.

Ulmer's group is also interested in developing synthetic versions of nature's structural proteins like silk and wool. The powerful adhesive that anchors a barnacle to a rock is a protein. So is spider silk, a phenomenally strong material for its weight.

Inevitably costly, these synthetic structural proteins are unlikely to be used for shirts or curtains. But aerospace and other high-technology industries might be prepared to pay for their unique properties.

Genex and other companies have invested heavily in computer graphics. Genex's protein engineering group has two Digital Equipment VAX computers. An interactive graphics program called Frodo runs on the group's Evans and Sutherland PS300 colour graphics workstations. With Frodo, it is possible to build a geometrical model of a known protein (using data from X-ray crystallography), examine it on the screen from any viewpoint in space, measure all the angles and distances in the molecule, and tinker with its structure in any reasonable way.

What the engineer at the computer terminal cannot do is to determine, with confidence, how the real molecule will react to this tinkering. Even a few atoms changed might conceivably affect the entire shape of the molecule, making nonsense of the hypothetical structure displayed on the screen.

Software does exist which can partially predict the folding of a protein chain, but according to Ulmer, current techniques are too hit-and-miss to be useful in protein engineering. As far as Genex is concerned, the only sure way to determine the structure and properties of a newly designed protein is to go away and make it in the laboratory.

It is as if the designers of a new microprocessor had to order prototype chips without first running a logic simulation on their design. The protein engineers are attempting computer aided design of molecules, but a key component of CAD – simulation – is still missing. Ulmer believes that this handicap will slow down the progress of protein engineering but need not halt it. And he expects that protein engineering will itself generate the new knowledge needed for successful computer simulation of the protein folding process. Current theories of the folding process are based on observations of natural proteins. Now scientists can harden up their theories experimentally, testing their ideas with proteins made to order.

As those theories take shape, the goal of designing proteins by computer will come closer.

A year later Genex, for one, was little closer to the dream. Kevin Ulmer had left, to head the Center for Advanced Research in Biotechnology. After losing its main customer, G.D. Searle and Company, Genex pulled out of manufacturing. Contract research became once again its chief source of income.

33

Taking the universe to bits

In Stanislaw Lem's science fiction story *Non Serviam* an English computer scientist called Professor Dobb created an entire computer-simulated world complete with intelligent inhabitants. Professor Dobb eavesdropped as these 'personoids' discussed the possibility that their world might have a creator, whom they referred to as 'God'. Dobb was not alone in the field of 'personetics'. Similar work was in progress, in the Polish author's tale, at the Massachusetts Institute of Technology.

Lem's story carries a powerful hint that for all we know, our own universe might be nothing more than a vast computer program. I am not sure whether Lem was aware that there is a real-life MIT professor who believes this, or something very similar, to be the literal truth.

24 January 1985

While Princeton's Stephen Wolfram sees useful 'first approximation' models for physics in the highly parallel arrays known as cellular automata, Edward Fredkin of the Massachusetts Institute of Technology goes further. 'I believe physics is a cellular automaton,' Fredkin says. 'I believe that what goes on in the world, the basic phenomenon that underlies quantum mechanics and everything else, is the operation of a machine like a cellular automaton.'

He believes there is at least a remote possibility that his unproven assertion will one day be tested directly by scientific experiment. If Fredkin is right, and the universe is ultimately a 'digital information process', the implications for physics are astonishing.

Time's ever-rolling stream is portioned into discrete units, the individual ticks of the cosmic clock. Space is no longer a smooth and seamless web but a lattice of separate points, packed so closely as to be invisible even in experiments which probe the internal structure of subnuclear particles.

Some of the grittiest paradoxes of thermodynamics, quantum mechanics and relativity find novel solutions in Fredkin's universe. So does one paradox which dates back to the fifth century BC.

For Fredkin, a flying arrow does not move continuously like a Newtonian particle. It simply occupies a series of positions, like a 'sprite' on a home computer screen. He believes the Greek philosopher Zeno was correct when he argued, in effect, that a flying arrow could not occupy an infinite number of positions in a finite time.

What then gives the arrow its speed? How does it know where to appear next? 'There is no such thing as an instant in time,' claims Fredkin. 'Only *two* instants in time.'

What happens next is determined not only by the present instant but by the instant immediately past. So Zeno's arrow 'knows' which way it is flying, even though at any single instant it is theoretically motionless. Fredkin insists that this is not an artifice but 'a very beautiful thing that came out of the mathematics' when he and the physicist Richard Feynman recast the Schrödinger equation of quantum mechanics in discrete form.

Feynman won the 1965 Nobel physics prize for his brilliantly confirmed theoretical work in quantum electrodynamics. Not long after that he wrote (in *The Character of Physical Law*): 'It always bothers me that, according to the laws as we understand them today, it takes a computing machine an infinite number of logical operations to figure out what goes on in no matter how tiny a region of space, and no matter how tiny a region of time. How can all that be going on in that tiny space?'

One reply open to the physicist is that physics can do things computers cannot. For example, computers can handle only finite amounts of information. While in the conventional formulation of physics, it is possible for a finite volume of space to contain an infinite quantity of information.

Both Fredkin and Feynman found this idea uncomfortable. Both looked for ways to avoid the unnerving infinities. While Feynman dreamed of a physics without mathematical formulae, Fredkin played with the idea that some computer-like digital process underlies everything that happens, and that the amount of information in a cubic centimetre of space is actually finite.

'When I heard about cellular automata I realized right away that this was an idea that was both simple and powerful enough to be a good model for physical processes,' says Fredkin. 'So I started writing programs, and I discovered all kinds of interesting things.'

Cellular automata have a number of physically plausible features. For example, no influence can propagate faster than one lattice spacing per tick of the clock. So there is a built-in speed limit, analogous to the speed of light in Einstein's theory of relativity.

On the other hand, the cellular automaton universe has an absolute Cartesian frame of reference, namely the cellular array itself. This jars severely with the Einsteinian view that all measurements of position and velocity are relative.

Mention a Cartesian frame, says Fredkin, and most physicists will stop listening. 'If they only had earlids they would close them at that point,' he remarks. Fredkin saves the situation by postulating an additional layer of software between the observed universe and the underlying digital process.

'The answer,' he maintains, 'is that the spacetime that we live in is not that Cartesian lattice, but it's an information process that runs on the lattice.'

One of the great challenges for physics has been to explain why irreversible processes occur in a world where the basic laws are, with one or two provisos, reversible in time. Omelettes do not turn back into eggs. Yet there is very little in the basic laws to account for the 'arrow of time' and the obvious asymmetry between past and future.

The usual explanation is that the arrow of time comes not from the laws but from the initial conditions. The universe began in a state that was, in some sense, highly 'unlikely'. Ever since, the universe has been gradually settling towards a more 'likely' state. It is highly unlikely, runs this statistical argument, for the universe to return towards an earlier state.

Fredkin and his group at MIT (including Norman Margolus, Tommaso Toffoli and Gérard Vichniac) have been particularly interested in the class of cellular automata which evolve according to 'reversible' rules.

Unlike omelette-making, a reversible cellular automaton can be stopped and run backwards. An essential requirement for this is that no information is destroyed, though it may change its form as the system evolves.

Omelettes cannot be unmade, because of the difficulties (both practical and theoretical) of stopping every molecule in its tracks and precisely reversing its motion. The average computer program is irreversible for a somewhat different reason: information is destroyed as it runs.

Computer simulations of reversible cellular automata suffer from neither of these constraints. The researchers therefore enjoy the supernatural power of turning history around in its tracks. An orderly pattern may dissolve into apparent chaos as it evolves. But when the machine is thrown into reverse, order re-emerges from chaos in a seemingly miraculous fashion.

If, as Fredkin believes, the universe itself is a reversible cellular automaton, then no information is ever destroyed. From the point of view of an observer outside the universe, the entire past and the entire future could be deduced from the world's present state.

That is not to say that anyone *inside* the universe can enjoy similar omniscience. If the universe is a computer, then as Fredkin points out, 'You can prove that you can't in general solve what will happen in any experiment without performing that experiment.' In general, there is no short cut to knowledge of the future. In a similar fashion Fredkin deduces that it is difficult for anyone or anything inside the universe to monkey with the arrow of time.

Practical details aside, we could unmake an omelette if we had sufficient information about the omelette's past. But that information would have to be physically stored somewhere by some process which would be just as unlikely to occur (if the universe were left to itself) as the unscrambling of an egg.

Even if Fredkin's informational model of physics can be squared with relativity and thermodynamics, an impasse looms with quantum mechanics. The model is deterministic. Quantum mechanics is probabilistic.

Einstein argued that 'God does not play dice', and that the randomness observed in atomic-scale phenomena was due to the influence of some as yet undetected 'hidden variables'. But a series of experiments has given results that most physicists regard as incompatible with 'hidden variable' theories. It looks as though nature's randomness is no illusion. Fredkin rejects this interpretation. To simplify his argument greatly, he says that the confusion arises from the false assumption that the experimenter can make a random choice. In his view, not even the experimenter's actions can be random.

In one rather weak sense, Fredkin's position is uncontroversial. Some cellular automata are known to be universal computers, so if physics can be modelled with symbols at all, it can be modelled with a cellular automaton. 'There's no doubt for anyone that physics can be run this way,' says Fredkin. The only question, he adds, is what it takes in terms of computational resources.

Scientists look for elegance in their theoretical models. They are unlikely to buy an informational model unless it produces a lot of physics from relatively little computation. Fredkin has not yet shown that this is possible. He is, however, one of a growing band of researchers who are trying to build bridges between physics and computer science. They argue that computer science can throw light on questions in physics such as randomness and irreversibility.

Equally, they argue that computer scientists should pay more attention to physics since any real computer must obey physical laws. Fredkin's group has waded into the current controversy on 'dissipation-less computing'.

They argue that a computer can, in theory, run on arbitrarily small amounts of power. To support his case, Fredkin devised an imaginary computer where bits of information are represented by perfectly elastic billiard balls bouncing off each other and off fixed obstacles. This extraordinary machine has been simulated by an unusual cellular automaton, but argument still rages as to whether a zero-power computer could actually be built.

Further reading

Feynman, R. (1965). *The Character of Physical Law.* Cambridge, Mass.: MIT Press.

Lem, S. (1981). *Solaris: The Chain of Chance: A Perfect Vacuum.* Harmondsworth: Penguin. (This is one English-language volume in which the story *Non Serviam* can be found. It also appears in the anthology *The Mind's I*; see 'Further reading', Chapter 60.)

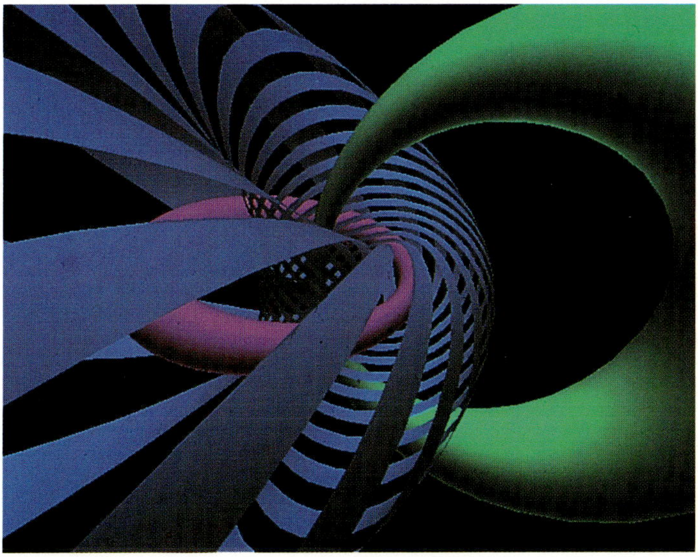

Plate 1 A computer-generated view of a four-dimensional object. The toroidal surfaces divide up a hypersphere in the same way as lines of latitude divide the spherical surface of the Earth. *See Chapter 8.*

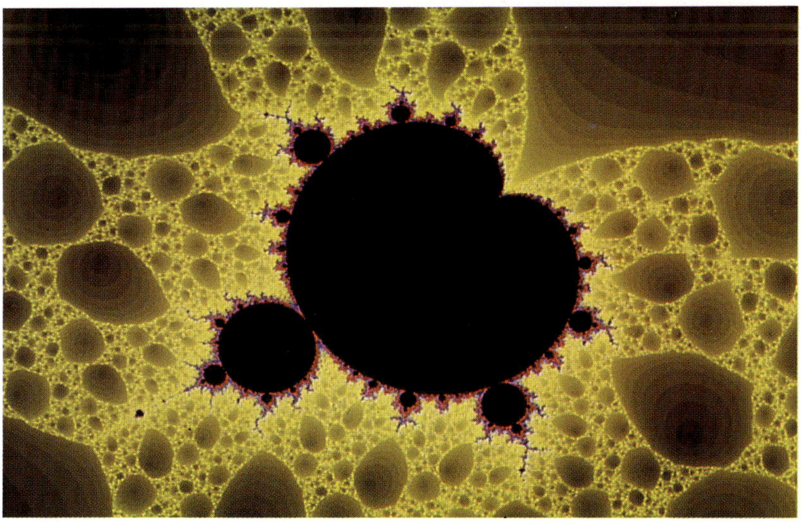

Plate 2 A tiny copy of the Mandelbrot set, discovered in a chart of the theoretical magnetic properties of an idealized solid. *See Chapter 30.*

Plate 3 Close-up of part of the Mandelbrot set, an infinitely complex object generated by a simple mathematical rule. *See Chapter 30.*

Plate 4 A fractal pattern generated by a one-dimensional cellular automaton, starting from a single 'seed' point. The vertical dimension represents time. *See Chapter 31.*

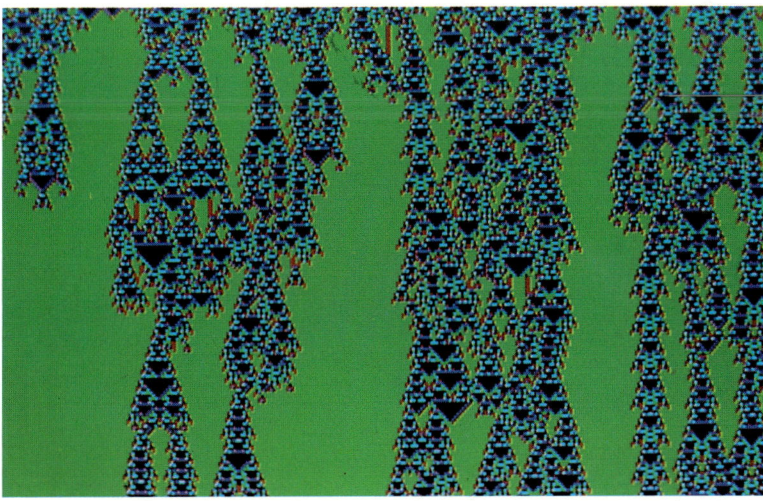

Plate 5 Complex behaviour of another one-dimensional cellular automaton. Although its behaviour is deterministic, there is probably no way of finding out what it will do, other than watching and waiting. *See Chapter 31.*

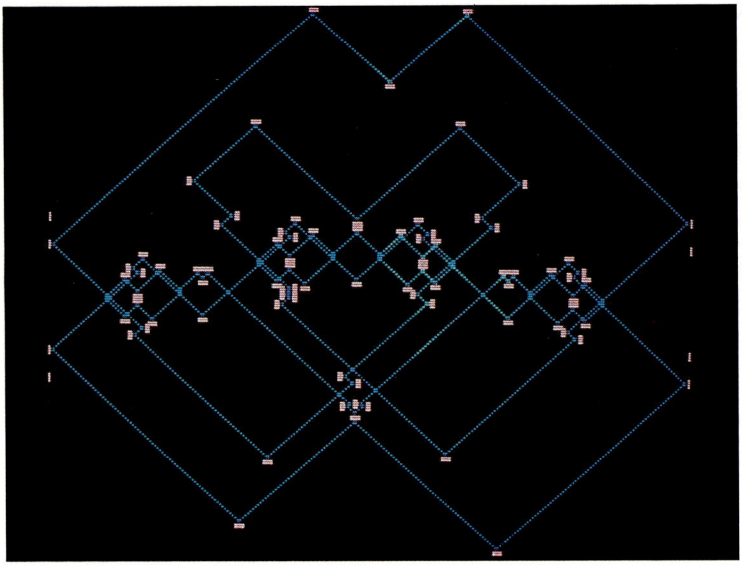

Plate 6 The Billiard Ball Machine in action. *See Chapter 33.*

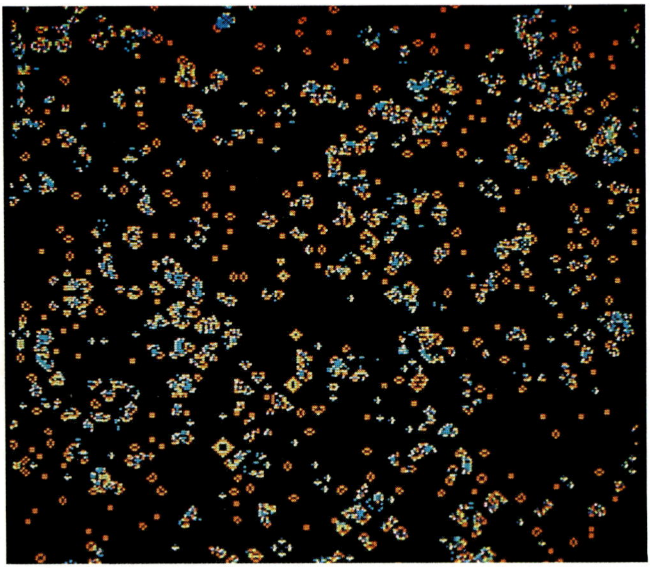

Plate 7 The game of Life, on Tommaso Toffoli's Cellular Automaton Machine. A few generations after a random start, some stable forms have emerged. Elsewhere, activity continues. Colours show the trace of earlier generations. *See Chapter 28.*

34

A program with a touch of Zen

While few Westerners have seriously studied Zen Buddhism (I certainly have not), millions have seen the film *Star Wars*. Perhaps the key Zen statement of the film comes at the moment when Luke Skywalker switches off his computer on the final bombing run. Whether you take your training with the Jedi knights or at a Japanese monastery, the object is to learn – or unlearn – enough to be able to rely on your own unconscious mind. This, surely, is what it means for the 'force' to be with you.

I am basically in sympathy with the director George Lucas's humanistic message, but I do think he missed a chance to give us a scene of triumphant human-computer cooperation. Of course, issues have to be kept simple in the movies, and if it had to be either the man or the machine that sealed the rebels' victory, then the man it had to be.

This article is about a computer program which plays Go. Let me just say that when I tried a few friendly games against the program, the force was definitely not with me. My clear impression was that it was hovering somewhere around the 6502 microprocessor beneath my keyboard.

28 January 1985

The Japanese are keen on computers and crazy about the game of Go. Why have they left it to Westerners to write Go-playing computer programs?

'They know its's impossible,' answers Allan Scarff, who soon intends to enjoy the satisfaction of selling a Go program to the sceptical Japanese.

At ICL, Scarff led projects on expert systems and intelligent databases. He left to set up his own software and consultancy business, Edge Computers Ltd. He did not mean to get involved in the risky business of games software.

An experienced Go player of *shodan* standard (it takes a thousand games, they say, to reach even this first rung of the nine-*dan* ladder), he was spurred into writing a Go program by a competition that Acornsoft ran last year. A condition of entry was that Acornsoft acquired the rights to the winning program. So instead of competing, Scarff raced to get his own program, Microgo 1, onto the market first.

Microgo 1 is available in versions for Acorn (BBC and Electron) and Commodore 64 machines. Other versions are planned, including one aimed at the Japanese market and running on the NEC 9801.

Probably the strongest competition comes from Nemesis, a Go program written by Bruce Wilcox of Cambridge, Massachusetts. It runs on the IBM PC.

Scarff's experience with expert systems convinced him that while many problems can be tackled with a body of knowledge expressed as rules, Go would not yield to this approach. Instead he tried to model the unconscious perceptual skill with which an expert player instantly sizes up a complex position on the Go board.

'Go is an Oriental game. There is a total split between Oriental thinking and Occidental thinking,' Scarff observes. He believes Western players spend too much time thinking. They lose the flow of their sequences of moves. Eastern players just look at the board and play where they feel is right. They can always produce elaborate explanations afterwards. 'But if you go to 20 different Go players, you get 20 different explanations,' says Scarff. He believes the real thinking is done unconsciously. 'I don't think they know how they do things,' he says. 'I think the explanation is just a theory.'

Go is a two-player game in which the main goal is to enclose territory. The standard board is a 19 by 19 grid. The players take turns to place their pieces or 'stones' on intersections. (Microgo 1 plays on a smaller, 9 by 9 board, to suit small screens and small computer memories. But Scarff says the program is actually stronger on a larger board.)

Once in position, a stone may not be moved. Stones, or groups of stones, may be captured by surrounding them. As in chess, the threat of capture is a major force in the game. But a Go game can develop without the slaughter that is inevitable as a chess game proceeds. In chess end games, the board is almost empty. The Go end game does not begin until the board begins to look crowded.

In chess, Go and similar games, it is theoretically possible to trace the consequences of any move and see whether it leads to a win or a loss. In practice this requires a search of an astronomically vast tree of alternative conclusions to the game. Neither a human player nor a computer can examine all of the possibilities.

A good chess program might look nine moves ahead. It cuts down the search by excluding obviously foolish moves. If it cannot find a quick and certain way to force checkmate, the program plays towards some position which it judges to be favourable.

Many game programs use an 'evaluation function' to judge the strength of a position. This function will reflect the programmer's intuitions about the game, or sometimes, the program's own experience.

Scarff's Microgo program relies almost entirely on a sophisticated evaluation function. In general it looks ahead only one move. If a program can be said to work by intuition rather than analysis, this one does. It makes tactical mistakes that might have been avoided by a little more logical analysis. But Scarff claims it is strong in strategy.

He reckons its strength at 15 *kyu*. A research version of the program plays, he says, at about 10 *kyu*. Human beginners play at about 25 *kyu*, and many never get into single figures. Fewer still reach the superior *dan* grades.

'Strong players like it because it has got some feel for the game,' Scarff says. 'It is playing Go. It's not mindlessly grinding out the moves.'

Scarff's algorithm evaluates a position by methods similar to those used in image processing or the early stages of computer vision. Its image of the board is an array-like data structure in which each cell corresponds to one intersection. On the board, each intersection can only have three states: it can be occupied by a black stone, a white stone, or no stone. The program, however, admits eighteen possible states for a cell. These additional states represent more abstract properties of the game position. For example, the program has a concept of 'eyefulness' which expresses how close a group of stones is to forming an 'eye' – an empty square safely surrounded by stones of one colour. Eyes are important because a group of stones with two eyes cannot be captured.

On each 'tick' of an imaginary clock the cell may change state, according to the inputs it receives from neighbouring cells. The array of cells operates as a cellular automaton. The automaton is run, typically for about five ticks, until it settles in a stable state. Each tick performs what Scarff calls a 'progressive abstraction' on the data. What starts as a raw pattern of black and white stones on a board is progressively interpreted as an actual game of Go.

Most of the information that the program extracts is hidden from the user. But Microgo has a 'beginner mode' in which it marks with crosses the areas of the board that it believes each side can influence. These may be very different from the areas physically occupied by each side's stones.

Designing a cellular automaton with the perceptual skills of even a modest Go player was understandably difficult. 'After many false tries I decided to evolve the game, and start from a proto-Go,' Scarff recounts. The proto-Go game had simplified rules and an infinite board. Edges and corners introduce complications that Scarff has still not solved to his satisfaction.

Since all the cells were to behave identically, the only freedom available to Scarff was in the choice of the rule which relates a cell's future state to its present inputs. He tried to devise rules which reflected important concepts in the game of Go.

The Go player's eye is sensitive to groupings of stones of the same colour. Scarff tried to model this skill by making his automaton fill in 'cell walls' round the edges of such groupings. Interestingly, the rule needed to do this is not unlike the rule of John Conway's well-known cellular automaton game, Life. Isolated or overcrowded stones die, others survive.

Scarff added further Go 'axioms' – axioms, rather than theorems, because they represent reasonable assumptions rather than proven results. Any potential conflict between axioms was suppressed by the very act of building them into a single cellular automaton rule.

A conventional rule-based program is not usually successful in Go, according to Scarff. The trouble is that the rich patterns of the Go board are open to many interpretations. Several rules may 'fire' at once, leading to conflicting advice.

Go players have many rules of thumb, known as 'proverbs'. But Scarff says: 'The proverbs for humans are absolutely useless when you come to program them. The biggest Go proverb of them all,' he adds, 'is don't follow Go proverbs blindly.'

Microgo may appear to follow rules. When two white stones lie alongside two black ones, the program often puts the next white stone exactly where a Go proverb says it should go. But the program does not know the proverb. It does not know that it should try to make that particular pattern. 'Certain cellular automata give rise to that happening,' says Scarff. 'The reason you make that move is not to make that pattern. It's a consequence.'

Suspicious as he is of theories, Scarff has had to use them, at least implicitly, in developing his program. He has even come up with some new theories which he believes have made him a stronger player. 'I play like a computer now,' he remarks drily.

Simple games like Nim, played with heaps of matches, can be played by a formula. A perfect evaluation function exists for Nim. There is no need to look ahead. For more complex games like chess and Go, it seems unlikely that there is any such formula. These games are probably computationally irreducible, like physics and Stephen Wolfram's cellular automata. There is no way to predict the outcome perfectly, short of a complete simulation.

But for both chess and Go, evaluation functions exist which, while not perfect, predict a game's outcome rather well. Indeed, in many chess end games it is possible to prove theorems about the outcome.

Scarff believes that in Go there may be principles of near-theorem status, which 'are very very useful and very very fundamental if not actually fundamental'. If such principles exist, they probably have little to do with the Go proverbs used by most humans, and the rules used by most computer programs playing Go.

Zen Buddhism teaches people to grasp a situation as a whole, and act without conscious analysis. Does it mean anything to say a computer program follows Zen principles? And are there other applications, besides the game of Go, where this might be the appropriate style of programming?

All this surely supports Douglas Hofstadter's view that pattern recognition is the essence of intelligence.

The big issue raised here is the validity of abstractions. Can one meaningfully divide a Go position into groupings? Do such groupings have sufficient independence to be useful? Can the goal of winning a game of Go be reduced to subgoals? Are there any general principles which help to identify good moves?

Scarff does not claim that groupings, subgoals, principles or theories are worthless. Rather, he is saying that there are so many rival theories, so many alternative subgoals, that none of them can claim any special status. Theories and subgoals seem to belong to a particular style of play, rather than to the game itself.

Alternative theories of the physical world have often coexisted. But science has always tested its theories against the touchstone of experiment, and usually one theory has been victorious, for a while at least. In a game like Go, a theory can only be tested in play against other theories. The results seem to have been inconclusive. Many theories work. No one theory is resoundingly right.

Artificial intelligence researchers often say of their work that 'the program is the theory'. This is merely an excuse for not stating a theory explicitly. Such researchers never say what question their experiment was meant to answer. This makes it conveniently difficult for others to say that the experiment has failed.

Scarff has no such pretensions. He is not trying to produce a theory of Go. He is trying to produce a program. It would be nice to find out why the program works, but it is not essential to do so.

This is not a program for extracting square roots or running a nuclear power station. It would be pointless to try to specify it formally. If you succeeded in formally specifying the task of winning at Go, you still would not have a clue how to implement the specification.

According to Scarff, it is not even particularly helpful to try to make the knowledge in the program explicit, as is usually done in expert systems. Microgo has no 'human windows', and cannot explain its own actions. Game programs like this simply evolve under their author's guidance. Author and program together constitute a powerful learning mechanism. It is sad, inevitable, but in a way exciting, that the program may succeed in acquiring knowledge in a form that is inaccessible to its author. We all see our children grow away from us.

At the end of 1985 Allan Scarff was working on an IBM PC version. He reckoned its strength at 10 *kyu* – much stronger than Microgo 1 – given one minute per move on a 19 by 19 board. His main complaint was the appalling inefficiency of running a parallel algorithm on a sequential machine.

35 The cryptological timebomb

The game is one metaphor for our dealings with the world. The code or, more properly, the cipher is another. In a game, skilful action ensures survival and leads to success. The reward for breaking a cipher, however, is knowledge. Scientists sometimes think of themselves as codebreakers.

Real ciphers are themselves part of a game, with one side setting ever tougher puzzles for the other to solve. The cryptanalyst merely carries on the story of human life, confronting complexity and trying to make sense of it. The cryptographer, however, is in the business of creating complexity and ensuring that any underlying sense is well hidden.

'God is subtle,' said Einstein, 'but he is not malicious', implying that the secret laws of nature can be laid bare by honest scientific toil. Mere subtlety, however, is not enough for cryptographers, and if they could make their secrets unbreakable, they would.

This is a poor example for designers in general, and for software engineers in particular. But cryptographers are not quite the agents of chaos and darkness they might seem.

There are elegant ciphers and messy ciphers. One thing I learned from Henry Beker and Fred Piper is that elegant ciphers are more reliable. There is no reason in principle why a messy cipher should not be secure. But it will be very hard to derive mathematical proofs of its security against specific types of attack.

Unskilled attempts to randomize a message often fail. Random-looking processes turn out not to be random at all. It is safer to tie your cipher to some solitary mathematical boulder that no one, so far, has managed to shift. You then know that it will resist known methods of attack. You only have to worry about the methods yet to be discovered.

10 November 1983

There are rumours that the best known and most widely used cipher system for computer data, the Data Encryption Standard (DES), has been cracked. Two Americans based in Geneva have said that 'a known general solution exists' but they have neither described nor demonstrated the alleged solution.

British cryptologists are sceptical of the claim but have not dismissed it out of hand. Donald Davies of the National Physical Laboratory commented, 'We were aware of weak keys, semi-weak keys and other interesting properties of the DES, but none of these had shown any flaw that could be exploited.'

Fred Piper of Westfield College, London points out that DES was never expected to have more than a limited life. The standard was published by the US National Bureau of Standards (NBS) in January 1977. At two workshops held by the NBS soon afterwards, the consensus was that DES would be a satisfactory standard for the next 10 to 15 years. Much of that time has already passed.

With lucrative prospects in data communications, electronic mail, software protection, banking and finance, cryptology is attracting more and more of the world's best research brains. One result of this is that any cipher system soon comes under attack and may eventually succumb.

'Unbreakable code' is a phrase used often by the Press and rarely by cryptologists. In 1949 Claude Shannon proved that a message can be sent with perfect secrecy only if the 'key' to the cipher is as long as the message itself. Any cipher which uses a more compact key is theoretically vulnerable. This means not only DES but virtually any commercial cipher you like to name.

There are two distinct threats. One is predictable and arises from the steadily falling cost of computer power. The other threat is more capricious and comes from the rapid intellectual advance of cryptology itself. Overnight, a problem which defeated a Cray can succumb to a better algorithm running on an Apple.

Buried like timebombs under the entire edifice of cryptology are a number of unsolved mathematical problems. One small one blew up last year when Adi Shamir of Israel's Weizmann Institute found a solution to the simplest form of the 'knapsack' code invented by Ralph Merkle and Martin Hellman.

The knapsack code was proposed as a public key (PK) system. PK systems are intrinsically no more or less breakable than other codes, but they have one unique, fascinating and potentially useful feature. In a PK system, knowing the key that was used to encipher a message is of little or no assistance in deciphering the message. This contrasts with DES, for example, where the two keys are identical.

The operator of a PK system can publish the enciphering key. Anyone can then send him secret messages which only he, using the private deciphering key, can read. The owner of a private key can also authenticate a message with a 'digital signature', which anyone can verify but no one else can fake.

Shamir's attack has shattered confidence in the knapsack code. 'Certainly there is no way that I would use it, or advise any commercial company to use it,' says Henry Beker, who is research director at Racal Research Ltd, visiting professor at Westfield College, and co-author with Piper of the book *Cipher Systems*.

But Piper argues that all Shamir has done is 'something we all believed was possible'. He points out that Merkle and Hellmann always believed that the knapsack code in its simplest form was open to attack, and recommended that the process for disguising the key should be repeated two or three times over before the key is published.

Another, less celebrated PK system has also been cracked. In the October 1980 issue of *Cryptologia*, Martin Kochanski gave a solution of the 'Lu-Lee' code proposed by S.C. Lu and K.N. Lee.

So what does that leave of PK systems? There are one or two obscure, uncracked ones like that proposed in 1978 by Robert McEliece. And there is the celebrated 'RSA' algorithm devised by Ronald Rivest, Adi Shamir and Leonard Adleman. To break the RSA cipher you must find the prime factors of a very large number. Though trivial in principle, the task of factorizing a 100-digit number by any known method requires a vast amount of computation.

Numbers of 60 decimal digits can now be factorized at a reasonable cost in computing time. 80-digit numbers may be brought within reach by the new Schnorr-Lenstra algorithm published earlier this year. Other groups are building special add-on factorizing hardware for already powerful supercomputers. But the RSA system is well placed to fight off this kind of attack.

The reason for this is that all the known methods of factorization are 'exponential-time' algorithms. This means that the time required for factorization can be doubled by adding a modest number of digits to the key, then doubled again by adding the same number of digits again. The complexity of the problem simply explodes as the key is lengthened. Sheer brute computer power can never keep up. Currently 512 binary digits, equivalent to 154 decimal digits, is considered a secure length for an RSA key.

The real timebomb under RSA is the possibility that someone may discover a 'polynomial-time' factorization algorithm. Polynomial-time methods show a far less explosive growth as the numbers involved get bigger. If a polynomial-time method exists, a problem is much easier prey for the code-breaker.

Meanwhile at the back of every cryptologist's mind lurks a deeper anxiety. This is the biggest timebomb of all. Factorization is just one of many problems which could lose their exponential status overnight. No one has ever proved that any problem actually needs exponential time for its solution. There are plenty of problems we think are tough. But they may not really be tough at all. As Henry Beker says, 'It could be that every problem is polynomial.'

Some of the tough-seeming exponential problems may be picked off one by one. But there is an elite group among them, known as NP-complete problems. The most general form of the knapsack problem (not the Merkle-Hellman instance) is NP-complete. So is the well-known problem of the travelling salesman trying to minimize the length of his tour. It has been proved that if any one of the NP-complete problems has a polynomial-time solution, then so has *every other problem* that one might consider attacking with a computer.

If that particular timebomb explodes, there will be no 'tough' exponential-time problems left to be used as the basis of highly secure ciphers. 'Cryptographers would have an enormous problem,' Beker explains. 'It really would be an incredible breakthrough.' But it is not something he expects to happen.

Beker considers it more likely that someone will prove that the NP-complete problems cannot be solved in polynomial time. This would assure the supply of tough problems to be used as the basis of ciphers. But cryptographers could still be caught out. It is not enough to choose a 'tough' problem. You have to choose a tough instance of that problem. That is why the Merkle-Hellmann knapsack code was cracked, even though it was based on an NP-complete problem.

A resolution of the NP-complete question does not seem imminent. The 'arms race' between code-makers and code-breakers is likely to continue. Those with sensitive information to protect will arm themselves with the available cryptographic weapons, even though these, like other weapons, can potentially blow up and injure the user.

Following the London University reorganization, Fred Piper is now at Royal Holloway and Bedford College, London. Henry Beker is now (November 1985) at Racal-Chubb Security Systems Ltd. Donald Davies has retired from the National Physical Laboratory.

Nothing more was heard to suggest that DES had been cracked. The issue is losing its importance since DES is in any case due for replacement.

The NP-complete question remains open.

Further reading

Beker, H. and Piper, F. (1982). *Cipher Systems*. London: Northwood Books. (Currently available from Van Nostrand Reinhold, Wokingham.)

Deavours, C.A. (1983). 'The view from across the pond: an interview with the Geneva Management Group' *Cryptologia*, **7**, no. 2, April, 187–190.

Lewis, H.R. and Papadimitriou, C.H. (1978). 'The efficiency of algorithms', *Scientific American*, January.

36

A physical assault on software piracy

Copy protection of software offers a neat application for public key cryptosystems. But encryption alone does not solve the problem.

17 November 1983

Software pirates may be about to meet their match, in a new program-protecting formula prepared from equal parts of pure mathematics and good old-fashioned physical security.

The physical security will be provided by tamper-proof modules, or perhaps ultimately by microprocessor chips with secret codes burned into their memories. The mathematicians have made their contribution by devising the ingenious one-way ciphers, public key (PK) cryptosystems.

Any cipher based on clever mathematics could be made vulnerable by future mathematical discoveries, but perhaps this is a risk that software producers can take. Many successful packages have been sold with no protection at all. One hundred per cent protection is neither feasible nor necessary.

Some cryptologists still say that the best way to protect secrets is to use a secret algorithm both for enciphering and deciphering. But it is hard to quantify the chance that someone will guess your algorithm. So another school of thought says that you must assume your algorithm is publicly known.

One widely publicized algorithm is the Data Encryption Standard (DES). The functioning of the algorithm is controlled by a 64-bit number called the 'key'. (The effective length of the key, however, is only 56 bits.) Users of DES obtain secrecy by not letting their enemies know which of the 72,000 million million possible keys they have chosen.

In PK systems it is safe to publish not only the algorithm but the enciphering key. Deciphering requires a separate key which (for practical purposes, anyway) cannot be deduced from the enciphering key. In the Rivest-Shamir-Adleman (RSA) system the deciphering key is a pair of large prime numbers. The enciphering key is the number obtained by multiplying them together. The security of the system rests on the extreme difficulty of finding the factors of a large number.

When a PK system is used for software protection, the supplier of the software and the supplier of the protection need not be the same person. For example, the protection company (or public authority) can give each user a public enciphering key, and a private deciphering key. There is no way the public key can be abused, and no one will mind if the user prints it on his letterhead or broadcasts it on prime time television. The software supplier will need to know the enciphering key when he prepares a uniquely encrypted copy of a program to sell to the user.

The user's private key, however, is extremely sensitive, and not even the user himself will know it. If he did, he could give or sell it to his friends, so enabling them to run illicitly copied programs. This is where the need for physical security arises. There is nowhere on a floppy disk where you could hide the private key from technically sophisticated professionals. It is safer inside a physically tamper-proof box.

A great many variations on the basic scheme are possible. Backed by the British Technology Group (BTG), the National Physical Laboratory is trying to develop a cost-effective software protection scheme which will almost certainly be based on the combination of a PK cipher and a tamper-proof module. Derrick Grover of BTG hopes that the cost of the necessary hardware may come down to £20 to £30. The NPL is forming a consortium of UK companies to fund the necessary research. Two have joined already; another dozen are being wooed.

Many existing protection techniques depend on some special coding or 'fingerprinting' of floppy disks to prevent copying. 'They provide protection against the amateur copier,' says Grover, 'but there are various systems coming onto the market which enable you to copy them.'

Disks 'protected' by non-standard formatting can often be copied in a few minutes, using one of the commercially available software utilities such as Locksmith or Back-it-up. The Snapshot card for the Apple II will copy any program which loads to memory in one piece, without overlays or further disk accesses. Even if none of these will work, the determined pirate can in principle comb through the program, identify the 'traps' and either figure out how they work or simply bypass them.

Indelible 'fingerprints' or 'watermarks' introduced during disk manufacture may prevent bit-for-bit copying of the disk but are not immune to more intelligent copying techniques.

Even a hardware module of the 'dongle' variety may not offer complete protection. It may be possible for the pirate to find and excise the instructions in the program which test for the presence of the dongle, or to write a routine which simulates the dongle's operation and allows programs to run without it.

This is the basic weakness of any protection method which works by introducing 'traps' into an otherwise unaltered application program. One kind of dongle is a bit cleverer than this – it actually contains and executes part of the program itself. This is impractical if the user wants to run dozens of different programs on the same machine. But there is another way of hiding the application code from the user, and that is by encryption.

Obviously it is no use encrypting the software, if the first thing the user's system does is to decrypt it and store the plaintext program in its memory where all and sundry can inspect it. On the other hand, if each instruction has to be fetched, decrypted and then executed at run-time, there is a danger that the program will run at only a fraction of its normal speed.

The NPL project will be looking for ways out of this dilemma. For example, it may not be necessary to encrypt the entire program. Even a small amount of encryption could leave so many holes in the program that it would be impracticable for a pirate to reconstruct a working copy.

The hardware module is likely to play a more active role than that of a 'black box' decoder. If parts of the application program are actually executed out of sight inside the sealed box, no one is likely to work out how the program functions by analysing traffic on the system buses. Brian Wichmann of NPL points out that many microcomputers have space for a second processor. This could be a physically hardened unit performing a mixture of decryption and application processing duties.

David Everett was already thinking on these lines over two years ago, and his company Open Computer Security has probably achieved a world first with its Padlock software protection scheme. Padlock uses an ingenious combination of DES and the RSA public key system.

The software is encrypted with the DES algorithm. But the DES key used in a particular instance is disguised from the user by means of the RSA algorithm. The Padlock box only has to use RSA once, to find the DES key. It then decrypts and executes the software in real time. By using the fast DES algorithm for the bulk of its decryption task, Padlock runs much faster than a 'pure' RSA system would.

The entire application program runs inside the Padlock module. 'You never see a plaintext copy of the software outside our tamper-proof module,' says Everett. To make this possible, the module must contain a good deal of hardware including a processor, real time clock, decryption circuitry, random access memory, and its own power supply. (An energy source is usually required in any such device, so that it can auto-destruct if tampered with.)

Evidently the Padlock module is almost a complete computer in itself. It costs £250, but Everett claims the price could fall as low as £50. This would probably mean using a small number of large custom or semi-custom chips, which presupposes a volume market.

It is possible to imagine the whole lot integrated into a single chip, pin-compatible with an industry standard such as the Z80 or 8088 but able to run encrypted software. Such a device could be retrofitted, even to computers with no second-processor option. Each microprocessor (cryptoprocessor?) coming off the production line would be unique, with a private key burned electrically or by laser into its read-only memory, and no doubt a public key number (for use by software houses) ink-jet printed on its packaging. That is a little way off, though. Perhaps the biggest technical problem is to devise an auto-destruct mechanism for the chip.

A more immediate prospect is that major software packages, protected by public key cryptography, will be distributed at near-zero cost on video disks, by telephone line, cable television or broadcast telesoftware. Users will pay nothing for the package itself but could be charged £10,000 for the 200-digit magic number which unlocks it. Hopefully they will pay rather less for the X-ray-proof, screwdriver-resisting, auto-destructing black box which performs that particular piece of magic.

The NPL did develop a tamper-proof microcomputer chip very much on the lines described here. Ironically, with this physical protection, encryption was found to be unnecessary.

Most suppliers of microcomputer software, if they use copy protection at all, still depend on disk based methods. Some offer a choice of unprotected disks, or protected ones at a lower price.

The most elaborate protection methods were devised to deter professional crooks (or dishonest dealers) from selling unauthorized copies for profit. But there do not seem to be many big rackets of this kind. Almost certainly, most copying is done casually by users themselves.

Someone who only wants to make one or two copies will be deterred by quite simple protection methods. If it takes a week to crack the protection, you might as well go out and buy the package. Many people who acquire pirate copies probably do not want them so badly that they would be willing to pay the full price, so they could argue that they are not robbing the supplier of potential sales. This seems unlikely to succeed as a defence in court.

At least one American company has put encrypted software on videodisks. The method has not taken off yet, because the videodisk player is still rather a rare computer peripheral. Interactive video is used mainly in education and training, not in business where the big software markets lie.

PART 4

Software

37

Code and chips on the Inmos menu

If designers intend to keep things simple for their customers, they can start by keeping things simple for themselves. It seems obvious that designers should not reinvent the wheel. Nor should they preinvent it: in designing a vehicle it may be wise to leave the method of propulsion undecided till a later stage. Tracks or an air cushion might be better than wheels.

General Motors, of course, would laugh at that idea. They are in the business of selling cars, not hovercraft. And there are people who argue that in computers as in personal transport, we should be thinking about the physical implementation even as we formulate the abstract design. Geoffrey Hinton and other 'connectionists' believe that artificial intelligence systems should be designed from the bottom up, beginning with hardware. That point of view, which becomes increasingly plausible as computer hardware approaches absolute physical limits, will be explored in the fifth part of the book.

One can never completely ignore the physical, but it may be safe and, indeed, liberating to postpone thinking about it. Most of the people interviewed in this fourth part of the book are concerned with the design of software or, more generally, the design of systems. Some of them, particularly those who use structured or formal methods, can be regarded as practitioners of the top-down approach. Not all: in the Lisp culture (and its educational branch, the Logo culture) there is a strong tradition of structured, but bottom-up design.

In practice no one works entirely top-down or entirely bottom-up. The important thing is to structure the design task so that you can think about one thing, or a small number of things, at a time. When Inmos designed its innovative 32-bit microprocessor, the transputer, the company made extensive use of top-down techniques. The top-level specification was for a component that could be used to build concurrent or parallel computer systems. But it was pure bottom-up, physical thinking that dictated that the next big advance in computer power would come from concurrency. Now where did the demand for more computer power come from? It was from the top-level, abstract need of various engineers and scientists for some thing that would perform certain computations at high speed. The would-be users of this thing did not care whether it was physically made of silicon or greengage jam. I suggest that behind many good pieces of top-down design there is some bottom-up thinking. But behind *every* good piece of bottom-up design there is top-down thinking. It is quite possible that the top-down thinking takes place before the design process has even begun. But it cannot be left out altogether. The danger of bottom-up is that you will end up with something very clever but not at all useful.

The 'Software' part of this book begins with a discussion of the design of a piece of hardware. This is not a mistake.

---

19 January 1984

Everyone knows the difference between hardware and software. Hardware is a physical product and software is an intellectual one. But as with good and evil, you rarely find one without some admixture of the other. Is microcode software? Is a mask read only memory hardware?

Take even the simplest digital electronic component and you can formulate an abstract description of what the thing does. This is usually called a specification but it could equally well be called a program. On the other hand, that which we usually call software exists only in a Platonic sense, until it is physically embodied in electricity, magnetism or ink. Try again – a pragmatic definition this time: if it is designed on a computer aided design system, it is hardware. If it is written in a programming language, it is software.

What then is Inmos up to? No question that this is a hardware company, a chip maker. But in designing the family of powerful and unconventional microprocessors known as transputers, Inmos has adopted the software industry's techniques. Its own programming language, Occam, is not only used to program transputers. It is used to specify the function of the chip itself, as it appears to the programmer and to other devices.

The microprocessor design team at the company's Bristol headquarters uses a computer aided design system which fosters a style of work more like that of a software house than that of a traditional silicon foundry. The techniques are essentially those of structured programming. The chip area is divided into modules and these are subdivided hierarchically, right down to the physical details of the circuitry. Simulation tools are available at each level. Logical design and physical design are not kept separate. They develop in parallel and mirror each other.

The division of labour resembles the 'work group' system pioneered at the Volvo car factory. Instead of doing a particular job (say, logic design) on the whole chip, each designer works on a small part of the chip, handling all aspects of its design.

There is relatively little hierarchy as far as people's jobs are concerned. This is possible precisely because the CAD system itself is hierarchical. It includes a Hierarchical Design Language, which is said to allow designers to specify a chip fully, from functional to transistor level. On their interactive colour displays, Inmos designers can zoom in on a single transistor in one screen window while keeping a view of the whole chip in another.

Inmos has still not made a complete transputer chip. All its subsystems have been fabricated on the same wafer, but they have not yet been joined to form a single functioning unit.

Transputers will be available during 1984, Inmos says, but the company has not named a month or even a season. In November it released details of the 32-bit, 10-mips (million instructions per second) T424, first of a family of transputer devices. The family will also contain 16-bit devices, beginning with a graphics controller and a disk controller.

These last two will be 'tailored' devices, derived from the standard transputer by putting a relatively small amount of special circuitry on the chip. In the disk controller, for example, circuits will be added to perform serial–parallel and parallel–serial conversion, and the cyclic redundancy check.

Additional tailoring will be made possible by the controller's on-chip read only memory. This, with the transputer's spare processing power, could be used to implement a disk filing system, taking the load off the central processor.

The designers seem to be confident that they can merge the existing modules to make a working transputer, and then carry on to produce tailored versions soon after. They are confident that their CAD system, which is designed for this sort of thing, will pull them through.

To illustrate how tailored transputers might be used in practice, Inmos engineers have sketched a rough design for a personal computer using three transputers. A standard transputer would run application programs and handle the keyboard, with one tailored transputer to handle the screen and one as disk controller. Cheaper, and less powerful versions of the design might get away with two transputers or even with a single one.

This is the essence of the transputer concept. It should be possible to distribute work between a number of transputers, for maximum performance, or just as easily, to load all the work onto a single transputer, subject to capacity. All this with minimal changes to the program.

Most attention has been given to the possibilities of concurrent processing, with thousands of transputers working in parallel in 'fifth generation' machines. Certainly the transputer is well adapted to this role. Its four high-speed serial links can be connected to neighbouring transputers in a rectangular array on a printed circuit board. Ultimately it might be possible to integrate an array of transputers on a single silicon wafer, if yield and cooling problems can be overcome.

One scenario is for a database machine, with 128 transputer chips on a single board, providing 0.5 megabyte of random access memory and an aggregate of 1 Gips (one thousand million instructions per second) processing power. It is estimated that it would take this machine 1.3 milliseconds to search a database of 25,000 16-byte records. By pipelining requests through the system, one million searches could be performed every second.

An Inmos brochure quotes Carver Mead, America's master of silicon design: 'Sequential systems will not be adequate for the future. There are an additional four orders of magnitude in computational capability available through concurrent systems.'

But that is only half the picture. One does not always need supermainframe performance. If necessary, a single transputer chip can share its time efficiently between a number of tasks. The programmer can still treat these tasks as though they were being run concurrently.

Two innovations make this possible. One is the hardware scheduler, a piece of circuitry which allows the transputer to switch tasks in as little as two microseconds. This is one or two orders of magnitude faster than a conventional microcomputer operating system.

The other is the 'process' model of computation, supported by the hardware and embodied in the Occam language. A process is a sequential computation with a beginning and an end, which can send messages to other processes. Within any process there may be other processes, executed sequentially or concurrently, and sending messages to one another.

An Occam program is composed of nested and communicating processes. The programmer can postpone the decision as to where each process will be physically executed. If the system contains more than one transputer, the program is annotated, so as to assign each process to one of the available chips. This should make it easy to port programs from one transputer system to a larger or smaller one. Occam programs are not tied to any particular word-length, and Inmos says that 16- and 32-bit transputers can be mixed in the same system.

Designers who use transputers will be able to choose flexibly between high performance, hardware-intensive solutions, and software-intensive solutions which must always ultimately be cheaper in a volume market.

Inmos has adopted a design philosophy which denies that hardware and software are chalk and cheese. Perhaps the transputer, when it arrives, will trigger a new cross-fertilization of ideas between those who think of themselves as 'programmers' and those who think of themselves as 'engineers'.

On 5 April 1984 Iann Barron, one of the founders of Inmos, gave a lecture at the Royal Society in London. In the course of a lucid exposition of the Inmos philosophy, Barron made one particularly striking remark. 'Our circuit engineers write better programs than our computer scientists,' he said, explaining that the engineers naturally think in terms of concurrent processes.

'Our computer scientists design better circuits than our circuit engineers,' he added. The computer scientists had the habit, not always well developed in engineers, of decomposing a complex system hierarchically into subsystems.

Barron was surely right that computer science has no tradition of concurrent thinking. For many years computer scientists lived in an overwhelmingly sequential world, and it was only the need to design operating systems and computer networks that forced them to confront that disorderly reality in which several things are always going on at the same time. Only a few brave researchers sought a theoretical understanding of concurrency – among them Anthony Hoare, the Oxford University professor whose work on Communicating Sequential Processes (CSP) led directly to the development of Occam.

The second part of Barron's observation is probably the more contentious. Agnes Kaposi, Gerald Sussman and Hal Abelson, all of whom we shall meet shortly, would I think argue that engineers need no lessons from computer scientists in the art of hierarchical decomposition. Clearly there are engineers and engineers. No one has a monopoly on the techniques of good design, and equally, no one should pretend that they have all the answers.

In June 1984 the 'Fat Freddy' design system was licensed by Inmos to Racal-Redac, a company in the Racal electronics group which specializes in computer aided design. Racal-Redac developed the system into a product called Isis which was launched on 1 March 1985.

Inmos had decided to prepare the market for its novel product well in advance. But delays in the production of actual chips soon became an embarrassment. The T414 transputer (with only half the memory of the prematurely trumpeted T424) was finally declared to be available in October 1985. As important as the chip itself is the range of evaluation boards, compilers and other development tools which will provide some support for those customers who wish to practise the Inmos philosophy of design.

The tale of the company's financial ups and downs and its acquisition by Thorn-EMI has been told elsewhere. Transputers are to be used in a number of research projects part-funded by the British Government's Alvey programme. But one of the nicest events of 1986, for Inmos, was the announcement of the T series of supercomputers made by Floating

Point Systems of Beaverton, Oregon. A respected and successful supplier of high-performance computing hardware had designed its new range of machines round the transputer. This was exactly the kind of powerful and massively concurrent system that Inmos had said could be built with transputers. Not only that: Floating Point Systems could have dressed up the T series as just another FORTRAN engine, but instead it took the brave step of asking customers to program the machine in Occam.

38

Controlling complexity

Complexity is like fire: fascinating, dangerous, and very useful. Conway's Life, blazing away from a random start and dying down to embers. The colourful pyrotechnics of the Mandelbrot set. These things appeal to something in the human spirit, but they also warn of the chaos that can be spread by complexity untamed.

Engineering without complexity is as unimaginable as civilization without cookery, pottery or metallurgy. Often, extremely complex methods are required to achieve a simple effect. Consider the depth of technology required to produce a large single crystal of silicon, which is, from the physicist's point of view, a very simple object.

Information technology, in particular, seems condemned to deploy ever greater complexity in its efforts to deliver systems that are simple and easy for human beings to use. Observe how microcomputer software has evolved in ten years, from hair-shirt 4-kilobytes BASIC, to friendly environments like Smalltalk-AT which requires a megabyte of memory to run effectively. If a piece of software seems simple on the outside, it is nearly always complex on the inside.

Fine for the user, but what about the poor programmers, who have to concern themselves with the complicated guts of the system? Is there any way in which something can have very many parts, and very many possible behaviours, and remain comprehensible?

Is there? Yes: Do not expect to be told how it is done in the next sentence. Control of complexity is a simple, noble goal. But the path to it, as you might guess, is long and winding. Indeed, there are many alternative paths.

The bad news is that things which seem simple on the outside are almost always complex on the inside. The good news that stems from this is that if as an engineer or programmer you are compelled to deal with complexity, you can usually wrap it up into easily managed bundles. You need to know what the bundles do, how they fit together, and ultimately, what is inside each one. But you do not have to think about all these things at the same time.

This is structured design. The wonderful thing is that while you are thinking about how the bundles fit together, you only need to consider the function each bundle performs. You can ignore its inner workings. Mechanical engineers would go crazy if each time they used an electric motor they began worrying about coils and magnets and commutators. What they need is a *model* of an electric motor which describes its function but hides the details. The model might be some mathematical relationship between current, voltage, speed and torque.

Of course, the people who design electric motors would go equally crazy if their heads were full of washing machines and cranes and clocks and potter's wheels. That is the other marvellous thing about structured design. When you want to look at the details, you can ignore the grand scheme.

This has its dangers, and some would say it leads to tunnel vision and unintelligent design. That may be so, but at least structured design provides a safety net. It is just a mechanism for making clear what each part of the system is meant to do, and how they fit together. Which bit is designed first, how changes in the design are handled, what happens when a specification turns out to be unimplementable – these are management issues which can be handled in many different ways. There are top-down, bottom-up, and middle-out approaches. The choice will depend on the kind of project and the characteristic style of the organization and the individuals involved.

None of these insights is particularly new. Structured methods, however, are only the beginning of the new discipline of software and systems engineering. There is still much to be learned about the management and organization of projects; the technology can certainly strengthen old-fashioned authoritarian management, but it could also support a more democratic, cooperative style. Automation is important: a whole new range of power tools is becoming available for programmers and designers.

But all this needs a firm foundation. The power of structured design will be enhanced by an injection of mathematical rigour. Mechanical and electrical engineering acquired their mathematical foundations many years ago. The mathematics of information engineering is young and still growing.

Programmers develop intuitions and hunches about software, just as carpenters and scaffolders develop intuitions about geometry. Some of these intuitions may turn out to be insubstantial. Others can be captured as mathematical concepts of tremendous power. The characteristic of mathematical reasoning is that it tells you useful things that you would never have guessed.

What can mathematics tell us about software? Not least, mathematical reasoning can verify that you have actually written the program you intended to write, and that it will do the things you wanted it to (and only those). That is the chief burden of so-called 'formal methods' in software engineering.

Another bunch of mathematical tools are known as 'software metrics'.

Here we meet the powerful idea of complexity as something that can be measured, in the same imperfect but useful way as money measures economic value. If one is seeking to control complexity, it will surely help to have quantitative measures of one's success.

---

2 January 1984

In the late 1960s Edsger Dijkstra proposed that WHILE-DO and IF-THEN-ELSE were the only constructs needed, or indeed desirable, to control the flow of a program. At the time this appeared to be a pretty swingeing application of Occam's razor – the 'keep things simplest' principle rightly or wrongly attributed to William of Occam. Fans of the fourteenth-century Surrey cleric will be pleased to hear that Dijkstra was being unnecessarily indulgent.

Robin Whitty of the Polytechnic of the South Bank has recently observed that a single construct will suffice for all sequential programming. The construct has two paths from beginning to end, with a loop grafted into one of them.

It has something of IF-THEN-ELSE about it (the alternative paths) and something of WHILE-DO (the loop). But it cannot be split into these simpler elements because it contains an 'illegal' jump out of the loop. Technically, it is the unique irreducible CGK flowgraph with two tests. You will not find it ready-made in any programming language, it has no name other than C(2), and it is probably a little too cumbersome for practical use. Like a Swiss Army knife, it is versatile but not often the best tool for a particular job.

C(2)'s importance is symbolic. Logic designers already know that if necessary, they could build all their circuits from NAND gates alone. Now program design, too, can be reduced to its bare bones, though it is hard to imagine any programmer willingly adopting such an ascetic regime.

Whitty is a member of an interdisciplinary team which has recently completed a general mathematical theory of structured programming. The other members are Norman Fenton of Oxford University, and Agnes Kaposi, who is head of the South Bank Poly's department of electrical and electronic engineering.

Kaposi is a strong protagonist of the 'systems' approach. Both in research and in teaching, her department looks for underlying principles which can be applied to software, to hardware or, for that matter, to an organization's management structure.

It is all too easy, in this area, to develop grand theories which explain everything and solve nothing. Kaposi is alive to this danger. 'What we want to do,' she explains, 'is to ensure that while the methods we are developing are sufficiently general and rigorous, they are also applicable.'

The work on structured programming is one of a number of research projects launched in the past five years under the slogan 'control of complexity'.

'Structured programming,' says Kaposi, 'is not merely about writing programs. It is about the control of structural complexity.' She suggests, as a general hypothesis, that 'Poor lifecycle performance of a system stems from unreliable design'.

Often, undetected design errors lead to trouble much later. 'Subsequently the errors show themselves to originate from early decisions which were faulty,' says Kaposi. The aim is to eliminate unimportant aspects of design which distract from the major decisions, and 'to provide the designer with the opportunity of clean thought'.

One such stripping-down operation led to the invention of the Cowell-Gillies-Kaposi (CGK) flowgraph. This network of blobs and arrows is what's left if you take an ordinary program flowchart and edit out all the procedures, leaving only the tests. The loops and branches are all still there, but there is no indication of what the program actually does. Only binary choices are permitted – no multiple-case statements – and the graph must have a single entry and a single exit point. With trivial changes, any program can meet these requirements.

Since a CGK graph is a well-defined mathematical object, it has been possible to prove a number of general results which can then be applied to real systems. Once the bones of a program are exposed as a CGK graph, its structure can be analysed by mathematical techniques. Kaposi's group has a program which analyses other programs written in BASIC. Essentially it works on a plateful of 'spaghetti code' by trying to extract forkfuls which are connected to the main mass of spaghetti by no more than two strands. Formally these forkfuls are known as 'proper subgraphs'. They can be excised neatly by simply snipping them out and joining the cut ends. A program which is well structured, in Dijkstra's sense, can be taken apart completely by this method.

A further procedure known as unfolding takes care of sections of code with more than one entry point. The code in question is replaced by a number of single-entry copies. If the program still cannot be taken to pieces it must have a tangle in it. A tangle, or irreducible graph, cannot be separated without more drastic surgery. And once you have teased one tangle apart, you may find other tangles hidden inside it. There may be a hierarchy of irreducibles.

Kaposi points out that this analysis yields a number of objective measures of complexity. One possible measure is the number of nodes (a node, remember, is a test leading to a branch or loop) in the system's worst tangle – 'worst' meaning the one with most nodes.

Alternatively one can look at the hierarchy of tangles within tangles, and count the number of levels of nested irreducibles.

'The things that correspond to the prime numbers, the building blocks of this whole theory, are the irreducibles,' says Norman Fenton. One crucial result of the theory says that however you attack a flowgraph you always end up with the same set of irreducibles, just as factorizing a given number always leads to the same set of primes. So measures of complexity based on the irreducibles will be consistent.

An outwardly similar method of measuring complexity and diagnosing 'nonstructuredness' was proposed in 1976 by T.J. McCabe. But Kaposi claims that McCabe's method is inconsistent and incomplete. She is concerned at the spread, in industry and education, of methods of software structuring based on McCabe's work. She would like to see fully rigorous methods used instead.

Even tangled programs are not beyond redemption. Irreducibles can be teased apart and turned into well-structured code. But this can only be done by introducing additional tests and variables each time a loop is broken. The team at the South Bank Polytechnic has converted educational programs from unstructured BASIC into polished Pascal. An automatic untangling program has been written.

The method 'is a powerful tool of software maintenance,' says Kaposi. A demand exists for commercial software-restructuring services, as the New York firm Peat Marwick Mitchell has demonstrated with its Structured Retrofit.

Complexity control methods may be useful for putting right the mistakes of the past, but a more important objective is to avoid similiar errors in the future. Nor are the methods confined to software. Kaposi's group means to marry them with the new generation of system design tools which transcend the hardware/software barrier. Among these are the Occam language promoted by Inmos, and a computer-based design methodology called SADT which originated in the United States and is now used in Hungary to generate complete system designs for steel rolling mills.

Industry has much to gain from this kind of research, and also much to contribute to it. In one project on a mathematical approach to structure metrication, the Polytechnic of the South Bank is working with British Telecom.

An important Alvey project on 'structure-based software metrics' is being led by Norman Fenton. Robin Whitty, now at Goldsmiths' College, London, is also taking part. The industrial partners are Plessey, ICL and the Central Electrical Research Laboratories. This project offers a practical opportunity to try out some of the mathematical ideas on large industrial software systems.

According to the paper referenced below, the sufficiency of IF-THEN-ELSE and WHILE-DO was pointed out by C. Böhm and G. Jacopini in 1966. It was Dijkstra who argued the desirability of using only these constructs.

Further reading

Cowell, D.F., Gillies, D.F. and Kaposi, A.A. (1980). 'Synthesis and structural analysis of abstract programs' *Computer Journal*, **23** no. 3, 243–247.

Simon, H.A. (1969). *The Sciences of the Artificial.* Cambridge, Mass.: MIT Press. (An influential book by one of the founders of artificial intelligence. The essay 'The architecture of complexity' is particularly relevant, and discusses hierarchical and nearly decomposable systems.)

39

Teaching the technology of thinking

Controlling complexity is a central concern for Gerald Sussman and Harold Abelson. An inspirational team at the leading edge of the MIT culture, they encourage their students to think about thinking.

29 November 1984

Things don't get invented in a place, Gerald Sussman suggests. They get invented by a culture. Part of the power of being a professor, he observes, is that you can slowly influence the culture. He and associate professor Harold Abelson teach a particular cultural approach to the design of large systems. It is presented as computer science but the essence of it has nothing to do with computers.

Sussman acknowledges his debt to an ancestry of 'great wizards', among them Marvin Minsky and Seymour Papert, the pioneers of artificial intelligence at the Massachusetts Institute of Technology. John McCarthy, who left MIT to found the Stanford University AI laboratory in 1963, is another.

Loyal as they are to the MIT 'party line', Sussman and Abelson claim allegiance to a design culture that no one campus, or one country, can appropriate. Carver Mead of Caltech, and Lynn Conway, now at the US Department of Defense, are important prophets of that culture. Their ideas on the design of large systems were concretized as strategies for the design of very complicated integrated circuits. The two MIT professors also name three or four UK computer scientists among the 'wizards' of design. Functional programming is one area where British work has inspired the Americans.

Sussman himself, after making his name in artificial intelligence research, became deeply involved in integrated circuit design. Then, he says, he spent last year as an astronomer. While studying the stars at Caltech he led the design of a special purpose supercomputer for orbital mechanics problems, the Digital Orrery. Both he and Abelson, incidentally, were trained as mathematicians.

'Computer science is not a science and has little to do with computers,' they write in their newly published book *Structure and Interpretation of Computer Programs*. The book is the set text for a 13-week course they teach to first-year MIT undergraduates.

They try to teach their students strategies of design – technologies of thinking. They are not trying to manufacture hotshot programmers, but along the way the students pick up a knowledge of Scheme, a polished dialect of Lisp which reflects the Sussman-Abelson philosophy.

Scheme is presented as a notation for abstract procedures, and only incidentally as a language which may be executed on computers. Concepts like data abstraction and lexical scoping are introduced almost immediately. The starting point is the way one would like to think about problems. The limitations of real computer systems are kept in the background, though never entirely ignored.

Towards the end of the course, all 700 students are given the task of implementing Prolog. Students who three months earlier knew nothing about computing find themselves writing (in Scheme) a Prolog compiler. Yes, they get as much help as they need. Yes, they are all mathematically sophisticated. Yes, they are some of the brightest students in the United States. But it still seems a lot to ask of them.

It is no big deal to write a program, Sussman insists. It helps, of course, to have the large library of Lisp functions and programming tools that has accumulated at MIT over the years. But the main requirements are native intelligence and a few techniques which can be stated explicitly and involve no magic.

The MIT students learn three basic 'technologies of thinking'. All the techniques are well known to electrical engineers. And most computer professionals, especially those trained in 'structured' methodologies, will have some inkling of them.

The first technique is the use of 'black box' abstractions. You learn to break a problem up into pieces, find solutions for the pieces, and combine them to solve the problem. Abstraction, say Sussman and Abelson, is hiding detail. If you are going to assemble a system from black boxes you must have an abstract description of the behaviour of each box. You deliberately ignore the box's internal workings. Hierarchical design? It is not quite as simple as that. You are encouraged to look at the problem from different angles and break it down in different ways. Each of these multiple views is expected to add something to your understanding.

The second technique embodies the almost childish commonsense of

Meccano and Tinkertoy. 'Establish conventional interfaces.' That, say Sussman and Abelson, is the way to build families of things which can be reused and fitted together in many different ways.

The third key idea is that there will be more than one language in which you wish to express your ideas. All the languages may be formally equivalent, but for each part of a design task you should choose, or create, the appropriate language. This is a familiar thought in computer science, where interpreters and compilers perform translations between formally equivalent languages. But Sussman points out that the same concept applies in other fields like electrical engineering. Electrical engineers use a systems language, with primitives like 'amplifier', and a circuit language with primitives like 'resistor' and 'inductor'.

At first sight, the systems language seems to be 'higher-level', and the circuit language closer to physics. But that particular hierarchy can easily be turned on its head. Time was, that an amplifier was a thing you constructed from resistors, transistors and other parts. Now, Sussman points out, it is sometimes simpler to simulate an inductor with an operational amplifier, a couple of resistors and a capacitor.

The manufacturer's circuit diagram of the 'op amp', Sussman argues, is just a lie to help you understand how it works. Inside, it is quite different from the diagram. Even a resistor has a lot of internal structure. It is a black box, intricately designed to behave according to Ohm's law. 'Resistor' is an abstraction in just the same way as 'op amp' is an abstraction, according to Sussman.

The students implement Prolog in Lisp, to learn how ideas can be transferred from one language to another. Though MIT eats, drinks and breathes Lisp, Sussman and Abelson try to explain that the language is not as important as the ideas you express in it – ideas that could, in principle, be expressed in many other languages. Prolog is there in the toolbox. It just is not used all that much. Minsky's famous opposition to the use of logic to represent knowledge must have something to do with it.

The real lesson is that if you don't like the available tools you can and should build your own. Sussman believes that the core of any language should be very small, so anyone can understand it quickly. But he says there should also be extensive libraries of subroutines and utilities, standardized databases, standardized display drivers, windowing systems and so on. On top of that, you should be able to extend and customize the language for yourself.

Lisp is extendable in this way. So is Forth. The first thing you learn in Forth is to define a procedure, and that is the way Sussman and Abelson teach Lisp too.

Forth was invented by an astronomer, Sussman points out, not by a computer scientist. Lisp was invented by logicians; so was Prolog. APL was invented by a physicist. Languages are invented by people with problems to solve. It is difficult to think about thinking, says Seymour Papert, if you are not thinking about thinking about something.

Lately the two professors have been thinking a lot about hardware. Abelson explains how simply one can write a program to model electrical circuits; a few black-box abstractions like 'resistor'; a few simple procedures for combining them, like 'series' and 'parallel'. A page and a half of code, and you have the makings of a system for designing circuits of arbitrary complexity.

With three colleagues, in 1979 Sussman designed a single-chip microprocessor which directly executes the Scheme language. It was done, he says, by four people working part time for a month. And in that time, they not only did the design itself, they put together the computer aided design and simulation tools they needed.

It was not quite the impossible task it sounds. They already had a library of 'metadesign tools', one to handle geometry and layouts, one an abstract, general purpose simulator, and so on. They only had to bolt these together and customize them for the job. Also, they did not debug the chip nearly as carefully as would have been necessary, had it been a commercial product. In 1981, Sussman and five colleagues repeated the exercise. The redesigned Scheme chip had approximately 80,000 transistors.

Students regularly create their own chip designs, and have them fabricated through the Mosis scheme set up by Lynn Conway. Designs from universities are sent in through the nationwide Arpanet. Several semiconductor manufacturers participate. Costs are cut by combining a number of chip designs on one wafer. Fully packaged chips come back just one month after the designs are received.

The designs are software. They are Lisp programs. The chips are largely produced by automatic machinery, the chief human agent being the 'chef' who supervises the chemistry of silicon processing. Sussman and Abelson argue that it is now as easy to create hardware as it is to create software.

The Orrery occupies a cubic foot of space and calculates at approximately one-third the speed of a suitably programmed Cray-1 supercomputer. Sussman reckons it was designed and built in approximately the time it would have taken to write the programs for the Cray.

If hardware design is so easy, how come commercial projects still cost millions and take years? If assembling your own design tools is so easy, how come commercial CAD systems sell for five- or six-figure sums?

Why, Sussman counters, do people still program in FORTRAN? Not because something better doesn't exist, but because that's 'the way it's done'.

Sussman and Abelson have lately mounted a major expedition into the borderlands between physics and computation, scene of several other developments reported in this book. Their thesis is that scientific theories can now be couched as programs. So instead of deriving abstract mathematical results about the solar system or whatever, you *simulate* it.

They do not question the value of the traditional techniques based on algebra and calculus, but they suggest that these have been pushed as far as they can go. They intend to build software which can reason qualitatively or symbolically about physical systems and also, when necessary, launch into massive number-crunching 'thought experiments'. The system would act as an intelligent assistant to the working scientist.

Of course, with their experience of building special purpose supercomputers, they propose that the whole thing should run on a lightning-fast parallel computer which will be equally adept at symbolic and numerical computations.

PC Scheme, an implementation of Scheme for the IBM PC, XT, AT and compatible machines, is available from Texas Instruments, PO Box 655012, Mail Station 57, Dallas, Texas 75265, USA.

Further reading

Abelson, H. and Sussman, G.J. (with Sussman, J.) (1984). *Structure and Interpretation of Computer Programs*. Cambridge, Mass.: MIT Press. (This is a text book. It is hard work – at least, I do not suppose it gets any easier beyond the point I reached – but rewarding. If possible you should have a Scheme system to hand. For most of the exercises you could make do with another dialect of Lisp, but you will become acutely aware of its infelicities.)

40

Asserting the assertional style

An excellent meeting at the Royal Society, in London, brought together many of the leading lights of computer science in Britain and abroad. What follows is not a comprehensive report of the meeting. It omits many names and concentrates on one theme. Its role here is to introduce formal methods, logic programming, and functional programming.

Functional programming was mentioned in the previous chapter but not explained. In fact, Sussman and Abelson teach functional programming in Scheme. David Turner's scathing remarks about Lisp, reported below, were aimed at earlier and less pure dialects of the language. Turner and Sussman have the greatest respect for each other's work.

8 March 1984

Those who went to the Royal Society on 15 February expecting a verbal punchup between the advocates of functional and logic programming will have been disappointed.

Bob Kowalski of Imperial College remains loyal to logic programming, while David Turner of the University of Kent is as active a publicist as ever for functional languages. But at this meeting on mathematical logic and programming languages, the two campaigners pitted their forces against a common enemy. Both of them argued the superiority of the assertional style of programming, as opposed to the imperative style seen in most programming languages from FORTRAN onwards.

Programming, for most people, is telling the computer what to do and in what order. Imperative languages represent knowledge in a procedural form, sometimes described as 'knowledge how'.

Assertional languages characteristically use a declarative representation of knowledge, or 'knowledge that'. The Kent approach is to represent knowledge with a system of equations, which may involve numbers, truth-values, characters, lists, functions of course, and other, user-defined data types. The order in which the equations are written does not generally matter.

Logic programming is not all that different. Again there is a body of declarative knowledge. It is represented as a set of predicate calculus formulae, which express the truth or falsehood of various relations between things.

According to Kowalski, however, there is more to it than that. A statement such as 'If X is a human X is mortal' may look declarative but, he argues, it implies a procedure. The 'knowledge how' embodied in the statement might be expressed either as 'To show X mortal, show X human,' or as 'To find X mortal, find X human'.

'To say logic programming is declarative programming is only half the story,' said Kowalski.

Kowalski and Turner were united in the view that if you want a program which can rigorously be proved to satisfy its specification, you should use an assertional language rather than an imperative one. Of course, Kowalski would favour a logic language such as Prolog, while Turner is now promoting a new language called Miranda, developed from the better-known Kent Recursive Calculator (KRC).

One of the main criticisms of such languages has been that programs written in them execute slowly and inefficiently. Both Turner and Kowalski defended their methods against this charge. But neither of them would be drawn back into the old Lisp-versus-Prolog debate. Kowalski announced that 'Prolog is a great language but it doesn't live up to logic programming ideals.' while Turner bluntly stated 'I don't consider Lisp a functional language.'

'Lisp does have a functional subset', Turner admitted, but he claimed that most programs written in Lisp are imperative. Twisting the knife, he declared: 'I think Lisp probably delayed the development of functional programming by about ten years.'

In mathematics one assumes that the two sides of an equation are equal, and that equal quantities can be substituted for one another. 'In programming languages all this is altered by the introduction of the assignment statement,' said Turner. 'Now we can write statements such as $x = x + 1$.'

This, he argues, has impeded the application of formal reasoning and proof to programming languages. There are two ways to improve the situation. One is to develop languages without assignment statements. Both logic and functional programming take this approach. The alternative is to develop formal methods which can handle the peculiar implications of $x = x + 1$. This approach, too, has had its successes.

Don Good from the University of Texas, and Tony Hoare of Oxford, presented evidence that provably correct programs can be produced in imperative languages such as Pascal and Ada.

Good's group in Austin has used the Gypsy program verification system to create successful programs for some very demanding tasks. Experimentally at least, Gypsy has been used to generate proven 'correct' programs for computer networking, computer security, and air traffic control. And this was all done with an imperative language derived from Pascal.

But there can be little doubt as to which way the wind is blowing. Don Good said that the next development in Gypsy would be 'along functional language lines'. The term 'correct' is a convenient one, but not one that Good himself likes. 'I wish we hadn't ever used that term, correctness,' he said. 'It has a connotation of absoluteness to it that is inappropriate. All we are doing is, we are proving that a program satisfies a certain relation.'

The proofs obtained with Gypsy only verify the relationship between a high level language program and the specification which states what the program is meant to do. The Gypsy compiler, and the hardware for that matter, have not been proved 'correct'. 'At the moment we are assuming these things work,' said Good. In ten years' time, he commented, it may be possible to prove the soundness of the Gypsy compiler.

Ideally, a specification should be in a language that is naturally understood by the user. But ordinary English, for example, is too full of ambiguity. It provides no anchorage for a formal proof. Formal software specification languages exist, but there is now a strong school of thought which says that the specification should be in a language as near as possible to the language of the program. The peculiar consequence of this is that in principle at least, the specification itself can be executed by a computer. This raises obvious questions. What now is the difference between a specification and a program? What becomes of the activity of programming?

Kowalski's answer is that 'If we restrict ourselves to complete specifications then there is no difference between specifications and programs except for efficiency.' In computation, of course, efficiency is no laughing matter. Kowalski took a simple sorting program as an example. The specification might be written:

sort (x,y) IF permute (x,y) AND ordered (y).

This logical formula means that list x can be sorted into list y if list x can be permuted to list y and the items in list y are in order. It is a commonsense description of what sorting achieves. No thought has been put into how the sorting will be done.

Kowalski says that this specification can also be interpreted as program. But what a program! A Prolog system would take the statement at face value and test every permutation of list x until by chance it hit upon the sorted list y. This must be the ultimate inefficient sort algorithm.

The program proper is more complicated, and it takes a little thought to see that it does correspond to intuitive concepts of sorting. It is still declarative in form. That is, it is stated as if it were simply a definition of what sorting achieves.

Once again a Prolog system would initiate a search procedure. But this time the search is more purposeful. By only looking at pairs of items, and swapping them if necessary, the system performs an efficient bubble sort.

Turner provided an even more impressive example in the context of functional programming. It was a perfectly sound specification for the so-called Hamming numbers problem which, regarded as a program, was not merely inefficient. It was non-executable. As stated, it required the sorting of an infinite list.

The fact that some specifications are executable does not mean that programming is abolished. The programmer's job, as ever, is to turn the specification into something which is not only runnable but efficient.

The final step is to show that the code is reliable. This is where conventional software testing may gradually be replaced by methods of formal proof.

41

Prologue to what?

Knocking Prolog is a popular sport. Perhaps Prolog's trouble is that it seems too clever for a mere programming language, and people then rationalize their irritation in other ways. As the former Australian Prime Minister Malcolm Fraser used to say, 'Life wasn't meant to be easy.' Prolog threatens to make life easy.

It can reason forwards – if this, then that, therefore the other – which does not seem too surprising. It is the backward reasoning that can astonish when it is first encountered. Here is an addition sum. Most of the digits have been replaced by Xs. Now go away and work out what the Xs stand for – Prolog can. It looks like creativity. In fact it is trial and error, but efficient, purposeful trial and error, of a kind that did not have to work at all. In the late 1960s Alan Robinson (Chapter 45) proved that it would work; logic programming followed. Prolog (as Bob Kowalski and others always remind us) is one manifestation of logic programming. There is nothing perfect or final about it. Surely stronger branches will spring from the same tree.

5 April 1984

Prolog is to Japan's Fifth Generation Computer Project, what the VW Beetle was to the California beach buggy industry. It is promising raw material, a good chassis on which to build more exotic vehicles.

Recent publications from the Institute of New Generation Computer Technology (ICOT) in Tokyo reveal that the Japanese are busy reshaping and extending the logic programming language they acquired from Europe and so admire.

Robert Kowalski (then at Edinburgh University) helped Alain Colmerauer of Marseille to create Prolog in the early 1970s. Kowalski has been one of Prolog's leading advocates ever since. But in February he told a London meeting, 'Prolog is a great language, but it does not live up to the ideals of logic programming.'

In no sense did this signal an abandonment of Prolog, for like the Japanese, Kowalski's group at Imperial College is working on a number of projects aimed to build on Prolog's strengths and make good its deficiencies. The current and planned developments include the introduction of 'higher-order' functions, improved methods of handling changing data, a related language called Parlog which will run on parallel hardware, and a friendly user shell called Apes.

Apes is about to be launched commercially by the campus spin-off company Logic Programming Associates. It provides special facilities to help relatively inexperienced users to construct expert systems.

Prolog is, in theory at least, a general purpose programming language. In principle one could use it for engineering calculations or business data processing, but neither of these exercises would be particularly efficient on today's hardware. Prolog comes into its own when the task is naturally expressed as a process of logical inference. The obvious application, though by no means the only one, is in expert systems.

What Prolog does, in essence, is to take a set of facts and rules and use them to deduce further facts. The facts and rules are expressed in a particular form of logic called first order predicate calculus.

Logic, like mathematics, is a toolbox full of different formal systems. These systems use different symbols and different ground rules. No one system of logic is any more or less valid than another, and most of them are powerful enough in themselves to tackle any problem. Choosing a logical system is like choosing a programming language: you look for one which will express the problem elegantly and solve it efficiently.

For the subset of predicate calculus used by Prolog, there are efficient automatic methods to test whether a particular consequence can be deduced from the facts and rules given. But some of the things you might want to express are not readily expressed in Prolog.

Facts are expressed as predicates. For example the fact that John is alive might be represented by giving the predicate LIVING(JOHN) the value 'true'. Relations are readily expressed by predicates such as LOVES(JOHN, MARY) or PARENTS(JANE, MARY, JOHN).

But in Prolog you cannot say that John is not living. You could introduce a new function, DEAD(X) but Prolog would also need new rules to the effect that a person living is not dead, and vice versa.

Nor can you state directly that John lives in London OR Vancouver. Again the Prolog programmer has to 'hack' round the problem by writing extra rules. Rules in Prolog resemble the IF . . . THEN . . . statements of other programming languages but there is an important difference. A rule says that one fact implies another. It does not instruct the computer to perform a test and select a course of action.

Another peculiarity of the Prolog environment is that propositions (like guilt in the courts) are assumed false until proved true. Strictly speaking, one cannot ask Prolog, 'Is X true?' The proper question is, 'Can you prove X to be true?'

This reflects the origins of Prolog in research on the automatic proof of theorems. It is arguably a sound principle in expert systems. Usually an expert system is expected to be able to provide reasoned justification for its pronouncements.

A Prolog program is static. It describes one state of the world. 'Destructive assignment' is prohibited, that is to say, the value of a variable is never overwritten by a new value. This makes it easier to prove, formally, that a program is correct. It also eliminates some of the synchronization problems that occur when conventional languages are run on parallel processing hardware. On the other hand, it means that special methods have to be used to handle, say, a frequently updated database.

The logic toolkit of Prolog could be extended in two possible directions. One would be to incorporate more expressive forms of classical logic. Higher-order predicate calculus, for example, is a form of classical logic which brings greater powers of generalization. Specifically, it allows functions like LIVING, or predicates like LOVES(X,Y) to be manipulated in the same way as constants like JOHN and MARY.

Attempts to compute with higher-order predicate calculus have not been entirely successful. But Keith Clark at Imperial College is working on a language called Lambda-Prolog which will embody a more modest 'higher-order' capability.

Lambda-Prolog will attempt to match, within the Prolog framework, the higher order facilities found in functional languages such as the University of Kent's Miranda. In Lambda-Prolog, for example, a function can act on another function. So instead of defining GRANDPARENT, GRANDFATHER and GRANDMOTHER as three new relations, you could define a new function GRAND which turns the function PARENT into GRAND(PARENT), FATHER into GRAND(FATHER) and so on.

Marek Sergot is working to extend Prolog to handle non-classical logic. A number of non-classical logics have been devised for special purposes. Some use the standard connectives such as AND, OR and NOT but with non-standard meanings. Others alter the laws used to derive one expression from another; for example, a logic can be constructed without the law of the excluded middle which says that a proposition must either be true or false.

Logics have also been devised which use entirely new operators. For legal purposes, it is useful to have ways of expressing prohibitions, obligations and entitlements.

A number of difficulties revealed themselves when the Imperial College group set about rephrasing the Nationality Act in formal logic. Phrases like '. . . and his mother is, or if male would have been, a British citizen' were hard to translate. Prolog as it exists today cannot temporarily assume, for the sake of argument, that a lady is male. Lawyers and parliamentary draughtsmen apparently can.

Parlog, developed by Keith Clark and Steve Gregory, is a manifestation of logic programming designed to exploit multiprocessor architectures. Essential for logic programming's fifth generation credibility, concurrency presents certain technical difficulties. Transient messages must flow between processes. An ingenious method is used to represent these messages in a Parlog program without resorting to destructive assignment.

Prolog implementations now exist for many machines. Micro-Prolog has brought Prolog within reach of microcomputer users, and there is even a version for the Sinclair ZX Spectrum. But like Lisp, the favoured language of the US artificial intelligence community, Prolog really cries out for specialized hardware.

Lisp aficionados have the Symbolics machine and the Xerox 1108. Imperial College, Logic Programming Associates, and Cambridge Consultants are now collaborating on the design of a Prolog machine. The first hardware is likely to be a microcoded version of an existing bit-slice processor. Later Prolog machines are likely to contain specially designed VLSI (very large scale integrated) circuits.

The commercial development of Prolog has come late, but the language could still ride to success on the expert systems boom. Apes, developed by Peter Hammond and Marek Sergot, is a suite of software modules which form an environment for building expert systems or for general logic programming. Anyone with Micro-Prolog and a machine with 128K of memory will be able to use Apes. A cheap and friendly entry-level system could help prepare the market for the high-performance Prolog machines and advanced Prolog-derived languages when they come along.

Not all the developments mentioned here have reached successful conclusions. Frank McCabe shelved his work on Lambda-Prolog and instead implemented LPA's MacProlog for the Apple Macintosh. The Imperial College collaboration with Cambridge Consultants foundered. Work on Parlog, however, has stepped up. Interest in the language is likely to increase, now that parallel computers have become a normal article of commerce. The Japanese are busy with it. They are also working with Concurrent Prolog, a similar language developed at the Weizmann Institute in Israel. An unpublished research report from Honeywell recommended that Parlog should be used for the company's Inference Storage Retrieval machine. There is also enthusiasm for the language at America's Argonne National Laboratory.

Several new projects, approved at the end of 1985 by the Alvey Directorate as part of its logic programming initiative, enabled Imperial College to take on approximately ten more research assistants. Parlog is featured in several of these projects. For example, it will now be implemented on the Flagship machine. Flagship is one of Alvey's star projects – a £15 million industry/university effort to develop declarative languages, software tools, and parallel hardware.

The expert system shell Apes is now available from Logic Programming Associates Ltd (Studio 4, Royal Victoria Patriotic Building, Trinity Road, London SW18 3SX, England). LPA also supplies Prolog implementations for Unix systems, the IBM PC range, the Apple Macintosh and some other computers.

42

The program changes, the variables remain the same

Occasionally one is reminded, with a jolt, of the everyday miracle of software. Miracle? The miracle, as I see it, is that machines can be built from symbols. A computer program is a machine. It has been designed and assembled to perform some job, and it performs it. But unlike machines built from lumps of iron, software can change its form without losing its potency. It can be sent along wires, recorded on disks or tape, printed out on paper and read back into the computer by optical character recognition.

Programming languages are the Meccano kits from which these soft machines are constructed. Essentially we ask two things of a programming language. It should be possible, indeed easy, to use this kit to build a symbolic, abstract engine to solve the problem we want to solve. And it should be possible to build a physical engine of some kind which will power the symbolic engine. Software alone can do nothing. In computer-speak: the language should be implementable.

That physical engine (a computer) delivers the raw computing power that a program will harness to some useful purpose. Often the computer will itself be built partly of abstract, symbolic stuff which is hidden inside it and usually ignored by its users. This stuff is called microcode. Pursuing the metaphor of computer as motor, the microcoded computer is like one of those electric motors which have a gearbox incorporated inside the casing. Of course the gearing has to be right for the motor's intended application.

Some computers (for example the Norsk ND500, the Symbolics and LMI Lisp machines, and the High Level Hardware Orion) allow the user to get at the microcode and alter it. One can therefore tune the machine to deliver its power in a suitable form for running some particular programming language.

Computer scientists have always enjoyed inventing new high level languages which express algorithms elegantly, succinctly and clearly. They are now also experimenting with new low-level or machine languages and the unusual computing motors which will drive them. The domination of the von Neumann machine is broken. Experiments with microcode can be the preliminary to the design of entirely new types of computing engine. Indeed, the microcode implementation may be the final one.

The work on first order predicate calculus as a high level language has encouraged researchers to develop physical devices (such as content addressable memories, and hardware unifiers) which directly execute parts of first order predicate calculus.

Other logics, too, are being examined as possible machine languages. David Turner, a professor at the University of Kent, has been particularly interested in combinatory logic, a formalism invented in the 1950s by the logician H.B. Curry.

Turner's work has shown that combinatory logic is not only implementable as a machine language, but implementable with reasonable efficiency. The miracle has happened again. An unlikely-looking set of symbols has become a machine capable of a vast range of information-processing tasks. Of high level programming languages, the functional languages are particularly well matched to combinatory logic as a machine language. Turner's work in functional programming (like that of John Darlington and Peter Henderson) is influential both in Britain and in the USA.

---

10 May 1984

'Do more with less' is a sound engineering principle that has often been fruitful when applied to the development of programming languages.

Few other languages can be as powerful and succinct as Miranda. Miranda has been developed by David Turner of the University of Kent from the earlier versions St Andrews Static Language (SASL) and Kent Recursive Calculator (KRC). For example, a five-line Miranda program will find all ways of placing eight queens on a chessboard so that no queen threatens another. An 'almost complete' Miranda compiler, itself written in Miranda, is just 374 lines long.

However, Turner is aiming to do more than merely to develop a very high level language. The work on Miranda is closely linked to the development of a new kind of computer called a combinator machine. And the functional or applicative style of Miranda will, in Turner's view, greatly ease the task of proving formally that programs meet their specifications. For Turner it is essential that these proofs should themselves be performed on a computer. 'Program proving is just a game until the proofs are computer-based and machine-checked,' he maintains.

Interest in functional programming has burgeoned since the 1977 Turing lecture by John Backus. Backus declared that the future of programming lay not with FORTRAN, COBOL and their descendants but with a quite different style of programming exemplified by the list processing language Lisp.

Functions, as in school mathematics, are things with one or more 'arguments' or unknowns. The function will return a value when values are given to the unknowns.

A Lisp program is built up by defining various new functions in terms of existing ones. This establishes an environment in which some quite simple expression may stand for a great big complicated function. When you press the button, the machine evaluates the great big function and, possibly after hours of computation spews out the answer. The answer may be a number such as '42' or it may be a list, or list of lists, which occupies a mile of printout.

In 'pure' functional programming (and Turner points out that virtually all serious Lisp programs are impure), the role of variables is subtly different from the role they play in FORTRAN and similar 'imperative' languages.

In FORTRAN or BASIC, a variable is really a name for a memory location, whose contents may be changed during the running of the program by an instruction such as $x = x + 1$.

Functional programming returns to the mathematical concept of a variable as an unknown. 'Variables do not change their value in mathematics and logic, as they do in a programming language such as FORTRAN or Algol,' says Turner.

Miranda statements take the form of equations. This makes a Miranda program or 'script' more legible than its Lisp equivalent. (Lisp thrives on massive expressions with parentheses nested dozens deep.)

A system of equations is also a comfortable environment for attempts to prove the correctness of the program. 'The method of proof depends heavily on the properties of equations,' explains Turner. 'These proofs are all substitutions of equals for equals.'

Miranda programs are compiled to an unusual kind of code called combinatory logic. 'Combinatory logic,' Turner explains, 'is a very simple language which has the property that it is completely variable-free.'

It is a remarkable fact that any functional language that uses variables can be translated into a code which contains constants only. There is a procedure for squeezing all the occurrences of a variable such as x out of an expression. Once x has been abstracted, the process can be repeated for y, and so on. As this is done, the expression itself changes shape in a dramatic way. New constants called combinators are introduced. They do not represent numbers or any other familiar quantity. Essentially they are markers which show how the expression has been rearranged, and thereby preserve its meaning. Three combinators, known as S, K and I, will suffice. But Turner and others have introduced about half a dozen additional combinators in the interest of efficient execution of the code.

The small instruction set contains the combinators and little more, apart from a conditional operator equivalent to IF, a data structuring operator which adds items to lists, and the usual arithmetic operators such as PLUS and TIMES. Remarkably, this simple code can represent nested conditionals, local variable definitions, recursion, and complicated data structures. A fairly simple machine can execute it. It is, however, virtually incomprehensible to human beings.

The combinator expression is made up of letters, numbers and masses of parentheses. As such, it is pretty opaque to the human intellect. But its logical structure can be represented as a binary tree, with branches forking into two at each node, and with constants as its leaves. (Combinators, numbers, and the basic functions such as PLUS, count as constants.) If recursion is present, a branch may lead back to an earlier node. The structure then is strictly a graph, rather than a tree.

Execution of the program is a pruning process. The tree is simplified, and unnecessary bits are lopped off and removed by a 'garbage collector' routine. This process of graph reduction is utterly different from the execution of a conventional computer program.

We are accustomed to the idea of a fixed program, which works on variable data. But here there is no distinction between program and data. The program is actually destroyed during execution (though a copy would usually be kept somewhere else). Execution is complete when the program has been simplified down to something that can be printed.

A crucial innovation ensures that execution is fast and efficient. If the run-time system (the real or abstract 'combinator machine') attacked the graph like a mad axeman, it might well give itself more work than necessary. Instead, the system uses a method called lazy evaluation. This only evaluates functions when it absolutely has to. When it suits the system to do so, it will pass unevaluated functions – intact branches of the the tree – from one part of the program to another. This not only avoids unnecessary work. It may sometimes prevent the system tackling an infinite task and becoming trapped in a loop for ever.

The safety and efficiency provided by lazy evaluation can be felt, indirectly, by the user. The programmer can use infinite data structures, such as the list of all prime numbers, secure in the knowledge that the system will only do any actual computing of primes as and when they are needed.

Miranda also uses a very powerful set notation. It deals comfortably with sets of all the objects which satisfy some condition, even though those sets may be infinite.

Turner's group at Canterbury has two three-year grants from the Science and Engineering Research Council. One grant, worth £120,000, is for the development of a combinator machine and a complete operating system written in a functional language. The combinator machine is being created by microprogramming an Orion supermini computer made by High Level Hardware of Oxford.

Turner was working on this project with Waldo Watkins. Tragically Watkins was killed in a road accident in April 1984. Simon Thompson, a logician, has joined Turner for another project which SERC is funding to the tune of £130,000. Its aim is to derive formal, machine-checked proofs of software.

Combinator machines and more general graph reduction machines are being developed at several other centres. The university-based Cambridge Processor Group built a machine called SKIM (from the names of the first three combinators) in 1980. They are working on a new machine which will perform between 50,000 and 100,000 combinator reductions (basic tree-pruning operations) per second.

Turner also collaborates with the Burroughs Corporation's research centre at Austin, Texas. Burroughs is building a very fast combinator machine which will perform up to 250,000 reductions per second.

All these are sequential machines. In principle the reduction process could be carried out in parallel, with pruning proceeding on several branches of the tree simultaneously. Turner believes that future reduction machines will use many processor chips working in parallel. But certain questions, including that of memory organization, have yet to be resolved.

John Darlington at Imperial College is building a general purpose, parallel reduction machine called Alice which could, among other things, handle combinator logic.

Logic programming languages such as Prolog have much in common with functional languages like Miranda. There are also important differences.

Prolog has established itself as a suitable language for expert systems and knowledge based systems generally, a field where impressive performance is achieved with large bodies of facts and rules. Miranda is perhaps better suited to the representation of a different kind of knowledge, the knowledge embodied in clever algorithms.

The market for this at the moment is limited, and the artificial intelligence community seems to be moving in the opposite direction. But it is hard to believe there is not a use somewhere for a language which produces code ten times more compact than Pascal, and offers the prospect of software that is formally proved correct.

Without attempting a full explanation of graph reduction, it is worth pointing out that I oversimplified things by calling it a pruning process. The reduction process does not continuously make the graph smaller. It may actually expand parts of the graph as a preliminary to pruning them. Other parts will stay expanded and appear in the result as data structures.

That is how those mile-long printouts can happen.

The impact of John Backus's Turing Award lecture was so great because Backus, of IBM, was himelf the inventor of FORTRAN. It was as if Issigonis or Pininfarina had stood up and said 'cars are dead, the aeroplane is the coming thing.' In his lecture, Backus described a functional language called FP which is elegant and terse but lacks the power of recursion.

Other functional languages have found favour in the British research community. Hope and ML both originated at Edinburgh University. Cambridge is developing a language called Ponder.

David Turner is now working full time on research, thanks to a grant from a computer manufacturer ICL which relieves him of teaching and administrative duties for four years.

The article as it appeared in *Computing* did not properly distinguish Miranda from Turner's official University of Kent research projects. In fact Miranda was from the start a commercial project, backed by venture capital. Towards the end of 1985 it made a very quiet entry into the market. Miranda runs on most Unix systems and is available from Research Software Limited, 23 St Augustine's Road, Canterbury, Kent CT1 1XP, England (telephone 0227 471844, international +44 227 471844).

Turner says that about three quarters of the early sales were to universities and colleges. There is a demand for a modern functional language for teaching. At least one customer has been using Miranda to write an expert system. ICL has used the language to write an executable specification for a commmunications protocol.

Keith Hanna of the University of Kent has written a theorem-prover in Miranda, which he uses to verify that designs for digital circuits meet their specifications. Actually the program was written first in Lisp, over a period of two years. Hanna then rewrote it in Miranda in a fortnight. Before concluding that Miranda multiplies programmer productivity by a factor of 50, bear in mind that writing a program is not just a matter of expressing your perfectly formed ideas in your chosen programming language. The ideas themselves have to take shape. After this, paraphrasing the program in a new language is not all that difficult, provided the new language is at least as rich and expressive as the original one.

When will Miranda run on a parallel reduction machine? Perhaps by the end of 1987. The machine in question should result from Alvey's GRIP (graph reduction in parallel) project, led by Simon Peyton-Jones of University College, London. High Level Hardware Ltd, Research Software Ltd, and ICL are the industrial partners.

GRIP will use symbols called supercombinators, which are, as the name suggests, an advance on Turner's combinators. They were invented by John Hughes while he was at Oxford University. He is now a professor at the University of Glasgow.

By late 1985 Burroughs Corporation in Austin, Texas had built three prototypes of its Norma combinator reduction machine. A leading supplier of computer systems to banks, Burroughs is, like ICL, a large and outwardly boring computer company with some clever and far-sighted individuals tucked away in its research and design departments.

Norma is a sequential machine like SKIM, but it has been built in custom-designed VLSI (very large scale integration) circuitry. So it runs that much faster than SKIM, which was assembled from ordinary off-the-shelf chips. The long-term goal of the Burroughs research is to build a machine which performs many reductions in parallel.

The world's first reduction machine would appear to have been the one built in 1976 by Werner Kluge and his colleagues at West Germany's national computing laboratory, the Gesellschaft für Mathematik und Datenverarbeitung (GMD). In a friendly office crowded with desks, chairs, people and plants, the machine still stands in a corner, cherished but permanently *kaput*. Kluge's group, too, hopes to build a parallel reduction machine, and has been using software to simulate possible designs.

Further reading

Backus, J. (1978). 'Can programming be liberated from the von Neumann style? A functional style and its algebra of programs' *Communications of the ACM*, **21**, no. 8, 613–641.

Byte, August 1985. (Several articles on declarative languages.)

Turner, D.A. (1979). 'A new implementation technique for applicative languages' *Software – Practice and Experience*, **9**, 31–49.

43

A logical route to the parallel world

Another unusual machine code, another unusual machine. This time the machine, of its essence, is massively parallel. It deploys vast numbers of very simple processors to tackle problems which are regarded as intractable on conventional computers. This intractability, however, is only held at bay. It reaffirms itself once the problems become big enough to saturate all the processors.

To bring problems of arbitrary size under control, one has to assume that as many processors as necessary will be provided. Surprisingly, this is not an altogether unreasonable assumption. Computer scientists already habitually assume that unlimited supplies of memory will be available, which on the face of it is just as implausible.

The instigator of this tough research programme is better known for his writings on less grave subjects. As a result he sometimes has trouble getting other computer scientists to take him seriously. This article, as it first appeared in *Computing*, may not have helped the situation. To put the record straight I must stress that this article is about research on novel computer languages and architectures. A column in *Scientific American*, and a work of imaginative fiction, do not impinge on this research in any direct way. They are mentioned because they show another side of a creative scientist.

24 May 1984

Alexander Keewatin Dewdney is moving into the public eye this month. Pan Books has published his book *The Planiverse* and Dewdney has also just taken over the monthly *Computer Recreations* column in *Scientific American* magazine.

The Planiverse is a kind of twentieth-century *Gulliver's Travels*. It describes a two-dimensional world called Arde where there is up and down and east and west but no north or south. When two travellers meet, moving in opposite directions, one must climb over the other. When it rains, the world becomes a river and the inhabitants seal themselves into their underground houses. They have balloons, rocket ships, and a computer, but no wheeled vehicles.

Contact with Arde is made when a computer simulation called 2DWORLD mysteriously meshes with Ardean reality. Despite numerous hints (for example, the language of Arde is based on Maltese), some people are inevitably going to believe the whole thing really happened.

Dewdney is an associate professor of computer science at the University of Western Ontario. He sometimes worries that his light-hearted public activities will lead academic colleagues to dismiss him as 'not a real scientist'.

In fact, when he is not trying to figure out how Ardeans mate or build steam engines, his main interest is in complexity theory, the branch of computer science concerned with the inherent toughness of problems and the efficiency, or otherwise, of algorithms. At the moment he is investigating a unique approach to programming based on symbolic logic, and a novel computer architecture which could execute the programs. Programs are prepared to run on the envisioned machine, by a compiler called Transat. This is short for 'translation into satisfiability'.

In keeping with the spirit of the times, Dewdney has adopted a declarative programming style which breaks with FORTRAN and COBOL traditions. A program in his Nondeterministic Parallel Language (NPL) does not instruct the computer to do things in a particular order. It merely defines what would constitute a solution to the problem at hand.

Like other declarative languages, NPL is ill-matched to the conventional von Neumann computer architecture, which allows unlimited memory but only a single processor. Dewdney, like others, has read the writing on the wall which says that processors and memory now cost about the same, and that the next big speed-up in computer performance will be achieved with large numbers of processors working in parallel. So NPL programs are compiled to run on a highly parallel machine which Dewdney calls a logic grid. This does not yet exist as hardware, but it can be simulated in software.

The 'machine code' of this abstract machine is a subset of symbolic logic. This intermediate code plays a role analogous to that of predicate calculus in Prolog, or of combinator logic in the functional languages developed by David Turner at the University of Kent. Dewdney's code is drawn from propositional calculus, the simplest form of symbolic logic. It is less expressive than, say, predicate calculus. But a remarkable theorem shows that even the toughest computational problems can be translated into this deceptively simple formalism. Every problem becomes an instance of what logicians call the satisfiability problem.

Essentially every problem one could hope to solve with a computer falls into the class known as NP. Strictly speaking, NP only includes decision problems, where the answer is either yes or no. But as Dewdney points out, 'Almost every decision problem has a search version.' The decision problem asks whether a solution exists. The search problem says, 'OK, then find it'.

Complexity theorists rate the difficulty of problems according to a surprisingly simple criterion: how long it takes to solve them. This has to be related to the size of the problem. The actual time required to sort a list of, say, ten items is not very important. What matters is the way that the computing time increases as you go to a list twice as long, or ten times or a thousand times as long. This time is said to be 'polynomial' if it ultimately grows no faster than some power of the size of the problem. (That power might be the third power or it might be the thirty-third, but that is a relatively minor detail. At least the problem is not exploding exponentially.)

The nondeterministic polynomial (NP) problems are those which can be solved in polynomial time on a nondeterministic computer – one with an unlimited capacity for parallel processing. Since every real computer has physical limits, membership of NP does not imply that a problem can actually be solved in polynomial time.

Within NP, however, there is a class P of problems which can be solved in polynomial time on a deterministic machine like the one that may be on your desk. It is conceivable that one day all NP problems will be proved to belong to P, but most mathematicians regard this as highly unlikely.

In 1971 Stephen Cook, then a student at the University of California at Berkeley, proved that any decision problem belonging to class NP can be translated into a corresponding problem in logic, known as satisfiability.

Satisfiability became the first of the NP-complete problems, so called because an NP-complete problem can stand for any other problem in class NP. Around 2000 NP-complete problems are now known. Their existence is generally taken to be a strong indication that some problems are inherently intractable.

Cook's translation process yields a formula called a conjunctive form consisting of a number of bracketed expressions called clauses. Within the brackets are variables linked by logical OR operators. These variables may be negated. The clauses themselves are linked by AND operators.

The expression is said to be satisfiable if there is a way of assigning a value, TRUE or FALSE, to each variable so that the whole expression is true. In other words, the variables must be juggled until there is at least one true literal in each clause. If such as 'satisfying assignment' exists, we have a YES answer to the original decision problem. But Dewdney has ingeniously extracted, from Cook's theorem, a method of solving problems where more than a yes/no answer is required.

Cook's transformation not only transforms the decision problem,' he says, 'it also transforms the search problem. That's not used in the theorem, but I take advantage of it in this particular system.'

Cook's method, never intended for practical computation, is inefficient and throws up enormous clause systems from quite simple problems. For the purpose of a mathematical proof this did not matter. Dewdney, on the other hand, will consider he has succeeded only if the method can be groomed into something fast and efficient enough to solve real problems.

He independently found a very efficient (linear-time) algorithm for translating problems into conjunctive form clause systems. He then discovered that Mike Robson of the Australian National University had reached the same result a year earlier.

Even when the problem has been 'compiled' to a clause system, there remains the tough, NP-complete problem of testing the clause system's satisfiability. Fortunately the clause systems thrown up by the Transat software seem usually to be highly structured, and easier to solve than the general problem.

Parallel processing should also help cut the problem down to size. Dewdney's proposed parallel machine still exists only as a software simulation. It uses the 'divide and conquer' strategy that is often used to build efficient parallel processing algorithms. The problem is divided into two smaller problems, these are divided again, and so on.

The machine has two main components. There are the processors themselves. And there is a sorting network which can route data from any processor to any other, rather like a telephone exchange. Each processor is either free or busy. As one processor splits its task into two subtasks, the network automatically finds a free processor somewhere else to take on the new subtask. Before splitting the problem in this way, a processor first tries the logical operation known as resolution. (Resolution is also used, in a somewhat different form, in the logic programming language Prolog.)

This can avoid unnecessary computation. 'If you use resolution,' explains Dewdney, 'you can often find out that an expression is unsatisfiable right at the beginning.'

His current system can only handle problems up to about 'size ten', such as sorting a list of ten items. With the help of a three-year, $60,000 grant from Canada's National Science and Engineering Research Council, he hopes to move up to problems of 'size 1000'. This, he believes, would establish his method as a feasible approach to parallel computing.

'Such a system, should it be successful, would automatically be a partial answer to the Japanese fifth generation challenge,' he says.

His chance of success? '100 to one against', is his surprisingly cautious estimate. Dewdney the computer scientist keeps his imagination firmly under control. Somehow, the level-headed scientist manages to share a brain and a body with the writer who dreamed up a flat world and its bizarre inhabitants. The symbiosis seems to be successful.

The successful symbiosis continues. I should stress that Dewdney remains first and foremost a computer scientist, since some people reading my original article may have formed the unfortunate impression that research is just a hobby for him. He has wound up his investigations of Arde, but in late 1985 he was working on a new book called *I, Robert*. It is about a man who thinks he is a robot.

The column in *Scientific American* continues triumphantly, with fresh delights each month. Dewdney's full postbag confirms a truth of which you will find little evidence in the mainstream computer press: that there exists at least a small community of Renaissance individuals who like to use computers to gain insight into other, more interesting matters.

The personal computer magazines provide copious fare for gadget freaks, and some genuine assistance for people buying or working with computers. But they provide little for those who wish to use their computers for intellectual exploration. The few articles of this kind that do appear tend to perpetuate the myth that the computer is a mathematics machine.

By contrast, Dewdney urges us to create electronic microworlds in which fish and sharks breed and feed, or he decribes devilish wooden puzzles designed with the aid of a computer program. There are mathematical curiosities too, but Dewdney encourages us to use our personal computers to assist mathematical thought, not to substitute for it.

Meanwhile the research on satisfiability has progressed sufficiently to make the *Computing* article thoroughly out of date. The total system, software and hardware, is now (late 1985) known as a generic reduction computer.

The envisioned hardware is now called the very large network (VLN), and is imagined to have one million processors. A software simulation of this machine is used to test actual NPL programs.

The name Transat remains, for the program which translates NPL programs into logical formulae. But Transat is not just a compiler, preparing programs for processing. It also translates the processed data back into a comprehensible form.

The machine code is still based on propositional logic but with an extended range of operators. Dewdney says that the logical expressions produced by Transat are now ten times shorter than before. They are also easier to solve. The simulated VLN processor can now handle problems up to size 100, which one might regard as half way to the target of size 1000.

Further reading

Dewdney, A.K. 'Computer recreations'. Monthly in *Scientific American*.

Dewdney, A.K. (1985). *Generic Reduction Computers*. Report no. 141, Department of Computer Science, University of Western Ontario, London, Ontario N6A 5B9, Canada.

Dewdney, A.K. (1984). *The Planiverse* UK: Pan Books, London; US: Washington Square Press.

44

Engineers and mechanics

No one states the case for formal methods better than Bernie Cohen. It is interesting that both he and the like-minded Tony Hoare of Oxford University spent many years in industry before becoming academics. Unlike lifelong academics, they have first hand knowledge both of the problems and of the opportunities that exist in industry.

31 May 1984

The claim that one can write software without a knowledge of mathematics is coming under attack. A software mechanic – someone who bolts together reusable pieces of code designed by others – may get by without a grounding in mathematical theory. A software engineer cannot.

This view is gaining a hold not only in the academic world but increasingly in industry. In the UK, active groups of 'formalists' are at work in a number of companies, notably GEC, STC and ICL. One of the meeting points of the formalists is the Formal Aspects of Computer Science group of the British Computer Society.

Racal has funded a new chair of information technology at the University of Surrey. Bernard Cohen, a leading formalist from STC, took up the post on 1 March. Surrey's new professor built his reputation in industry. Nit-pickers will note that he does not even have a doctorate. But for others, who do not accept that universities have a monopoly on intellectual excellence, his appointment is a breath of fresh air.

Cohen will be pursuing his consuming interest in formal specification and design techniques. What distinguishes formal techniques from those which are merely 'structured', according to Cohen, is a strong and explicit link to mathematics. But it is not the kind of mathematics most of us learn at school. It is not even the mathematics traditionally taught to mechanical and electrical engineers. The search for a theoretical foundation for information technology has led to such disciplines as set theory and predicate calculus, or in the higher reaches, model theory and category theory. Collectively, these disciplines are known as discrete mathematics.

Cohen says that these disciplines are alien to the average engineer. But he maintains that many subjects in discrete mathematics are actually easier than the traditional mathematical fare of engineering courses.

Traditional engineering mathematics revolves round the differential and integral calculus. It assumes that quantities can vary continuously – that is, they can change by infinitesimal amounts. But this is not a very useful model of information-processing systems, which generally do one thing, or another, but not something in between.

In the mid-1970s, when STC was part of the ITT empire, the company began looking at the available design methodologies. It spent approximately £1 million in trying out one technique, Softech's Structured Analysis and Design Technique (SADT). But, says Cohen, 'We were very concerned that many of the claims being made for structured design methodologies were not justified.'

In 1979 STC ran a symposium on formal design methods, in Cambridge. Seven speakers were invited, each putting the case for one of the methods then available. Cohen and his colleagues felt that all the methods fell short of the ideal. 'Our conclusion after that conference,' he says, 'was that there was really no alternative to mathematical formalism.'

'Pseudo-mathematical' methods do not impress Cohen. Of database-derived techniques, with their entities and relations, he comments: 'It looks as though what you're doing is defining relations in a mathematical sense. But if you're not very careful you lose soundness, so you can no longer draw conclusions about the behaviour of the system.'

Another major approach is structured systems analysis, based on the data flow graph. Here too, Cohen detects pseudo-mathematical trappings. This is a pictorial approach, with arrows showing the flow of data through the system and boxes representing operations on the data. These boxes (themselves defined by further flow graphs) beg comparison with mathematical functions. 'It looks as though you are defining a function,' Cohen warns, 'but you cannot reason about its composition with some other function.'

These methods, according to Cohen, share the weakness of the common flowchart, which shows the flow of control rather than the flow of data. The flowchart's failing is that there is no powerful reasoning method attached to it. The only way to draw reasoned conclusions from a flow chart is to execute it mentally.

Cohen believes that any serious method for developing software, hardware or systems must address itself to the entire product lifecycle. He points out that often 80 per cent of the cost of a software development goes on testing, after the code has been written. 'The trouble is that nobody ever estimates that, so projects over-run, naturally.' This points to a need for more effort in the project's early stages. 'The more revision and checking you could do early in the development, the lower the cost of the development.'

It is usually impossible to test a system early in the development, of course, because nothing yet exists that can be executed. Software prototyping, and the concept of 'executable specifications', have been proposed as remedies. But Cohen counters that 'execution as a form of test is actually useless for the kind of complex programs that people are demanding today'. The problem is, quite simply, that the possible behaviours of a program are counted by a number which probably runs to hundreds of digits. There is no way to test all the possibilities within the lifetime of the universe.

'The statistical approach to testing is also flawed,' he adds. The problem is to choose a representative set of test conditions out of the possible billions. One can test software to the point where it is, in a statistical sense, very bad luck if a bug has slipped through the net. But there is no theoretical basis for thinking that one net will trap bugs better than any other. With hardware it is much easier since one can assume that a transistor, say, has a continuous transfer function. If it works at 4.9 volts and at 5.1 volts it almost certainly works at 5.0 volts.

A software bug can be regarded as a discrepancy between a program and its specification. A goal of formal methods is to prove, in the mathematical sense, that a program and a specification are equivalent.

A variety of proof methods are being developed. Many of them depend on the use of programming and specification languages specially designed for provability. All of them require that the languages and methodologies employed should be underpinned by powerful mathematics.

Naturally those who design these tools will need a deeper knowledge of mathematics than those who use them. But Cohen believes that the users – practising software engineers – must grasp the essential underlying theory of the tools they use. He appeals to an everyday analogy: 'You've got to have a feeling for the way arithmetic works, even when you're using a calculator, or else you do silly things.'

A few years ago British Telecom set up the Joint Curriculum Development Team, with GEC, Plessey and STC, to draw up a software engineering curriculum to be used in industry. 'It's a fairly shocking document,' says Cohen, 'because it makes no compromise about the degree of mathematical exposure that the engineer requires. Basically it says that the maths won't go away. You can't hide it.'

He observes a similar trend in many other new curricula, both in industry and in higher education. For example, discrete mathematics takes up 11 per cent of a curriculum drawn up by the Philips group in 1981.

At the University of Maryland, Harlan D. Mills of IBM's Federal Systems Division gives a one-semester, first-year undergraduate course called 'Structured programming using Pascal'. It is a good fashionable title, guaranteed to draw in students.

As Cohen describes it, the course constantly digresses into mathematical concepts – sets, predicates, relations, functions and lists. Apologetically Mills explains that these must be dealt with before coming to the main subject. The end of the course approaches, and Mills still has not taught any Pascal directly. He has used it in examples, and the students have absorbed a fair amount by osmosis. But much more important, they have been taught the underlying principles which never emerge when structured programming is taught as a craft skill.

Cohen agrees with Oxford's professor of computing, Anthony Hoare, who maintains that a software engineer has to be an engineer in all the senses that a civil or mechanical engineer is. The engineer needs a huge bag full of intellectual tools. Many of them may never be used, but one is not an engineer without them.

Further reading

Cohen, B., Harwood, W.T. and Jackson M.I. (1986). *The Specification of Complex Systems.* Wokingham: Addison-Wesley. (Written by three former colleagues from the golden days of formal methods at Standard Telecommunications Laboratories, this book shows how it is actually done. Intended for practising software developers, it presents the material clearly and attractively: But as you would expect, it does not dodge the mathematics.)

45

Programming's grand unification

The idea of combining the two great paradigms of declarative programming has already been mentioned in connection with the logic programming research at Imperial College, London (Chapter 41). That particular attempt was abandoned, at least temporarily; though John Darlington, also at Imperial College, has brought concepts from logic programming into the functional language Hope (which he and Rod Burstall devised). The highly expressive language which resulted, 'Hope with unification', is executable but perhaps not yet suitable for use as a programming language. It might be a suitable language for specifications.

Several other research groups, in the US and elsewhere, have tried to unite functional and logic programming. It is significant that Alan Robinson, inventor of the resolution algorithm which underlies most logic programming, believes this is the right direction to be going in.

23 May 1985

Grand Unified Theories (GUTs), which wrap up gravity and all the other forces of nature together, are the hot subject in physics at the moment. Something of the same excitement now exists among computer scientists, who are attempting their own grand unification between logic programming and functional programming.

For physicists, the final unification is at last in sight. Computer science, however, is still divided between the imperative style of programming (typified by Algol, Ada, and Occam) and the assertional style associated with pure Lisp and pure Prolog. It is within the assertional camp that the barriers are being broken down.

Alan Robinson of Syracuse University, whose work on theorem-proving prepared the way for Prolog, has spent the past few years trying to combine the best of Prolog and the best of Lisp in a single language. 'Prolog and Lisp are cousins,' he maintains. 'They descend from and exemplify the same idea, which is: to be computational formalisms governed by an underlying logic.'

In the case of Prolog, Robinson observes, the underlying logic is a subset of predicate calculus. Lisp's underlying logic is the lambda calculus. 'To call Prolog logic programming and to deny that to Lisp,' he says, 'is simply to miss the point, and not to see the deeper relationship.'

Another group with similar aims is led by Nachum Dershowitz at the University of Illinois. Both Robinson and Dershowitz reported on their independent projects at the Machine Intelligence 11 workshop, held at Strathclyde University during March. Dershowitz mentioned similar projects in progress at several centres, including the Centre de Recherche en Informatique at Nancy in France, and the University of Utah and the California Institute of Technology in the USA.

Superficially, Lisp and Prolog are quite different. Lisp is like a factory, with materials (data) going in at one end, to be processed by various machines (functions) so that products (results) come out at the other end. Prolog is more like a vast warehouse full of goods (individuals), with a very clever cataloguing system (predicates) which swiftly finds exactly the items, if any, which will satisfy a customer's order (user's query.)

Lisp's machines can be used to build or modify other machines in the factory. Functions or entire programs can be treated as data objects. Programmers find this a very nice feature of Lisp and other functional-style languages. In the Prolog warehouse, by contrast, the goods and the catalogues are kept on separate shelves. Predicates cannot be treated as individuals. Facts and rules about things cannot be treated as things in their own right.

But to the Prolog way of thinking, Lisp's powerful machine tools have their own limitations. A machine for making gizmos out of widgets cannot be run backwards to fashion widgets from gizmos. A warehouse catalogue, however, can be used 'backwards' to find items which do not appear in the main index. When Prolog cannot find an immediate answer to a query, it resorts to 'search'.

Leafing through a catalogue page by page may seem an inefficient way of finding the widgets, but Prolog has a number of time-saving tricks. Different implementations use different tricks, but all of them derive from the algorithm that Robinson developed in the early 1960s, which uses a method called 'resolution' to prove theorems in predicate calculus.

Dershowitz sees Lisp and Prolog as occupying different points on a spectrum of methods, languages and algorithms. At one extreme is pure 'computing', the production-line approach which efficiently churns out answers in a completely deterministic fashion. At the other extreme is pure 'searching' – often the only way to be sure of solving a problem, but potentially very inefficient.

Exhaustive generate-and-test strategies lie at the 'searching' end of the spectrum. Heuristic theorem-provers like Boyer and Moore's sacrifice a little completeness (they sometimes fail) in the interest of efficiency. Languages like Prolog and Planner, which backtrack when a subgoal fails, come next. Lisp lies fairly close to the pure 'computing' end of the spectrum.

Lisp and Prolog have already been united at a superficial level in some programming environments. Sussex University's Poplog, for example, allows the programmer to combine Prolog, Pop-11 and Lisp code in a single program. But Dershowitz, Robinson and other researchers have been trying, in different ways, to establish a more intimate union of functional and logic programming which provides the best of both worlds. Robinson's Loglisp interpreter can handle Lisp-like and Prolog-like constructs within a single expression or program line. Dershowitz has abandoned both Lisp and Prolog syntax, and instead uses so-called 'conditional equations', which are a kind of hybrid of a function definition and an IF-THEN rule.

Lisp plays two roles in Robinson's Loglisp system: a visible one and an invisible one. In its visible role, Lisp evaluates functions and performs any other Lisp-like tasks required while Loglisp is running. Logical operations are passed to a Prolog-like component, but this too is written in Lisp. Lisp's second, invisible role is as the underlying implementation language of the whole of Loglisp. 'We could have programmed the whole thing in Pascal or in C,' Robinson explains. But he adds: 'In fact, when we type something at Loglisp, it is Lisp that is listening.'

Prolog already has some Lisp-like features including arithmetic and list processing. But Robinson stresses that the argument is not about what can be done in a language, but what can be done naturally and easily. 'I think perhaps one has to make the comment that is always made in discussions of this kind,' he says, 'which is that any universal computing formalism can do the whole job, whatever the whole job may be. And Prolog in particular can, but it's very much the hard way. Prolog lacks some features that are very handy.'

It may not be all that difficult to combine logic programming and functional programming in a unified syntax. But the real challenge is to define a consistent way of reading programs, which unifies the contrasting 'functional' and 'logic programming' viewpoints. One of the main attractions of a programming language based on a formal logic or algebra is that one can reason mathematically about programs. It may be possible to prove, by hand or with machine assistance, that a program meets its specification. This advantage would be lost if one were to link functional and logic programming at surface level without firmly welding together their semantic underpinnings.

Robinson believes the semantic problems can be solved, probably by extending predicate calculus to include the 'functional' idea that an expression may be replaced by a simpler expression with the same value. Expressions with the same value would be gathered together into equivalence classes. 'For example,' says Robinson, 'you would have an expression "3 + 2" in the same class as the expression "5". They are equivalent because they denote the same thing.'

The Loglisp experiment has now ended. 'We have learned what was to be learned and we are now doing something else,' says Robinson, 'but there are people who might find Loglisp useful. It's a laboratory device and it is not polished for users, but there are some users.'

Robinson claims that the logic programming component of Loglisp is in some ways superior to Prolog. For example, it is less likely to get trapped in infinite loops. It is relatively slow, however, reaching a peak speed of around 1000 logical inferences per second (LIPS) compared with, say, Edinburgh Prolog's 45,000 LIPS. 'Our speeds are respectable enough for smallish problems, but we do not pretend to be competing on performance,' Robinson comments.

The group's efforts are now going into a completely new language called Super Loglisp. Functional languages are commonly executed by the process known as reduction, in which the program – effectively a single large expression – is progressively simplified by repeated application of a collection of 'rewrite rules'.

Reduction has no obvious connection with the resolution process that is the main engine of Prolog. Resolution operates on a collection of clauses, taking two at a time to generate a new clause by 'cancelling' a shared term, until the required result is reached. A process called unification decides whether two terms match and can be cancelled.

Robinson says he has found a way to re-express resolution and unification as a system of rewrite rules for a reduction engine to administer. 'It's not at all obvious, so I'm kind of pleased that I've finally been able to figure it out,' he says. 'One of the immediate things that follow from that concept,' he adds, 'is that you have a very natural way to do it in parallel, since the rules can be applied more than one at a time. In the general case there are many places in the huge expression where a sub-expression can be rewritten.' Robinson believes that if the architectural problems were solved, Super Loglisp would run efficiently on a reduction machine with 100 or 1000 processors working in parallel.

John Oldfield and Charles Stormon, also at Syracuse University, are designing a special co-processor which is expected to speed up the unification process in Loglisp, Prolog or other logic languages by a factor of 100. Normally, unification occupies anything from 20 to 90 per cent of a logic program's execution time.

According to Stormon, the Syracuse Unification Machine (SUM) may be built round an Inmos transputer chip running an Occam program. It would perhaps be unfair to regard this as evidence that inside every assertional language there is an imperative language trying to get out.

46

Eliminating discontinuities

The point has already been made, that engineers use complex means to achieve simple effects. A 'more is different' principle operates as systems grow larger or strive for higher performance. Functions became separated; structures become specialized. The same thing happens in organizations. As a company grows, you no longer find the same person designing the products and doing the accounts.

Of course, this burgeoning complexity is always presented as progress.

Many quite ordinary people are now proud of their mastery of MS-DOS (the operating system on the most popular personal computers). How many of them ever ask: why do we need MS-DOS? Why all this fussing with disks, files and directories? Is the computer serving me, or am I serving the computer? The things that I have on my screen right now – why cannot they simply *be there* when I need them again?

To which a programmer (head aching from figuring out the naming, binding, scoping and typing rules in Pascal) might reply: 'So you think you've got problems?' When really the programmer and the user should be finding common cause.

Computer systems are full of 'features' that were introduced for cost or performance reasons, and became fossilized as part of the dead weight of artificial stupidity that oppresses programmers and end-users alike. Meanwhile technology has moved on, and the original need has probably vanished.

A team at two Scottish universities (no longer the same two – a nice example of dynamic binding) has been thinking with great clarity about these issues. To its credit the computer manufacturer ICL (now part of the STC group) is supporting the research. It is to be hoped that commercial computer programmers and users will one day wake up to find their world marvellously simplified. As usual, they will wonder why it was not always like this.

File handling is one of the basic skills of the programmer's trade. So much so, that programmers may sometimes forget that the need for file handling arises from the physical limitations of computing machinery.

There must be a better way? There is. Ideas from Xerox's Smalltalk system, from functional programming, and from a possibly under-rated feature of ICL's 2900 architecture, have all helped to shape the concept known as persistent programming. But persistent programming is not available to anyone using BASIC or COBOL or other major languages. The full concept only works if certain important features are built into the programming language at ground level. Like many of the new programming concepts around at the moment, it really calls for changes in hardware if it is to function efficiently. But these changes might be achieved by microcoding and modifying an existing processor. There is no need for a totally new kind of machine.

Teams at the universities of Edinburgh and St Andrews are working on persistent programming with support from ICL and the Science and Engineering Research Council. Some members of the Edinburgh group will accompany Malcolm Atkinson when he moves to Glasgow to take up a newly created chair.

'The persistence idea is extremely simple,' explains Ron Morrison of St Andrews. 'You treat all data the same way. If I have something that lasts for 100 years, or lasts for one millisecond, I program it in exactly the same way.'

This idea has been implemented in a language called PS-algol. As the name implies, the language falls into the Algol family and will therefore be reasonably accessible to anyone familiar with other 'Algols' including Pascal. But Morrison hints that with Pascal, language development took a wrong turning. He and his colleagues are looking back to the ideas for simpler programming languages that were proposed in the mid-1960s by Christopher Strachey and Peter Landin.

'The popularity of Pascal somehow killed off these ideas,' says Morrison. 'In the late 60s and early 70s people were still very concerned with efficiency.' Computer power was treated as a scarce resource, as in many areas it still is today.

Persistent programming is likely to eat up a fair amount of computer power. But the cost of this may be more than offset by savings in the cost of developing and maintaining software. 'The saving over the software lifecycle will be enormous if we get this right,' comments Morrison.

Most programming languages distinguish between short-term data and long-term data. Short-term data is manipulated with the language's facilities (variables, arrays and so on) while long-term data is handled by a filing system or database management system which uses different data structures. An IBM study found that in a sample of programs, 30 per cent of the code was there purely to shuffle data between the short-term and long-term structures. It is this 30 per cent of code that persistent programming aims to abolish.

Persistent programming may be implemented on a system which has separate short-term storage (main memory) and long-term storage (usually disk). But the movement of data between the two is hidden from the programmer. That may sound like a description of conventional virtual memory, but according to Morrison, 'There are a number of reasons for saying we haven't reinvented virtual memory. What we're really working towards is an object-based addressing system, which is what segmentation was about.'

Paging, the basic virtual memory technique, works by swapping temporarily unwanted pages of data from main memory to backing store. It creates the illusion of an expanded main memory but does not usually conceal the existence of the backing store. A page has a fixed size of, say, 512 bytes which reflects the structure of the hardware. Segments are similar to pages but their size is flexible and reflects the structure of the data rather than the peculiarities of the machine.

Segmentation is supported on the ICL 2900 series and some Burroughs machines. But the segments are generally too big and too few to allow one segment to each of the 'persistent objects' created by PS-algol.

A more suitable virtual memory organization was developed in 1975–76 for the Smalltalk software system at Xerox Palo Alto Research Center. In its first version it held up to 64,000 objects on disk, and at any one time about 4000 of them would be held in memory. Objects called but not found in memory were fetched automatically from disk. Objects not recently used were systematically returned to disk.

Smalltalk was a landmark, but Morrison points out that it is a single-user system. The work at Edinburgh and St Andrews is based on the assumption that many users will have access to the database. Morrison foresees the need for large databases, containing many billions of objects. No available processor has a large enough address space to support such a database.

He suggests that the ideal hardware for persistent programming might use addresses as long as 128 bits. This would create an astronomically sized logical address space, to be mapped (by processes invisible to the programmer) onto the much smaller physical storage space. The huge address space would allow any object, on any computer in the world, to be uniquely identified. But little work has yet been done on persistent programming in the context of networking and distributed databases.

Another feature of persistent programming, not found in conventional virtual memory systems, is its transaction mechanism. 'A very important part of it is that the transactions are secure,' says Morrison. 'You can undo all your actions.'

Data is not changed permanently until the system receives a 'commit' instruction at the end of the transaction. Record lockout is an integral part of the system. Any number of users can read an object at one time, but only one can write to it.

There are guards against the accidental destruction of data. But there is a garbage collection mechanism to prevent the system becoming clogged with temporary 'scratchpad' information. It works by the rule that an item can be erased if there is no longer any path by which it can be reached.

Like most developments which give greater power and security to the programmer, persistent programming will make the hardware work harder. How much harder remains to be seen. There is always the danger that what works in the laboratory will bog down under the strain of running a real-time transaction system on a large database.

'We've run it against 30 megabyte databases and it seems to work,' Morrison reports, but he would like to try the system on a really large database of 30 to 100 gigabytes. He believes there is no substitute for a practical test. 'We've run some simulations,' he says, 'but I'm very sceptical about the results.'

PS-algol is derived from the earlier St Andrews language S-algol. It inherits the principles that all data types are checked at run time, and all have equal 'civil rights'.

'If you want to break the type structure in Pascal,' Morrison points out, 'you just have to write out a number as a real number and read it back in as two integers.' This is impossible in PS-algol.

S-algol and PS-algol have higher-order functions, that is to say, functions which can return another function when evaluated. Functions have the same 'civil rights' as other data types in some functional programming languages, but according to Morrison this feature is both unusual and difficult to implement in a 'store' language based on the conventional von Neumann model of computation.

Giving all data types equal rights eliminates one of the anomalies in conventional languages which limit what the programmer can do. Another inelegant feature disappears when main memory and backing store are given identical treatment. Programming a mainframe is no longer so different from programming a small micro.

This tidying-up of the programming environment continues. 'I see it as identifying where the discontinuities are in programming languages, and eliminating them,' says Morrison. 'After this one we'll hit the next.'

The Edinburgh team has now moved to the University of Glasgow as planned. ICL has put additional hardware, cash and effort into the research. The Alvey Directorate approved the £2 million Pisa (persistent information space architecture) project which began on 1 January 1985, and will produce a successor to PS-algol.

The first of five principles expounded in a paper by Malcolm Atkinson, Ron Morrison, and Graham Pratten of ICL, reads as follows:

> Controlling complexity: the complexity of the system must be kept under control, so that developers and users can concentrate on the application rather than the complexity of the system. This depends on establishing consistent rules which apply throughout the design and being parsimonious in the introduction of new concepts into these designs.

Further reading

Landin, P.J. (1966). 'The next 700 programming languages' *Communications of the ACM*, **9**, no. 3, 157–164.

Strachey, C. (1967). *Fundamental Concepts in Programming Languages.* Oxford: Oxford University Press.

I have not read either of the above, but I pass on the references for those who are interested in tracing these ideas back to their roots.

Kaehler, T. (1981). 'Virtual memory for an object-oriented language' *Byte*, August 378–387.

47

The programming of an apprentice

Artificial intelligence, software engineering, and the human-computer interface are often studied in isolation. A unique project at MIT draws all these areas of computer science together.

6 December 1984

Charles Rich, Richard Waters and their colleagues at the Massachusetts Institute of Technology chose automatic programming as the subject of an artificial intelligence project. They thought they would have a head start since they were programmers themselves.

Rich dates the intellectual origin of the project to 1973. He and Howard Shrobe drew up the main outlines in 1976. The Programmer's Apprentice project at the MIT artificial intelligence laboratory has had its own funds since 1980. The developing project has drawn in ideas from seemingly remote areas of computer science. Today's live issues in expert systems, in human–machine interaction, and in software engineering are all reflected in it. Much has been achieved. Much more waits to be done.

Rich states uncompromisingly that the long-term goal is automatic programming. 'We really believe,' he says, 'that much of the programming process, certainly the low-level part of the programming process, can be automated.'

The metaphor of the apprentice has helped Rich's group to define what they are trying to do. 'Our first idea is, let's try to build an assistant programmer, not a chief programmer,' Rich explains.

The apprentice need not be as skilled or as knowledgeable as an experienced human programmer. '80 per cent of programming is very routine,' says Rich. 'It's just like automating the Ford motor plant. You automate the routine jobs first.'

Users are encouraged to think of the apprentice as an agent. Tough decisions about the design of the system and its interface have been settled by asking, 'How would you interact with the assistant if it were another person?' 'It's really a very powerful metaphor,' Rich comments. 'It answers a lot of questions.'

For example, it was clear that the user, taking the role of chief programmer, must be able to review the apprentice's work. Incomprehensible binary code would not do. The apprentice must produce readable source code.

It was equally obvious that the system must allow the code produced automatically by the apprentice to be intermixed freely with code that the user enters by hand. The apprentice must also have full access to the computer. It must be able to use the compiler, run programs, and read error messages. Also true to its role, it automatically writes basic documentation for the programs it invents.

The whole concept rests on the belief that there is a natural division of labour here. It must be worthwhile to delegate work to the apprentice. 'It must not be easier to do it yourself,' says Rich.

The apprentice provides a 'knowledge-based editor', which knows a number of programming 'clichés' by name. Waters has written that typical knowledge-based editor commands are similar in tone to the directions a chief programmer might give to an inexperienced assistant, but 'more detailed and pedantic'.

The following commands were used to implement a simple program, which searches for an occurrence of a given integer among the terms of a vector:

> Define a program LOCATE with a parameter V.
> Implement the program as a Sequential_Search.
> Implement the Enumerator as a Vector_Enumeration of V.
> Implement the Failure_Value as '0'.
> Implement the Test as a Positive_Test.
> Implement the Success_Value as 'I'.

It should be clear from this example that the effort to date has gone into building the editor's knowledge of programming clichés. Future versions of the editor may sport a more flexible and English-like syntax.

The apprentice works happily with incomplete specifications. It will make a guess at what the user meant, offer up some code, and wait to be corrected. But according to Rich, this does not mean that the editor's input language can be regarded as ambiguous. 'The right way to put it is, you've left some decisions to the apprentice,' he says. No mystery is permitted about these decisions. The user can ask the apprentice to give an explanation for every line of code it produces.

Accountability is often presented as one of the ten commandments of expert systems. Here, the need for accountability follows naturally from the metaphor of the apprentice. Apprentices are asked to account for their decisions more often than experts are.

Users of a compiler generally treat it as a 'black box'. They do not wish to know about its interior workings, and ask only that it is reliable. By contrast, Rich does not expect the apprentice to succeed every time. Every novice programmer has some failures. 'When a compiler works 90 per cent it's zero useful,' he comments. 'When the apprentice works 90 per cent it's perhaps 50 per cent useful.'

Two different ways of thinking are reflected in the programmer's apprentice. Rich characterizes them as the 'expert systems' approach, concerned with superficial knowledge, and the formal approach which brings 'deep' knowledge about programs to bear. 'There must be a mathematical foundation,' he maintains, 'so you can prove properties of programs.'

The knowledge-based editor maintains two representations of a program simultaneously. One is the program text, in Lisp or Ada. The 'deep' description of the program is maintained in a specially invented formalism called plan calculus.

In a 'plan', a program is represented by a network of boxes joined by arrows, technically known as a directed graph. This graph resembles a conventional flowchart, but with a second type of arrow added to show how the data output from one operation becomes the input of another operation. The plan is hierarchical. A box may represent an entire subroutine, in which case another graph can be drawn to show the subroutine's internal structure.

Abstraction is the key concept. The plan representation hides inessential detail. For example, the plan does not indicate exactly how data will be passed from one process to another. The same net data flow could be implemented with variables, or by passing parameters, or by nesting expressions. Different methods would be attractive in different programming languages.

The concept of data abstraction is becoming well known. The idea is to define a data structure (a vector, say, or a stack) entirely in terms of its behaviour and the operations that can be performed on it. The definition says nothing about memory usage or the way that the data structure is to be implemented in a particular programming language.

As an informal method, data abstraction makes software more portable and maintainable. Applied with formal rigour, data abstraction brings an additional and more profound benefit. When the behaviour of a data structure is described formally by an algebra, properties of programs become amenable to mathematical proof. Proofs about programs usually aim to show that the program satisfies some formal specification.

Data abstraction is not yet fully supported in the programmer's apprentice, but this will be remedied, according to Rich, in a new version of the system that is nearing completion. 'The next system has a full formal logic theorem proving capability,' he says.

Better developed in the current system is the concept of control abstraction. The knowledge-based editor has access to a library of standard control abstractions. These include a number of different types of loop, each of which is a programming cliché. Again, what matters is the visible effect of the loop, not the precise manner in which it is implemented.

A human programmer can read programs, as well as writing them. The automated apprentice has an 'analyser' module which can look at a program text and decompose it into programming clichés. The current version works with a fixed set of clichés. The next version of the analyser will be able to use any cliché in the continually growing library. So when the user (in the 'chief programmer' role) amends the apprentice's program text, the apprentice can make corresponding changes in the plan which it uses to represent the program. Program analysis complements program synthesis.

Rich is not the only MIT researcher who believes AI programs should have this two-way flow between low-level and high-level representations. The same concept motivates David Levitt's work on music (Chapter 22).

There are many parallels between the MIT work on automatic programming and work initiated by Cordell Green at Stanford University in the late 1970s. The West Coast work has dealt with certain aspects such as the efficiency of programs, which Rich's group has yet to tackle.

But the MIT project is remarkable for its instructive use of the agent metaphor, its use of program analysis to support progam synthesis, and its determined attempt to build formal methods into an expert system.

Computer aided software engineering, as it is now called, is moving swiftly from the laboratory into commerce. Chuck Rich remains at MIT but is also working with Bachman Information Systems. This is a new company founded in Cambridge by Charlie Bachman, a pioneer of database technology. Bachman is incorporating ideas from the Programmer's Apprentice into a software product due for release late in 1987. It will have a program analysis or 'reverse engineering' feature, giving users the very important ability to use the new tools on old programs. There will be no need to start with a clean sheet.

On the research front, Rich is extending the apprentice metaphor to other parts of the software lifecycle. Existing software tools mostly support the design and coding stages. They help software developers to turn a specification into a usable program. Arriving at an appropriate specification is still problematic, and there are few software tools, if any, which aid this process without also, to some extent, committing the developer to a particular design. There is now an increasing awareness of the 'requirements problem'. Chuck Rich has begun work on a companion to the Programmer's Apprentice: the Requirements Analyst's Apprentice.

48

New tools for the software factory

This is the last chapter about mainstream software engineering. After this we shall examine the underlying themes of algebra and abstraction from two fresh viewpoints: robotics, and computer algebra.

3 January 1985

Formal methods of software and system development cannot work without a firm mathematical foundation. But for an organization which decides to adopt formal methods, teaching set theory to engineers who did not learn it at college is the easy bit. The big task is to bring in an entirely new way of managing people and projects.

Standard Telephones and Cables (STC) is one company where a small group of crusading 'formalists' has begun to make converts among hard-nosed project managers with deadlines and budgets on their minds. The goal is to reduce the lifecycle costs of projects by detecting and correcting errors at the earliest possible stage.

Bernard Cohen was the leading formalist at Standard Telecommunications Laboratories (STL) in Harlow, but he left to become a professor at the University of Surrey in March 1984. STL's work on formal methods, and related work in artificial intelligence, continues in the systems and software technology division led by Tom Cox.

STL has provided expert advice on formal methods to the European Community, the Alvey Directorate and the Department of Trade and Industry. Its courses on formal methods and discrete mathematics, developed for STC's own engineers and managers, are now run commercially for industry by STC Idec at Stevenage.

Vienna Development Method (VDM) is the method selected by STL and increasingly used on actual projects by other STC divisions. It was invented at IBM but never widely adopted by that company. Cox claims that STL has proved VDM's capability, upgraded it from a university environment and established it as an industrial tool.

STL has had contacts with VDM's two leading proponents, both of whom left IBM. In 1983 STL collaborated on an Esprit preparatory study with Dines Bjørner of the Danish Datamatics Centre. The laboratory also has an important contact with Cliff Jones at Manchester University, author of the definitive book on VDM.

STL's software technology division has links with Edinburgh, Oxford and a dozen other universities and polytechnics. It worked with DNL, the Netherlands PTT laboratory, to build a-small library of data abstractions – reusable software modules – with formally defined properties. Recently, for British Telecom, it produced a formal specification for part of Mchapse, the Minimal Chill Ada Programming Support Environment.

Now STL is engaged in a more ambitious attempt to produce a unified set of tools to support the entire software lifecycle. This time there is an important difference. A major feature of the new project, known as Nimbus, is that it is not linked to specific programming languages such as Chill or Ada. The researchers believe this approach will be more cost-effective than trying to develop specific tools for each language.

Conventional projects commonly go through a series of design stages: requirement, specification, high-level design, low-level design and coding. There is nothing testable until actual code has been written. As a result, Cox argues, the earliest errors are located last.

'The later in the lifecycle that you discover an error, the more it costs to correct it,' he says. 'Half of the total cost can be spent after you have installed the system on the customer's premises.' The last, biggest and most expensive shock comes when the customer powers up the system and explains that it is not quite what he had in mind.

Cox and his colleagues propose a quite different framework for the design process, which they call the 'contractual methodology'. The project still goes through the same stages, but each stage of the work is checked for correctness before it is passed further down the chain.

The process begins when a customer comes to the supplier with a requirement, which may be vague or unsatisfiable. Typically the requirement will be expressed in ambiguous, everyday language. An analyst works with the customer to turn the requirement into a formal specification. This is now recognized as one of the most difficult and important stages of a software project. It is also the stage which poses the toughest challenge for formal methods, since the customer's requirement is not itself stated formally. It is, however, possible to check that the formal specification drawn up by the analyst is consistent and complete. Flaws disclosed at this stage may enable the analyst to go back to the customer and say 'This is not on' or 'This is unreasonable.'

STL uses various ways of 'animating' a specification to demonstrate how it would work in practice. 'Part of this animation activity is creating a rapid prototype,' explains Cox.

Once both analyst and customer are satisfied, the analyst moves from the 'supplier' role to a 'customer' role. The high-level design team now takes on the role of 'supplier'. Designs are developed, verified against the specification, and modified if necessary. This process is iterated until both parties are satisfied. Then the 'customer' in the contractual relationship 'signs off' and the 'supplier' becomes a 'customer' in turn. A whole series of customer-supplier relationships is established within the supplying organization, as the project is passed on down the chain.

The contractual model suggests that the different design stages have more in common than one might suppose. What leaves one stage as a design becomes a specification as it enters the next.

The task of building an integrated project support environment (IPSE) becomes more tractable if this commonality between design processes is exploited. Will Harwood, who is working on STL's Nimbus project, points out that it should be possible to build many of the necessary software tools round a core of shared code. In addition, he says. 'You should be able to make the system very uniform from the user point of view.'

Users will probably write specifications, executable code, and system documentation in different languages. But all could be edited with broadly similar tools. However, it is not enough for the tools to observe the syntax of each langauge. They must, Harwood argues, preserve correctness as one language is transformed into another. 'Anything you do is semantics-driven,' he says. 'Basically you must know what you're talking about, and not just the surface form you use to talk about it.'

Harwood demonstrated the unfinished Nimbus 'structure interface'. This software tool is essentially a universal, programmable editor. Given a description of the syntax of any language it allows the user to develop programs or texts which automatically observe the language's syntax.

The obvious use is as a smart editor for a programming language. But supplied with a suitable syntax, the same tool could be used as an outline editor or 'ideas processor' like Brainstorm or Thinktank. Equally, it could be used to implement a powerful word processor with unusual features.

The structure interface uses the mouse, screen windows, and pop-up menu facilities of the Xerox 1108 workstation. It gently compels the user to write syntactically correct material, by only offering 'legal' alternatives on its menus. Later, a parser will be included, to check free text entered from the keyboard.

Harwood explains that the structure interface, driven by the user, constructs a 'syntactic object' or high-level representation which can then be viewed in different ways. Different views might be displayed simultaneously in a number of screen windows. One view of a program might only show type declarations, another might only show variable declarations, another might display the program as a diagram.

Other Nimbus tools will transform texts from one language into another, or support proofs that a program and a specification are equivalent. These tools will need to be furnished with a description of the semantics of each language, as well as its syntax.

Proof rules, used to prove that a program or specification has desired properties, will have to be described explicitly. So will transformation rules, which show how one language is related to other languages. Harwood points out that proofs will still need human intervention. 'There's really very little hope of getting fully automated theorem-provers that can handle a significant amount of the software activity,' he says. But software tools can ensure that the proof strategies chosen by the human user are valid and legal. This is essentially a clerical operation.

The STL group has been influenced by Robin Milner's LCF system, where a low-level 'object language' ensures correctness, while the user expresses proof strategies, which may or may not succeed, in a high-level 'metalanguage'. LCF does not let you imagine you have found a proof when in fact you have not.

Tim Denvir and Mel Jackson are working on other components of a proposed project support environment which would contain a wide range of software tools, and a library of abstract data types as software building blocks. Nigel Seel is working on artificial intelligence techniques which may be used to provide a friendly user interface.

Seel believes there is a role for artificial intelligence in formal methods. He is also engaged in an ambitious attempt to bring the two disciplines closer in another way, by describing a formal, mathematical foundation for artificial intelligence.

This piece of history is included because it presents some ideas about formal methods which are still highly relevant: notably, the point that management is as important as mathematics.

During 1985 there were major changes at STL. Many new staff were recruited to work on software technology, and the whole direction of the work changed. Will Harwood, Tim Denvir and Mel Jackson went to work for Praxis Systems, a software house in Bath. With Bernard Cohen, Harwood and Jackson wrote a book (see 'Further reading', Chapter 44) which contains, among other things, a fuller explanation of the contractual model of software development.

An IPSE called Istar, based on the contractual model, has been developed and marketed by Imperial Software Technology.

49

Arms and the machine

Designers of software and other things often emphasize that decisions should be postponed as long as possible, that parameters should be left open till the last possible moment. The principle is sometimes called 'late binding'. It means that instead of manipulating constants, you may have to manipulate unknowns. Your reasoning about the task is irresistibly shifted from the domain of arithmetic into that of algebra. It may be a little harder, but there is a payoff. You can change things without invalidating all your reasoning. Now even when the design of a program is fixed, one thing remains unknown: the data. If you want to reason about the behaviour of a program with unknown data, you have to use algebra. To observe how it behaves with known data, you could just run it; but what have you learned?

A commitment to solving each problem in its most general form, binding the unknowns as late as possible, may be noble but it could be misguided. Faced with dynamical problems which he assumes have no analytic (i.e. algebraic) solutions, Gerald Sussmann attacks them numerically with all the computer power he can muster. But there are other scientists of a more Quixotic bent, who continue to search for a general, analytic solution to their chosen problem.

28 March 1985

Joe Rooney opens a cardboard box and pulls out a floppy chain of seven tetrahedral blocks. It looks like a child's puzzle on the lines of Rubik's Snake or the Shinsei Mystery. A specialist in kinematics, or how things move, Rooney believes that one of the central problems of robotics is contained in this innocent-looking puzzle.

A rigid object moving freely in space has six degrees of freedom. Three relate to its location, and three to its orientation. So a robot manipulator needs at least six degrees of freedom or independent movements if it is to move a tool or workpiece to an arbitrary position within its workspace.

One important type of robot manipulator is a jointed arm with hinges or bearings. If the arm has at least six of these 'revolute joints' it can, in general, achieve full freedom of movement. Rooney's puzzle is a model of a general kinematic system with six revolute joints. Understanding it has become, for him, 'the Everest of kinematics'.

Jointed arms are not the only kind of manipulator. Some 'multiloop' designs have as many crosslinks as a Workmate or a baby buggy. Their parts move together in concert. Multiloop systems, according to Rooney, tend to gain positional accuracy at the expense of dexterity. But some of them have interesting properties. Rooney and his colleagues at the Open University have devised a complete topological classification for multiloop systems, which should help designers to be sure they have not overlooked any possibilities.

Most commercial robots have been 'serial' systems, with each segment joined to the next, and no loops. Like the human arm, designers thought. 'Actually the human arm is not a serial system, despite all these systems that have been copied from it,' says Rooney. 'It has got a loop in it,' he observes, twisting a skeleton's forearm to demonstrate the intricate motion of the radius, the ulna, and the wrist bones that close the loop.

Playing with the seven-block puzzle one discovers that even a serial system – a jointed arm with no loops – can show fiendishly complicated behaviour. In some positions a tiny movement of one of the ends induces an enormous convulsion of the middle joints. Sometimes an extra degree of freedom is gained, and the middle joints flop, no longer constrained by the positions of the end joints.

Industrial robots, too, have positions where they gain or lose a whole degree of freedom. According to Rooney, the manufacturers' leaflets do not tell the whole truth when they depict the envelope of the robot's workspace. There are regions within the workspace where the manipulator becomes clumsy or hard to control. Avoiding these regions is seen as a task for the person who programs the robot. The robot's control system usually knows nothing about them.

Given the set of joint angles, it is a straightforward, if tedious, task to calculate the position of the gripper. Rooney represents spatial rotations with mathematical entities called dual quaternions, which he finds more elegant than the usual matrix notation.

But to control a robot one must perform the reverse calculation. What joint angles are needed to achieve a chosen gripper position? To find out, one must solve a formidable set of non-linear simultaneous equations. 'Forward kinematics is trivial. Inverse kinematics is extremely difficult,' says Rooney.

There are usually several solutions, and this makes the problem if anything harder. The Unimation Puma has a choice of up to eight different 'postures' of its joints for a single gripper position. For a general six-axis arm, Rooney has proved that there are at least 16 postures. It is known that the number cannot be more than 32. But according to Rooney, 'It is still in dispute whether or not it is always possible to get 32 real solutions.'

The equations can be solved, in a given instance, by numerical methods of successive approximation. 'If you look at any proprietary robot system available,' argues Rooney, 'they work in a suck-it-and-see way.' One could pursue an artificial intelligence approach and try to develop more adaptable rules or heuristics for homing in on a solution.

But Rooney resists all suggestions that the problem can be solved by applying more computer power. 'I think it's opting out,' he says. 'There is a school of thought that information processing can achieve anything you want. I don't think it can.' His aim is to find a once-and-for-all analytic solution, an algorithm which calculates the required joint angles directly, without repetition, deviation or hesitation.

'I don't think there is any need to resort to heuristic approaches if one can end up with an algorithmic approach,' he maintains. 'It would be a cop-out to do that before we know what's going on. Where do we get our heuristics from if we don't know what it's possible to do?'

It is a view that would be echoed in some sectors, at least, of the AI community. Computer vision research is much influenced by the views of David Marr, who stressed the need for a principled computational theory of vision. Marr sought to discover what is theoretically possible in vision, before developing specific algorithms. And among researchers who program computers to do algebra and symbolic mathematics, a strong contingent argues that programs should use deep knowledge and very general methods, rather than a collection of rules of thumb.

A 'deep' understanding of the general six-jointed arm would enhance both the control and the design of robots. At the moment, only a few special types of arm are at all well understood. 'If you can analyse the general one, then all the other ones are special cases,' Rooney says. He draws hope from the fact that though no one has shown how to solve the equations, no one has proved them insoluble, either. This contrasts with certain other equations, for example a fifth-degree equation in one variable, that are known to have no analytic solution.

Ignorance of kinematics has made robot designers unadventurous, Rooney argues. 'What people do is, they either copy human anatomy or they copy what has been done before.' He hopes his theoretical work will lead to a better understanding of the largely unexplored 'design space', the space of possibilities within which the robot designer works. 'Hopefully what will come out of it will be a classification scheme so we can map out what's possible,' he says.

'People just design *ad hoc* when it comes to kinematics. For a start they use two-dimensional ideas.' Many robots are designed so that several of their rotation axes are parallel, and a large part of the structure moves within a plane. This simplifies the calculations needed to control the robot, because the motion can be broken down into a number of simpler, two-dimensional motions. But it also closes off many design options.

The general six-axis arm has no special alignments of axes. It is a fully three-dimensional system, with no easily analysed two-dimensional subsystems. 'It is a highly coupled dynamic system which is theoretically difficult to analyse,' Rooney explains. That, of course, is precisely why robot designers have stuck to simple, special cases.

No single design will get rid of the 'problem patches' where the robot gains or loses a degree of freedom. But if the general case is understood, designers will be able to see why a particular designs runs into trouble in certain positions. And they will be able to select, systematically, a design which gives the minimum of trouble in a chosen industrial application.

Rooney believes that robot control systems should know about the problem patches: and they should know where it is possible to flip from one posture to another. Taking an anology from computer hardware design, Rooney suggests that 'It may be possible to define certain paths through the workspace as kinematic "buses".'

He does not insist that all six-axis arms should be of the general type. On the contrary, the better the tough general case is understood, the more systematically one can search for tractable special cases. 'One of the main thrusts of the work is to look for modular solutions,' Rooney says. He and his Open University colleagues are designing a range of robot components. Individually the modules will have simple kinematic behaviour, but assembled they will permit a great variety of manipulator designs.

Another practical spin-off might be a hardware box to do fast arithmetic with dual quaternions. It could be built into robot control systems. The unusual dual quaternion notation might also prove useful in fast three-dimensional computer graphics.

Rooney's work in kinematics concentrates on movement and ignores the forces acting on the manipulator. Forces are the province of the sister subject of dynamics, and of course they are of great importance to the engineer. But the mathematical representations used in dynamics are similar to those used in kinematics. 'In some ways it's easier,' says Rooney. 'I would say kinematic design is the hardest part of manipulator design.'

He hopes that the study of robot arms will lead to a better understanding of the machines' fingers and legs. A gripper, he says, can be regarded as a group of cooperating 'armlets'. And legs? 'Kinematically,' he explains, 'a walking device is a gripper turned upside down, moving the earth along relative to itself.'

One could preach a sermon on Joe Rooney's string of tetrahedra. A system of simple structure but extremely complex behaviour; a trivial forward problem; a formidable inverse problem. The inverse problem requires backward reasoning from a goal to a series of actions. But search (such as Prolog might use) is too inefficient. More knowledge must be brought to bear on the problem if we are to home in faster on the solution.

Something might be learned about this kinematic problem from simulations or 'experimental mathematics'. Perhaps this is a case for one of Gerald Sussmann's special purpose supercomputers. Perhaps the multidimensional space of joint angles – for a chosen robot arm design – could be explored with Thomas Banchoff's graphics. But to search the space of all possible arm designs would be a mind-boggling task, no matter what computer aids were available.

It is impossible to deduce general conclusions from simulations. Bernard Cohen's objections to software testing are equally applicable to simulation: one can only ever explore a few of the possible cases. But simulation does help us to observe patterns and form hypotheses or conjectures. It stimulates the not inconsiderable human capacity for inductive reasoning. And one can then go back to the mathematics, as Banchoff does, as Peitgen and Richter do, and try to confirm the conjecture by formal, deductive proof.

50

Computer algebra: realizing a Victorian dream

The artificial intelligence community tends to lose interest in a problem, once a straightforward way of solving it has been discovered, and heuristics give way to algorithms. This is the direction in which Joe Rooney would like to push his area of robotics. This has been the fate of computer algebra. Why does AI, unlike any other discipline, disown its greatest successes?

27 June 1985

Exactitude is better than approximation, principled theories are better than rules of thumb, insight is better than slogging, and a general solution to a problem is more useful than a solution for one special case. That, in a nutshell, is the case for doing mathematics with symbols rather than numbers: for algebra as opposed to arithmetic.

Augusta Ada, Countess of Lovelace, who devised some of the programs for Charles Babbage's difference engine, wrote in 1844 that the machine 'Might bring out its results in algebraic notation, were provisions made accordingly'. Her foresight was astonishing.

Since the 1960s, a small but dedicated international community of researchers has been developing computer programs which manipulate algebraic formulae. The programs can integrate a function, sum a power series, or factorize a polynomial better than most human mathematicians. They can handle tasks involving enormous numbers, page-long formulae, and repetitive calculations which would take years to do by hand. Perhaps more significantly, they can also crack problems which humans find difficult even though the solution, when it is found, takes only a few lines.

Industrial scientists and engineers are learning that computer algebra systems can help them with their calculations, complementing and enhancing the power of the better-known numerical methods. The algorithms and methods used in computer algebra have improved dramatically in recent years. And at last desktop computers can provide the half-megabyte memory capacity that is reckoned to be the minimum for running full-scale algebra programs. The Mumath package for CP/M and MS-DOS machines, written at the University of Hawaii and marketed by The Soft Warehouse, is claimed to need as little as 40 kilobytes of memory.

There are a number of special purpose algebra packages. Relativity theorists use one called Sheep. (An earlier version was called Lisp Algebraic Manipulator or LAM.) The leading general purpose programs include Macsyma, developed at the Massachusetts Institute of Technology, SMP from the California Institute of Technology, Maple from the University of Waterloo in Canada, IBM's Scratchpad, and Reduce. Reduce is the collective product of work at many sites in North America, Europe and Japan. It is distributed on an at-cost basis by Tony Hearn of the Rand Corporation, Santa Monica, California. Once a mainframe package, it now runs on machines like the Hewlett Packard Integral transportable.

British contributors to Reduce have included Arthur Norman of Cambridge University, and John Fitch, James Davenport and Julian Padget of the University of Bath. Computer algebra, according to Fitch, is a mixture of very modern techniques and the methods of the pre-computer age. 'Some of it is actually finding old mathematics which has been forgotten,' he says, 'and some is really pushing the frontiers.' This certainly applies to the work that Fitch and his colleagues have done on integration.

Integration is a method of averaging, summing, or finding the cumulative effect of things, one simple application being to find the area enclosed by a curve. Nineteenth-century mathematicians developed many ingenious methods of integration. They looked for methods which would produce an exact, reusable formula, rather than an approximate numerical answer. They were interested in what would now be called symbolic integration.

When calculators, and then computers appeared on the scene, attention turned to numerical methods of integration. These methods will produce an approximate answer to almost any integration problem, including those for which no exact answer exists. Numerical methods involve much tedious, repetitive calculation, but computers are ideal for this.

In 1976, however, Bob Risch of IBM came up with a new algorithm for symbolic integration. Shortly before that Fitch and Norman, then both at Cambridge, had written a Lisp system suitable for algebra. Lisp was an unpopular language in Britain at the time, thanks to Sir James Lighthill's damning 1972 report on artificial intelligence. By good fortune Norman spent the summer of 1976 working at IBM, where he learned of Risch's algorithm. He brought that knowledge back to Cambridge, where he and Fitch implemented the algorithm on their Lisp system.

'The integration work meant we had a simple-minded, straightforward integrator within the year,' says Fitch. Tony Hearn, then a professor at the University of Utah, took the Cambridge integrator and incorporated it into Reduce. In 1977–78, Fitch joined the Reduce group in Salt Lake City, working on improvements in Lisp, which would help Reduce to run faster. He had been a reluctant convert to the flexible but slow-running language, and has mixed feelings about it to this day. 'One side of me says, if you don't do it in Lisp you can always make it run faster,' he says. 'The other side of me says, if you don't do it in Lisp you can never actually do anything interesting.' Algebraic expressions are easily handled because Lisp data structures can accommodate mixtures of variables like y, constants like 2 and functions like $+$.

Lisp is also a convenient language for handling big numbers without loss of precision. This is essential because enormous numbers may be generated in the course of some algebraic algorithms, even when no big numbers appear in the final answer. The digits may run into thousands, and sometimes the size of a number is crudely estimated as so many 'screenfuls'; but every digit matters. If two big numbers A and B appear in an expression like $Ax - By$, it is not safe to make any approximations until x and y are known.

The huge numbers can be kept under control by working in what mathematicians call finite fields – number systems which return to zero after a while, like a car's odometer, instead of carrying on to infinity. Reduce uses this approach systematically when it finds the greatest common divisor of two polynomials.

Every big number has an image in the finite field, and facts about big numbers project into corresponding facts in the finite field. Unfortunately some things which happen in finite fields are not true images of anything out in the world of big numbers. The results are suggestive rather than conclusive, so an algebra system must seek corroboration and then, if possible, check its putative answer.

Surprisingly, it is in a certain sense easier to factorize a polynomial, an expression containing terms like $3x^2$ and $9x^{15}$ than to find the factors of a mere number. All known algorithms for factorizing large numbers require 'exponential time', which implies that they are easily defeated by modest increases in the size of the number. Cryptographers make use of this fact. Reduce does not currently have an integer factorizer, but Julian Padget has written one which handles numbers up to about 30 digits. This will be a useful tool for scientists and mathematicians. But the James Bonds of this world can sleep easy unless they have ignored the advice of mathematicians, that ciphers should be based on numbers of at least 100 digits.

Factorizing polynomials is technically 'easier'. The best-yet algorithm requires an amount of time proportional to the thirteenth power of the size of the problem. On a sufficiently enormous problem it is bound to perform better than an exponential algorithm but, as Fitch points out, this is not necessarily the case for problems of practical size.

Fitch is cynical about theoretical measures of the performance of algorithms. He points out that you learn little by totting up the number of additions in a program, when one addition involves two small numbers, and another involves two colossal polynomials.

Complexity theorists, who deal with the efficiency of algorithms, generally look at the worst possible case. Many algorithms perform much better in practice than in theory, and there have been some attempts to measure 'average case complexity' instead of the worst case performance. This might seem more realistic, but as Fitch rejoins, 'What is the average case for a polynomial? The majority of polynomials don't factorize over the integers.' Yet as he points out, 'The ones that arise in problems tend to factorize.' This is mysterious. The problems we encounter in the real world seem to be precisely those that mathematics can solve. There are two rival explanations for the 'unreasonable efficacy of mathematics'. One suggests that we pick our problems to suit our tools, and simply ignore those aspects of the world which are mathematically intractable. The other view is that the world really is full of mathematical simplicity.

Fitch takes the first view. 'I think we model the world on our own mathematics,' he comments. 'I don't think the world is like that at all. I'm a born cynic.' James Davenport, on the other hand, finds it hard to believe that the world's apparent mathematical simplicity is all in our minds.

Computer algebra no longer depends on pattern matching, heuristic search, and similar AI techniques. Says Fitch: 'It started in AI and all the early work was in AI. It became more and more apparent that it wasn't AI. There were algorithms.' Heuristic methods are still used to check for obvious short cuts. As Fitch explains, 'We very often have a fallback position which we know is algorithmic but may be expensive.'

Algebra's true partner may be numerical analysis. 'There is not a big battle between algebraic and numeric methods,' says Fitch. Every algebraic formula is destined to have numbers substituted into it sooner or later. But if the formula is manipulated algebraically first, the final numerical calculation may be quicker and more accurate.

Approximation is a way of buying speed by throwing away information. Even algebra is not always exact. There are numeric approximations and there are algebraic approximations. As Julian Padget says, 'In algebra we do lose information because we do use approximation. But we choose when to use it. And we choose what we lose by using it.'

Further reading

Pavelle, R., Rothstein, M. and Fitch, J. (1981). 'Computer algebra' *Scientific American*, December, 102.

Wolfram, S. (1984). 'Computer software in science and mathematics' *Scientific American*, September, 140. (Stephen Wolfram (Chapter 31) writes about the SMP algebra package he wrote at Caltech.)

PART 5

Hardware

51

'Gt a gd jb qk' – but will your typewriter understand?

Hardware – the physical bits and pieces of computer systems – although often seen as the driving force of information technology, is really an enabler. Faster chips and better screens provide opportunities for a better human interface, more elegant system engineering, and increased use of AI techniques.

In the 1970s the excitement was about the cost- and size-cutting potential of the chip. The things the circuits did were not, on the whole, all that new. The ideas came from minicomputer and mainframe architectures. The novelty was to fit it all in a small box and sell it at a price that individuals or small businesses could afford. The rate of progress was dictated by the increasing speed and density of chips as the lines became finer and the individual transistors became smaller.

That underlying trend continues through the 1980s. It may begin to fail in the 1990s. But as we advance into the era of very large scale integration (VLSI) a new dimension opens up: architectures. New freedoms present themselves, for example the freedom to deploy processors almost as lavishly as memory, now that the price difference between the two has shrunk. On the other hand, new constraints are making themselves felt, notably the finite speed at which electromagnetic signals travel along a wire. Computer architects can experiment, as never before, with the logical organization of the machine; but increasingly they have also to think about its physical organization.

Computer scientists used to leave physical matters to the electronic engineer. They studied abstract machines. This approach has led to very important insights, but critics are now saying that computer science ignores physics at its peril. For example, 'wire' for most computer scientists is an abstraction, a conductor which transports signals instantaneously from A to B. Even this simple abstraction cannot be implemented in the physical world, where signals travel at a finite speed. In new proposals for faster and more powerful computing methods, the physical architecture of the hardware often plays an essential role. The challenge for computer science is to find new abstractions, which take account of unavoidable physical limitations but hide inessential physical details.

The word 'architecture' has a physical, bricks-and-mortar feel about it, but of course parts of any architecture may be implemented in software. The boundaries are always mobile. If there are software architectures, equally there are algorithms in silicon.

Designers are turning, once again, to biological models for inspiration. While self-assembling protein 'biochips' are still science fiction, machines like Hinton and Sejnowski's Boltzmann machine are actually being built to designs inspired by the wiring of the human brain.

Sensational press articles invariably suggest that artificial intelligence will flow from these brain-like architectures as night follows day. This is most implausible. Perhaps brainlike architectures do have a special enabling role to play, but constructing artificial intelligence from the bottom up is a long-term research project, likely to require at least as much effort as the established top-down approach.

There are, however, some capabilities of the living brain which seem to have very natural interpretations at the hardware level. Argument still rages over the mechanism of human memory, but it certainly does not behave as if all information were stored in numbered pigeon-holes, as it is in computers. For years it has been clear that content-addressable memory would be a useful thing to have, even for quite ordinary data processing activities. The article that follows looks very dated in some respects, but was reasonably prescient in others.

---

8 December 1983

Technology often reaches out too far, and falls flat on its face. But rising to its knees and brushing the dust off, it finds that it has at least advanced a little way. So it is with associative or content-addressable memory. Early attempts to simulate the learning and pattern-recognizing capabilities of networks of brain cells produced little of value to computer technology. The ideas were too big for 1960s hardware, and really called for very large scale integration technology, which was yet to be invented.

But the idea of associative storage lived on, and in the 1970s and early 1980s it has taken practical shape, first in ICL's disk-based Content Addressable File Store (CAFS) and more recently at chip level.

For the time being, the stress is not on quasi-human powers of recognition and recall, but on the simple and readily marketed virtues of speed and reliability. During the next few years, associative storage could facilitate rapid browsing through large databases on personal computers. Another possibility is a word processor which corrects the spelling of each word as it is typed.

Hewlett-Packard uses a small amount of associative memory in its

32-bit microprocessor chip-set. It is there to correct errors which may arise in the system's conventional random access memory. Essentially the chip learns to intercept certain bit patterns which correspond to faulty cells in the memory array. Without this protection it is unlikely that Hewlett-Packard could have achieved commercial yields and reliable performance in chips with one-micron geometry.

The experimental 4-kilobit associative memory chip revealed by Nippon Telegraph and Telephone (NTT) in September appears to be designed for rapid (and perhaps intelligent) searching of databases. Fabricated in complementary metal oxide semiconductor (CMOS) technology, it follows a 1-kilobit 'smart' memory chip produced in 1981 in *n*-channel MOS.

NTT's next target will be to produce a 16K version. But associative memory chips will never equal the storage density of random access memories because their task is inherently more complex. NTT's 4K associative chip uses approximately 18 transistors per bit. A 280K dynamic RAM produced at the same laboratory uses only 2.5 transistors per bit.

There are, broadly speaking, two ways to retrieve information without knowing where it is physically stored. One is to search sequentially through the whole database or a large part of it. The other is to use a memory with some built-in processing power which allows local searches to proceed in parallel throughout the store.

Associative memory chips embody the latter approach, with a high degree of parallelism. However, it is unlikely that the vast databases of fifth generation computers will be stored entirely in semiconductor memory. More likely, blocks of data will be moved very rapidly from magnetic or optical storage into the associative memory. A whole block will be searched in parallel, then another block, and so on. The bulk storage will not be associative itself, but it will appear as virtual associative memory.

The other extreme is represented by the TSIP package recently announced by Systems Designers (SDL). This is a pure software product which runs on Digital Equipment VAX machines. It searches sequentially through any free text database, with no need for any indexing. TSIP therefore emulates associative storage hardware, and does so at considerable speed, without any resort to parallel processing.

ICL's CAFS-ISP, the re-engineered and lower-priced version of the five-year old CAFS, falls between the two extremes. Each CAFS-ISP unit splits the data coming off the disks into 16 streams and searches them in parallel. Three units can be fitted to a 2900 series mainframe. CAFS-ISP represents an intermediate degree of parallelism.

ICL is now promoting CAFS-ISP as a general speed-up box for a wide range of applications. At the moment CAFS-ISP can only be used with the

Querymaster information retrieval program. But Hamish Carmichael, product marketing manager for CAFS, said 'There are going to be other software products using CAFS. There are going to be other interfaces to CAFS, so that users can write their own applications and software houses can write programs using CAFS.'

Further ahead, ICL is looking at the possibility of a further decrease in the physical size of the hardware, which could lead to another drop in its price. 'It would not at all surprise me if in a few years CAFS was a handful of chips rather than a handful of boards,' said Carmichael. 'We are looking at it very seriously.'

Fast, associative file searching could be a valuable feature on a microcomputer, and SDL has taken the first step in that direction. 'We have studied the possibility of putting part of the search suite into an outboard micro,' said Brian Smith, TSIP project leader. He and his colleagues have selected suitable micros and costed out the project, but they have gone no further. On the possibility of running TSIP on a standalone micro, Smith commented: 'In principle it is quite feasible to have a micro as the host. But when it will happen I'm not sure.'

As the cost of associative searching falls, applications which today might seem impossibly extravagant may become commonplace. Both Smith and Carmichael agreed that a real-time spelling checker was feasible, indeed Carmichael said, 'I think we could do one right now.' This is an interesting and demanding application for several reasons.

It requires an extremely rapid search of a database of some tens of thousands of words. Ideally the response time should be imperceptible. And if the program is to correct spelling, rather than merely rejecting impossible words, it will need to perform 'fuzzy matching' between the misspelt word and the possible correct spellings it finds in the database.

Imagine what it would be like to have a word processor which, no matter how bad your typing, made instant, intelligent guesses at what you really meant to say. Spelling words correctly, indeed even attempting to type them out in full, would be a waste of time. Why type out 'get a good job quick' when the machine could automatically add the missing letters to 'gt a gd jb qk?'

Associative search products face strong competition from the established, inverted file systems for information retrieval. Such products as IBM's Stairs, ICL's Status and ICI's Assassin all offer rapid retrieval of free text, using elaborate indexes instead of global searching. But updating the index consumes substantial computer time, particularly when the data changes rapidly.

ICL's Carmichael believes the two types of product are not mutually exclusive, and that the rapid searching power of CAFS could simplify the indexing in a Status system.

The original hope of the 1960s was that associative memories would have a built-in capability for fuzzy matching. Hopes were pinned on neural-network circuits which exhibit a holographic type of memory. In such a network an item of data is not stored at a specific location. Instead, it subtly modifies the overall state of the system. Nothing like this happens in CAFS or in the current generation of associative memory chips. This deficiency can be overcome. Fuzzy matching, for example, can be performed by software.

But now that simpler forms of associative memory have found a place in the market, the holographic and neural-network models are making a comeback. Researchers like John Hopfield of Caltech are reviving the old ideas from the 1960s. This time round, they are armed with the formidable capabilities of VLSI.

It is mildly laughable now, the suggestion that a mighty CAFS engine would be needed for real-time spelling checking. Borland International sells a memory-resident spelling checker called Turbo Lightning, for the IBM PC, which runs quite comfortably in the spare machine cycles that remain after a word processing program has grabbed what it needs. Of course Lightning does not search a flat, unstructured database as CAFS can. Presumably very clever indexing and data compression techniques have been used. That is the factor I failed to take into account.

Another interesting product is PC Type Right, from Xerox. This is a hardware unit. It sits between the keyboard and the system unit of an IBM-type personal computer and intercepts words it does not recognize.

I still hanker for a word processor with the 'left thumb key' that I first dreamed up in 1978. The idea is that the space bar is split in two, so the right thumb can type spaces as usual. As soon as you begin to type a word, the machine takes a stab at completing it. If it guesses wrong, you go on typing, and it immediately rubs out its first guess and flashes up a fresh one. If the guess is correct, you hit the left thumb key and do not bother to finish the word.

Building on this idea: if you type a non-word like 'jb', it spelling-checks and flings back 'job' or 'jib' or 'jab'. It will learn which you want next time. The guesses could be context-sensitive, perhaps using some rudimentary knowledge of syntax and/or semantics. The machine would remember any words that occurred frequently in a document, and favour these words in its guessing.

This is a tool for touch typists who want to boost their speed. It has to work almost instantaneously to save the user much time. I doubt if it could be done in software on today's microcomputers, though I could be proved wrong by a 386 or 68020 processor. Associative memory hardware or perhaps a dedicated transputer would be suitable. Some word processors will expand prearranged abbreviations. My view is that the machine and the user should develop a mutually agreed shorthand as they go along.

SDL merged with SPL and is now known as Systems Designers plc. ICL has produced more software for CAFS. On 5 March 1987 *Electronics* reported that AT&T Bell Laboratories had developed an associative memory chip of the neural network variety and had half a dozen start-up companies 'nipping at its heels'. This in itself is not surprising. However, the applications found for these components may be very interesting indeed.

Further reading

Longuet-Higgins, H.C. (1987). *Mental Processes*. Cambridge, Mass.: MIT Press. (Reprints some late-1960s papers on associative and holographic memory, and a proposal for a Computer Assisted Typewriter which pre-dates my own ideas on the subject by a decade.)

52

The transputer route to supercomputing

Once again the impetus for a new development in computing comes from physics. VLSI, in the form of the Inmos transputer (Chapter 37), is the enabling technology, and the development of a parallel architecture is the project's main business.

The architecture has to be considered together with the possible algorithms for the physical problems which are to be solved. Many physical computations have natural parallelism. The programmer's task is eased when the architecture fits the computation comfortably. When the fit is poor, parallelism ceases to be a benefit and becomes a source of appalling complexity.

It is impossible, or at least impracticable, to build a parallel machine which is perfect for every application. Software can hide a machine's architectural details, creating a 'virtual machine' quite different from the physical machine. But a mismatch between the algorithm and the underlying physical architecture will still reveal itself through poor performance.

A tempting alternative is to postpone some of the architectural choices by making the machine reconfigurable. A parallel computer can be physically rewired with plugs and cables, but electronic switching is quicker and more reliable. Of course this introduces an additional task for the programmer, who must now effectively redesign the machine for each problem. But will this really be such a terrible task? It is actually a much simpler task than designing a complete special purpose computer – which is the route Gerald Sussmann and Harold Abelson (Chapter 39) recommend for physicists.

If the concept is sound, and the implementation skilful, programmers (or physicists) may find that by the time they have reconfigured the hardware, there is very little more to be done. Most of the complexity of the algorithm will have been pushed down into the level normally regarded as 'architecture'.

An Occam program (Chapter 37) can be realized as an algorithm, an architecture, or any combination of the two. This is one decision that can usefully be postponed. Occam is therefore a natural programming tool for a reconfigurable parallel machine.

---

7 February 1985

An Alvey-supported project at Southampton University will test the claim that Inmos transputers can be used to build systems of 'supercomputer' power. The project's leaders believe it should be possible to assemble a machine with 1 gigaflops (a billion floating point operations per second) raw power, for under £1 million, as against £30 million for a commercial machine of similar performance.

Britain's state-launched semiconductor firm, now owned by Thorn-EMI, designed its innovative microprocessor to be used either singly or in larger clusters. The transputer, for those lucky enough to lay their hands on one of the long-awaited samples, has both physical and logical features to support parallel processing.

Physically, the Inmos chip has four dedicated input/output links which enable it to talk to other transputers. Logically, the programmer can use the Occam language to create processes which run in parallel and exchange messages.

The Southampton team is led by Tony Hey of the University's physics department, and Chris Jesshope of the Department of Electronics and Information Engineering.

A crucial chip for the project will be made on the campus. In the late 1970s the Science and Engineering Research Council set up two silicon processing facilities to develop silicon technology and make integrated circuits for the UK academic community. One 'clean room' is at Southampton. The other is at Edinburgh.

The Reconfigurable Transputer Array (RTA) is intended to handle the massive, repetitive number-crunching tasks that arise in physics. Tony Hey, and his colleague Denis Nicole, are planning an attack on one of the key problems of modern theoretical physics: quantum chromodynamics, or QCD for short. The problem is to understand the forces between quarks, particles which are believed to be the ultimate constituents of most of the matter in the universe.

Members of the team stress that their machine will also be useful in many other areas of science and engineering. They have resisted the physics community's current fashion for building 'problem-specific' hardware dedicated to QCD or some other single problem.

Some of these machines, according to Nicole, 'May be too problem-specific even to solve quantum chromodynamics'. A variety of algorithms can be applied even to this single problem. It is not yet known which will be the most effective. It is risky, therefore, to build a machine committed to a single algorithm or class of algorithms.

The RTA, however, is expected to be useful for a wide variety of physical computations involving flows, fields or large numbers of particles.

Nicole believes the machine will be broadly suitable for thermodynamic and 'Monte Carlo' simulations. He sees possible applications in plasma physics (the study of gases containing charged particles) and in geophysics (including oil exploration). He also notes that simulated annealing programs (Chapter 59) could probably be run efficiently on the machine. Simulated annealing has applications in physics, engineering and the investigation of perception and learning.

Jesshope sees several potential uses for the machine in his own field of electronic and computer engineering. It could simulate the behaviour of entire circuits or of individual devices.

Semiconductor engineers are also getting interested in 'process simulations' which tell them what they will end up with if they treat a silicon wafer in specified ways during fabrication. This involves heavy computations based on a model of the way atoms diffuse through solid matter. Another likely application is finite element analysis, a technique used by engineers to model the mechanical stresses and strains in structures.

Southampton has an Alvey contract to develop a 'supernode' containing a number of transputers. Inmos is acting as 'industrial uncle' on the project, under the arrangement which the Alvey Directorate adopted when it became clear that fully participating industrial partners could not always be found for deserving academic projects.

The supernode will itself be a building block for increasingly powerful machines of almost unlimited size. 'I should think a 64-supernode machine is on the cards as a viable proposition,' says Jesshope. Such a machine would have approximately 1 gigaflops of raw power, though performance on real problems would inevitably be somewhat less. There are a number of ways in which supernodes might be connected. These include linear chains, rings, or more exotically, n-dimensional hypercubes. There will probably be 16 transputers within each supernode. The data paths between them will not be hard-wired. Instead, signals will be routed through Southampton-built 'switch' chips which function like telephone exchanges. These semi-custom chips will use SERC's UK5000 gate array design.

The switch settings will be programmed at the beginning of each computation and then left alone. This contrasts with some other multiprocessor architectures where data packets are routed dynamically through a network.

The RTA will perform best in highly repetitive computations where the data flows can be planned and optimized in advance.

Physicists believe the laws of physics are the same at all times and everywhere. This is reflected in the kind of computing that physicists do. Typically, the same calculations are repeated for each of a large number of similar particles, or a large number of points in physical space, or (as in one popular approach to QCD) a large number of points in some more abstract space with four or more dimensions.

One way to attack such computations is to assign a processor to every point, and then run the same (sequential) algorithm on each processor. But since what happens at each point is influenced by neighbouring points and possibly more distant points, this requires a large amount of communication between processors. The thinking behind the RTA is different. The need for communication is reduced by assigning a fair-sized chunk of space to each supernode. The larger the chunk, the less surface it has in relation to its interior volume.

Many computations in physics are 'local', and require no long-distance signals. In this case a supernode will be able to compute values for all the interior points of its chunk of space, without fetching data from any other supernode.

While the transputer is better equipped than most microprocessors to communicate with other chips, it runs fastest when most of the data and instructions it needs are located in its own on-chip 4-kilobyte memory.

Within the supernode, each transputer will be assigned to a separate task. Some transputers will work on the problem, Jesshope explains, while others take care of 'housekeeping'.

Many of the algorithms which arise in theoretical physics provide opportunities for parallel processing. For example, in operations on the two-dimensional arrays known as matrices, it may be possible to carry out the same operation (a multiplication, say) on every element of the matrix concurrently. The idea is that data should flow smoothly within the supernode, always arriving where it is needed when it is needed. It is a more flexible version of the 'pipeline' principle used in supercomputers and other fast machines.

The exact pattern of flow will be determined by the programmer. 'The idea is that we should compile Occam code into switch settings,' says Jesshope. The idea of an intelligent optimizing compiler has been tossed around, but the problem is far from trivial and the general feeling is that it is worth going for the last ounce of speed that may be achieved with hand-crafted code. Physicists have traditionally been enthusiastic assembly language programmers, ever keen to pare another few machine cycles off an algorithm.

Southampton's RTA enters a battlefield where several different approaches to massive number-crunching are now fighting it out. There are the expensive commercial supercomputers from Cray Research, Control Data, and their newer competitors in the US and Japan. There are the add-on processors like ICL's DAP and the Floating Point Systems range.

There are the problem-oriented machines like Caltech's Cosmic Cube, often built by researchers for their own use. And there are the 'emulators', stripped-down boxes which run IBM code at high speed – fine if you also have access to a comfortable mainframe environment in which to write and debug your programs.

There is nearly always a trade-off between power and generality. The proposed Southampton machine promises to be very powerful – a 64-supernode set-up, for example, is expected to outperform any supercomputer available today. But the machine will also be relatively adaptable, at least by the standards of the highly specialized world of supercomputing.

The project has flourished with the help of £3 million of funding from the European Community's Esprit programme. Six partners have joined Southampton to design and build what is now called the Supernode Array. They are Thorn-EMI, its subsidiary Inmos, the French companies Telmat and Apsis, the University of Grenoble, and the Royal Signals and Radar Establishment, which is responsible for the project's overall management. Thorn-EMI and Telmat hope to exploit the development commercially.

Ferranti gate arrays were chosen instead of the UK5000 design. Control Data's supercomputer activities have been split off into a new company, ETA Systems. The Cosmic Cube turned out to be suitable for a variety of scientific and other applications. The Intel iPSC was the first of several commercial products to be based on its hypercube architecture.

The Alvey Directorate approved and funded a separate project in which Southampton is building an array of single-bit processors, reconfigurable to handle different types and sizes of data structure including arrays, trees, and strings.

53

Symbolic superchip

Regular data structures and intensive floating point arithmetic are the traditional characteristics of numerical computing. Symbolic computing calls for different capabilities such as pattern-matching, dynamic memory allocation and 'garbage collection', and rapid traversal of irregular data structures. This is the world of languages like Lisp and Prolog, and it is a wider world than that implied by the phrase 'artificial intelligence'. Lisp, for example, is a good language for writing software tools – programs which analyse or manipulate other programs.

Workstations optimized for symbolic computing did not appear on the market until the 1980s. The next step was to shrink much of the workstation's power onto a single chip.

13 June 1985

Texas Instruments claims to spend more on artificial intelligence hardware and software research than Japan's fifth generation computing programme – an astonishing statistic until one pauses to consider that the official fifth generation project, with a 1984–85 budget of $24 million is merely the spearhead of a much larger effort spread across Japan's great industrial laboratories.

TI's revenue in 1984 was $5.7 billion, and the company spent $364 million of its own money, and $324 million of its customers' money, on research and development in the same period. It therefore only had to allot a small percentage of its research funds to AI, in order to outspend with comfort the Japanese project which is supposedly such a threat to American technological supremacy.

With activities ranging from semiconductors to complete business, military and consumer electronic systems, TI is a vertically integrated company. It set up an AI group as long ago as 1978, but there was no obvious rush to build AI into products.

Speech synthesis appeared in products like the Speak and Spell educational toy. The Professional Computer, launched in 1983, could recognize spoken commands. With hindsight TI can claim that these were its first AI products, but at the time it seemed unremarkable that a semiconductor manufacturer with an interest in digital signal processing should turn out some products based on low-cost speech chips.

In the past two years, however, TI has offered natural (though not spoken) language interfaces for a number of software packages including Microsoft's MS/DOS operating system. Last year it launched Personal Consultant and Arborist, enabling users of the Professional Computer to build small rule-based expert systems and decision trees. And in the autumn came the US launch of the Explorer, a single-user workstation optimized for symbolic processing, which competes with broadly similar products from Symbolics, Lisp Machine Inc, and Xerox. The Explorer's sophisticated Lisp programming environment offers the choice of Zetalisp (a Lisp dialect originating from the Massachusetts Institute of Technology) or Common Lisp, which is the industry's best-yet attempt to agree on a standard, portable Lisp.

The Explorer's UK launch is scheduled for the third quarter of 1985, with a basic system priced around the £60,000 mark. Many customers will probably spend a further five-figure sum on a third-party originated knowledge programming toolkit such as Kee, Knowledgecraft or OPS5E.

Doug Johnson, from TI's computer science laboratory in Dallas, visited England at the end of May to demonstrate the Explorer. He said that TI is now engaged in research on expert systems and knowledge representation, natural language processing, speech, vision, AI programming environments, and advanced hardware design. Johnson manages the branch of the laboratory concerned with applications of AI. Several TI divisions are putting AI techniques to work in their own businesses. The geophysics group is looking for better methods of interpreting seismic surveys for the oil industry. The semiconductor group will be using AI to design very complex chips. Other groups are looking into advanced factory automation, and expert systems for fault-finding in electronic equipment.

AI programs are notoriously hungry for processing power and memory. As a major semiconductor manufacturer, TI sees very large scale integration as the key to an age of 'computational plenty' in which AI techniques at last become widely used in ordinary computing activities. Already the semiconductor industry delivers around 100 million million bits of memory per year, and the cost per bit has fallen to about one hundredth of a cent. AI has come along at the right time to stimulate demand for increasingly cheap and plentiful memory and processing power. It also represents a way of adding software value to hardware which, alone, could not guarantee a company's future income.

Addressing TI's computer user group in Copenhagen last October, senior vice-president George Heilmeier predicted that by the 1990s, only 10 to 15 per cent of computer power will be devoted to actual data crunching. The remaining 85 to 90 per cent, he forecast, will be devoted to making computers easier to use.

Johnson expounded the TI view that artificial intelligence, or symbolic processing (to use a more acceptable and perhaps more accurate term), will merge almost completely with conventional computing. 'Symbolic processing can bring two major things to conventional applications,' he said. 'One is dramatically improved user interfaces, where the application is easier to use, easier to understand by people who are not necessarily computer experts. The second is that you can bring a great deal more intelligence to an application, where that application can raise the level of the average user to somewhere close to the level of the best user.'

Nor will AI be confined to machines which are recognizably computers. It will be embedded in weapons, industrial machines, and consumer goods. The Defense Advanced Research Projects Agency placed a $2.6 million contract with TI for a symbolic processor chip which could, in principle, be built into 'smart' products of many kinds. According to Rick Morris, TI's international marketing manager for AI products, the chip will run at clock rates up to 40 megahertz. With approximately 500,000 transistor sites, Morris said the chip will have ten times the power of currently available symbolic processors, and 100 times that of typical chips on the market today.

The first language to be implemented on the chip will be the same Common Lisp superset that runs on the Explorer. 'Any of the symbolic processing languages could be implemented fairly well on it, including Prolog,' said Johnson. He revealed that the first chips have already been fabricated and tested. 'We are 14 months into a 27-month programme, and progressing on schedule, very satisfactorily,' he said. 'We have some test parts back, and they meet our expectations.'

The speed of the chip clearly makes it a candidate for 'realtime' AI systems which make complex decisions in split seconds. Whether on the battlefield or the factory floor, attempts to tackle time-sensitive problems of this kind with today's technology have been largely unsuccessful.

DARPA's prime concern is with military and aerospace applications, but at the right price a high-performance symbolic processing chip would have many uses in industrial and business machines. A desktop version of the Explorer is one possibility that must have occurred to TI's designers.

This is not the first time Lisp has been put on a chip. Twice since 1979, MIT computer scientists have designed chips to run the Scheme dialect of Lisp (Chapter 39). Both designs were actually put on silicon, but they were never debugged to commercial standards, and they lacked the go-faster architectural features of TI's far more complex design.

TI's commitment to Common Lisp is understandable. Common Lisp is also being promoted by Digital Equipment, whose VAX superminis have been the workhorses of the AI community. Efficient and reasonably complete Common Lisp implementations are now available for personal computers, including the ubiquitous IBM PC. The PC, and other personal machines such as TI's own Professional Computer, its new Businesspro and the portable Pro-light, may be selected as 'delivery vehicles' for expert systems developed on more powerful machines like the Explorer. People who write expert systems generally need a bigger machine than the people who use them.

The Explorer's Prolog is implemented in Lisp and therefore slow. According to Johnson, steps are being taken in Dallas to rectify the lack of an efficient Prolog. This has acquired more urgency with the impending launch of the Explorer in Europe, where Prolog is more popular than it is in the United States.

TI researchers are also interested in better languages within the Lisp family. Johnson stressed that at the moment this is purely a research interest, with no product implications, but he added: 'One thing of a great deal of interest to us is Scheme, as a simplified, cleaned-up language with several general concepts introduced into it, such as closures and continuations, that increase the power and potential of the language.'

Scheme is not available commercially, but since it is taught at MIT, a growing number of America's ablest young computer scientists are familiar with it.

TI's reputation has suffered a few knocks recently, with the revelation that some chips built into weapons systems had been incompletely tested, and the reports of the poor performance and alleged overpricing of the Harm missile. The synergy of superchips and symbolic processing is an important part of the company's strategy for the years ahead. The Lisp chip and the Explorer are the first fruits of that strategy, and it will be a severe setback for TI if either of them turns out to be a failure.

At the 1987 International Solid State Circuits Conference in New York, Texas Instruments revealed details of the symbolic processor chip it had developed for the Department of Defense. Other leading semiconductor companies working on similar developments were reckoned to be at least 8 to 10 months behind TI.

Symbolics, which pioneered the Lisp machine market, has squeezed much of its 3600 architecture onto a single chip which will be used in future products.

Scheme is now commercially available from Texas Instruments, whose address is given at the end of Chapter 39.

54

Lazy machine's turn of speed

The millions expended by Texas Instruments dwarf the modest budget on which Cambridge University researchers were able to construct their two Skim machines. But the spirit of the Cambridge effort would be understood in Dallas. The Skim architecture is optimized for a particular kind of programming language – specifically, for pure functional languages. Lisp may be regarded as an impure functional language. Texas Instruments wanted to develop marketable products, and this implied support for established programming languages. The Skim project was under no such constraint, and could explore a more radical model of programming.

Whether or not the fame of Skim has spread to Dallas, it has certainly reached Austin, Texas, where Burroughs has built its own combinator reduction machines. These have already been alluded to in Chapter 42.

14 March 1985

How can one write compact, reliable and comprehensible software which will, in due course, run efficiently on highly parallel 'fifth generation' machines? For many computer scientists the answer is 'functional programming'.

UK research in functional programming is respected all over the world, but hard-headed US observers use two-edged words like 'futuristic' in their praise. One problem is that the mathematically elegant functional languages run terribly slowly on most currently available computers. Another problem is that special tricks may be needed if a functional program is to handle inputs of data which occur while the program is running. (Logic programming faces similar problems, see Chapter 41.) It is not easy to write a purely functional operating system.

Evidence that the first of these problems can be overcome is provided by a small machine called Skim 2 that now sits on a Cambridge desktop. The second problem, too, is under attack. The Skim processor is being used in an effort to write a practical operating system in a purely functional language.

The Skim project was launched several years ago by an uncommonly adventurous undergraduate computer society. Thomas Clarke, who went on to design part of the Chase 68186 (a Unix-based supermicro computer), designed and built the Skim 1 prototype. Skim 1 was built on two cards, had 64 kilobytes of main memory, and a microcode memory of eprom (electrically programmable read only memory) chips.

Skim 2 was built in the university computer laboratory by Bill Stoye. 'Skim 2 is if anything, a simpler design than Skim 1,' says Arthur Norman, who supervised the project. It is, however, a more powerful and flexible machine.

It has 400 kilobytes of main memory, organized as 65,536 words of 50 bits. This, according to Norman, could at any time be expanded to 6 megabytes. In addition there is a 10 kilobyte writable microcode store (organized as 2048 words of 40 bits), which makes Skim 2 a 'soft' machine.

The processor box contains a power supply and just four double-size Eurocard printed circuit boards: the microcode memory, the main memory, a memory controller and the central processing unit (CPU). The largely empty box occupies about the same desk space as the Acorn BBC Microcomputer which serves as its 'intelligent front panel'. The prototype has not been built with leading-edge technology. The chip count of 230, which includes 92 memory chips, could probably be reduced dramatically by the use of large scale integration. The 24-bit CPU is based (like many commercial minicomputers) on Advanced Micro Devices 2901 processor chips. The 2901 is a 4-bit slice device, and Skim 2 uses six of them.

According to Stoye, the CPU is considerably less complex than a Motorola 68000 16-bit microprocessor, and would fit very well on a single chip.

The main memory is specially organized to support graph or tree data structures in which each cell, or node, may hold pointers to two other nodes. Lisp, which is the closest thing to a functional language in commercial use today, uses data structures of this kind.

'All of your programs and all of your data are stored as graph structures,' Norman explains. During the execution of a program, the machine follows chains of pointers, resetting some of them in such a way as to simplify the tangled data structure. This process, known as reduction, proceeds until the program has been simplified out of existence and only the desired result remains. Reduction succeeds because a functional program is in effect a single large and complex mathematical formula which may be simplified by substituting equals for equals. No such simplification is possible in conventional imperative languages.

Each 50-bit memory word is divided into a head and a tail. The head has one flag bit, four tag bits and 20 data bits, which may be the address of another memory location. The tail repeats this structure. The tag bits are used to identify the type of data that accompanies them. The flags are used to indicate which cells may be over-written. Flags are set by a garbage collection routine which marks a cell as 'dead' if no chain of pointers leads to it.

Before Skim can run, a microcode program must be loaded from a floppy disk, via the BBC host machine. The microcode is developed on an IBM 3081 mainframe. With different microcoding, Skim can effectively become many different machines. For example it could, presumably, become a dedicated Lisp machine. Skim's main role, however, is to run programs expressed in a notation known as combinatory logic.

Combinatory logic is just another way of writing functions. (A function is something which takes a number of arguments or 'inputs' and returns a value or 'output'. An entire program can be viewed as a function.) The extraordinary thing about combinatory logic is that it completely eliminates the use of variables.

Variables are normally used as a way of making the same data available to different parts of a program. The special symbols called combinators provide an ingenious way of piping a value from one part of a functional expression to another, without making use of a variable. Three combinators are sufficient. Their conventional symbols are S, K and I. (The M in Skim just stands for 'machine'.)

David Turner, now at the University of Kent, pioneered the use of combinatory logic in functional programming, and devised a number of additional combinators which increase the efficiency of programs (Chapter 42).

Combinators become the 'machine code' of the suitably micro-programmed Skim system. Type in:

S 1 2 3

The machine replies:

1 3 (2 3)

The S combinator has done its work and produced two copies of the number 3. Believe it or not, repeated use of combinators can clone any number of 3s, in the exact positions where you want them in a complex expression. Equally important, methods exist for combing all the 3s, or

Xs, or Ys out of an expression, leaving only combinators and the basic arithmetic functions +, −, *, /.

One can define a function SQUARE by typing in:

= SQUARE S * I

(This uses a second combinator, I.) Then type in:

SQUARE 4

and the answer comes back,

16

Any sizeable program soon becomes a thicket of brackets and other symbols in combinator code. But Norman argues that Skim's machine code is no more incomprehensible than that of the average micro. 'This appears to be a much nicer machine code than, for instance, Z80,' he says.

In fact the 'machine code' is both interactive and extendable. Serious programming is done in a high level functional language similar to Turner's SASL. It has the same syntax as the machine code. 'I'm still writing in machine code,' says Norman, 'but I'm writing in a machine code where a large number of extra operation codes are available.'

Norman estimates that Skim's performance, at about 80,000 reductions a second, is comparable to that of a typical 68000-based workstation, probably outperforming the 68000 on list processing but falling behind when handling arrays.

Response times tend to be good, because Skim uses the method known as lazy evaluation. Intermediate results are not evaluated until the program can go no further without them. 'Laziness means the entire machine's resources go into doing whatever's required to get the first character of your answer to you,' Norman explains. Lazy evaluation has other important consequences. It means that the programmer can happily invoke infinite data structures like the list of all prime numbers. Skim will not compute even a single prime until its value is actually needed.

Norman sees Skim as a step towards future machines with more than one processor. 'It provides a benchmark in terms of both absolute performance and price/performance, that the parallel machines can race against,' he says.

Parallel machines should be able to evaluate several parts of a functional program simultaneously, with a corresponding increase in speed. In FORTRAN or BASIC it is not so easy because the result of each section of the program depends in complicated ways on the 'side effects' of other parts of the program.

Parallel processing undermines the principle of lazy evaluation, since to keep the multiple processors busy it may be necessary to evaluate some results which may not in the end be used. Norman points out that one can analyse a program before it is executed, to identify those intermediate results which will definitely be needed. 'You can have your program lazy except where static analysis has shown that you can afford to be eager.'

Lazy evaluation also suggests a method of writing operating systems which can handle the input from a keyboard, a filing system or another computer. The idea is to treat the stream of characters from a keyboard, say, as an infinite list. One way to think of it is that every character that will ever be typed into the keyboard already exists – but the system in its lazy way has not yet bothered to examine more than a few of the characters in this infinite stream.

The stream concept may not in itself be sufficient for building efficient operating systems in pure functional style. Stoye is using additional constructs called 'processes' and 'messages'.

Why bother, when excellent operating systems have already been written in imperative languages? 'There is a sense in which functional programming languages are weaker than conventional programming languages,' Norman admits. But he adds, 'The view that goes with this is that a restriction or constraint is a good thing, not a bad thing.'

Specifically, functional programming creates opportunities for parallelism, and its mathematical basis simplifies the task of proving two programs are equivalent – an important requirement in the design of reliable software. Operating systems have to be particularly reliable, so there is not much point grafting functional application programs onto an imperative operating system.

The functional programmer sacrifices the freedom to alter the values of variables or to update data structures. Programmers who enjoy these freedoms may be able to make their algorithms fun faster. But as Norman points out, 'One also observes that the ability to update data structures enables you to make a whole class of mistakes'.

Stoye completed his PhD and left for the United States. Clarke continued as a research student in Cambridge, building on the experience with Skim-1 and Skim-2. Unwilling to claim miraculous properties for the systems, Norman comments level-headedly, 'We would not want to claim that pure functional code can do everything, and Skim operating system studies have shown us the hard edges rather clearly.'

55

A testbed for parallel architectures

Like reduction machines, dataflow architectures have a special affinity with functional or applicative languages. (If a distinction is made between the two, it is that applicative languages do not support user-defined functions. Full functional languages require a rather more complex dataflow architecture.)

One of the great attractions of dataflow is that it finds parallelism automatically. Unless there is a specific reason for performing two operations in sequence, the machine is free to perform them in parallel. This frees the programmer from thinking about the detailed mechanics of parallelism. It is important, however, to choose an algorithm which provides opportunities for parallelism.

Critics point to potential inefficiencies in dataflow. Since the machine schedules its own work at run time, it may have rather more 'housekeeping' to do than machines of other designs. Also, if no precautions are taken the machine may sometimes busily compute intermediate results which turn out not to have been needed. Most of the objections have been fairly well answered by the advocates of dataflow, and it is holding its place among the numerous alternative strategies for parallel computation.

A major dataflow experiment has been in progress at the Massachusetts Institute of Technology. Like the Supernode Array (Chapter 52), the system can be reconfigured to emulate many different interconnection schemes.

15 June 1984

Why are computers so slow? Because, runs an oft-rehearsed argument, the conventional von Neumann machine treats a program as a sequence of operations to be performed one after another. Programs would run faster if the machine could carry out many operations in parallel. But two things prevent this.

One limitation is imposed by the physical resources of the conventional machine. It only has one processor. Its memory can only handle one request at a time. In principle at least, these bottlenecks could be eliminated by expanding the machine's resources.

Another, more fundamental speed limit remains. Assume, for the moment, that the program is still seen as a body of operations to be applied to data. Each operation has inputs which may themselves be the outputs from other operations. Clearly those other operations must be completed first. They in turn must wait for the operations which compute their own inputs; and so on.

In the dataflow machine architecture, attention is focused on these data dependencies. In fact they largely govern the machine's behaviour. The programmer does not have to tell the machine the order in which instructions are to be executed.

In a dataflow machine, an operation may be executed as soon as its inputs are ready. The precise order in which instructions are executed may depend on physical details such as memory bandwidth, but the result of the computation will not be affected.

Dataflow machines are being developed in a number of centres, including Manchester and Toulouse. One of the most ambitious dataflow projects is led by Arvind, a professor in the Laboratory for Computer Science at MIT.

It has attracted $6.7 million funding from the Defense Advanced Research Projects Agency, it involves a dozen graduate students, many undergraduates, four IBM engineers, and one visitor from Ericsson, the Swedish-based telecommunications company.

Arvind's parallel machine will have 64 or 128 processors, each of which is a powerful computer in its own right. Its architecture is much coarser-grained than that of the massively parallel machine under development in MIT's Artificial Intelligence Laboratory (Chapter 56). That machine will probably have 4000 processor chips with 64 simple processors on each chip.

Arvind says he gave up the idea of designing a special processor chip three or four years ago. In his opinion 'there is no way that an interesting processor will fit on a chip'.

He looked at the possibility of designing a dataflow processor board, using commercial chips, as a building block. He decided this would involve too much work. Instead, Arvind's group has decided to buy ready-made, powerful processors which run the Lisp language. Their own efforts can then be concentrated on the problem of connecting the processors together. Software and microcode will be used to make the Lisp machines behave as dataflow processors. A big advantage is that complete programming environments already exist for such machines. The $80,000-plus Symbolics 3600 was Arvind's original choice, but now he says his group is thinking of using the recently unveiled Texas Instruments Explorer.

Packets of data called tokens will flow between the machines on a high-bandwidth network. Each token will contain 8 to 12 bits specifying its destination. Arvind plans to use a network in the shape of a 7-dimensional hypercube. In this highly symmetrical arrangement, a token can travel to any destination in, at most, seven steps. Many alternative, short routes are available.

Tokens will be routed by a specially designed board, plugged into the backplane of each processor. This board will handle the processor's own communications. It will also store and forward packets which are merely passing through on their way somewhere else. Each board will hold a table of routeing instructions. Altering the tables will make the hypercube behave like networks of various other shapes.

Arvind's proposed machine is described as a multiprocessor emulation facility. Its role is exploratory. It will not be a machine for end-users. It will be a testbed for parallel architectures.

Future parallel machines may be purpose-built for anything from signal processing to artificial intelligence. Their processors will be hard-wired together in specific arrangements which suit the application. It is argued that expensive failures may be avoided if there is a system on which new designs can be tested before they are built.

Until 1978, Arvind was at the University of California, Irvine. There he developed the Irvine Dataflow (ID) language. The original ID compiler generates Lisp code. It is still used for debugging.

A new compiler, written at MIT, generates dataflow machine language. Conceptually, a machine language program is a dataflow graph, in which boxes represent operations and arrows represent data dependencies. At the moment it is a machine language without a machine. But an abstract dataflow machine has been specified in approximately 300 pages of Lisp code. This code can be regarded as a hardware specification; it can also be run as an emulator, on existing hardware.

'We have a compiler, we have the emulator, and they work together once in a while,' says Arvind. Debugging the two programs has been difficult since they cannot be debugged separately.

Arvind's group has adopted a method of computing known as dynamic dataflow. It requires a more complex machine than Jack Dennis's original static dataflow concept; but it permits more parallelism in the computation, and allows the programmer to use procedure calls. Some observers think that dynamic dataflow machines may be suitable for artificial intelligence work, while static dataflow machines may offer higher performance in scientific computing.

According to Arvind, dynamic dataflow was invented by himself and Gostelow at Irvine, and independently by John Gurd's group in Manchester. 'In static dataflow,' he explains, 'there is a restriction which says you cannot have more than one token on an arc. In dynamic dataflow there is no restriction. You can have as many tokens on an arc as you like.' The problem is that tokens may arrive in the wrong order. Confusion is prevented by a system of tagging tokens which Arvind compares to colour-coding.

To exploit the available parallelism, the program (a dataflow graph) must be split up and distributed between many processors. Finding a good 'decomposition' of a program is a very hard problem, according to Arvind. 'These are things we want to study,' he says. 'We have lots of ideas, but we are not at all clear which is an acceptable one.'

He believes that the machine itself should decide the division of labour among its processors. This contrasts with the approach of Occam and other languages where the programmer can explicitly assign work to a particular processor. Instead, Arvind argues that one should choose a language which makes it easy to find parallelism in a program. Functional languages are the most suitable, he says.

A functional program is almost a software model of a dataflow machine, with arguments or inputs going into functions and results coming out of them, to be used as arguments by further functions. Of well-known languages, Lisp comes closest to the functional ideal.

All the arguments of a function can be evaluated in parallel, Arvind points out. 'When you write a program in a functional language you don't obscure the parallelism that was in your original algorithm.'

For the moment he is content to use the data-driven style of computation, in which the program computes all the results it might need later, even though some of them may prove to be unnecessary.

He admires the 'futuristic' work of British computer scientists like David Turner, John Darlington and Peter Henderson, who favour demand-driven computation. Here, the program computes only the results it needs. It can therefore handle infinite data objects without foundering in infinite computations.

But demand-driven computing requires extra book-keeping. 'The way demand-driven evaluation is usually done,' says Arvind, 'it's so inefficient that it doesn't have a chance of succeeding.' He has just written a paper suggesting a method of reducing the book-keeping.

Dataflow computers, like von Neumann computers, are stored program machines. The program itself does not change. Rather, it specifies operations to be performed on some data. But there is an alternative – to simplify the input expression (that is, program and data) by some kind of algebraic operation, until there is nothing left to do and the result simply falls into your lap. This is the method of reduction. In reduction machines, too, the program is represented as a graph. But no tokens flow along the graph. Instead, it is gradually pruned. This may be done sequentially or in parallel.

Arvind feels there may be deep connection between dataflow and reduction. He believes dataflow may be moving closer to parallel reduction, with the addition of data structure storage. When tokens become too big they can be stored in memory. Instead of the tokens themselves, pointers to their locations flow through the graph.

'If someone asked me to bet money today,' he says, 'I'd guess that hardware-wise, those two things will turn out to be the same.'

By November 1985, the project had eight Symbolics Lisp machines, and 17 Texas Instruments Explorers, all connected by an Ethernet network. There were plans to more than double the number of Explorers. A circuit-switched network was about to be installed; to be followed, in 1987 or after, by a packet-switched network with more than eight times its information-carrying capacity.

Further reading

Hankin, C., Till, D. and Glaser, H. (1986). 'Linking data flow and functional languages' *Byte*, May. (This article remains readable while explaining in some detail how dataflow works. It is taken from the authors' book *Principles of Functional Programming*, published by Prentice-Hall.)

56

Communicating at the speed of Lisp

While Arvind was planning to hook complete, powerful computers together for his experiments in coarse-grained parallelism, others in the same building were plotting what seemed the ultimate fine-grained parallel architecture: a giant memory, leavened with a quarter-million gossiping grains of processing power. In fact this was not the final subdivision. We shall turn shortly to those other smooth-textured computing structures which show no remnant of the von Neumann ancestry.

1 November 1984

'The difficulty in all parallel architectures is getting the correct data to the correct place at the correct time,' says Tom Knight of the Massachusetts Institute of Technology. 'Performing the computation is the easy part.'

That is why the highly parallel machine that Knight and his colleagues are designing in the MIT artificial intelligence laboratory is known as the Connection Machine.†

The idea for the machine springs from the work of Scott E. Fahlman in the late 1970s. Fahlman proposed a system for representing and using what he called 'real-world knowledge' – in other words, an artificial intelligence database. He also proposed a hardware architecture which would support the AI database. This 'futuristic' architecture was impractical at the time, according to Knight.

But after Fahlman left MIT for Carnegie-Mellon University, Tom Knight and Danny Hillis picked up and developed his ideas. They went to

†It was so known at the time. 'Connection Machine' is registered as a trademark by Thinking Machines Corporation, which has subsequently marketed a product of that name.

companies seeking funds to support the building of the machine. 'IBM never said no, but they never said yes,' Knight recalls.

Then came the split. Hillis abandoned the idea of collaborating with IBM, and went in search of venture capital for a start-up company. Thinking Machines Corporation was set up with $7.5 million of private capital, and with Sheryl Handler as president. The company is developing its own version of the Connection Machine for the commercial market.

Knight stayed on to develop another version independently at MIT. The academic and commercial versions of the machine are similar in concept but have diverged in matters of detail. Knight's descriptions refer to the MIT version.

Like earlier, sequential computers designed at MIT, the highly parallel machine is specifically designed to run the Lisp programming language. This does not preclude the use of other languages, since Lisp is regarded as a good language for writing compilers and interpreters for other languages. 'Lisp is not an AI language,' says Knight. 'It's a language for writing AI languages.'

Most American artificial intelligence workers are trained in Lisp and use it naturally, even on occasions when theoretically some other language might be more suitable. But there is also a tradition of building other languages on top of Lisp.

'This machine is not an architecture for AI languages,' says Knight. 'It's an architecture to support the languages that you're going to write AI languages in.'

Any substantial Lisp program calls for the construction of a large data structure. Most, or all of this data structure will consist of what is known as list structure. The basic element of list structure is called a 'cons cell'. It usually occupies one word of memory, and contains two pointers. These point either to further cons cells, or to Lisp 'atoms'. An atom, in Lisp, is a word, a number, or any other data item which is not itself a list.

'Cons' is the Lisp function which adds a new item (which may itself be a list) to the head of a list. Repeated application of the function can build up lists which are very long, or very complex, or both. Cons cells are the forks of the list structure tree; atoms are its leaves. A fair-sized Lisp package such as one of the major Lisp programming environments occupies many millions of cons cells. Future knowledge-based systems may run into the billions.

A conventional computer fetches one word at a time from memory to the central processing unit, examines it and decides what to do with it. Like other database machines, the Connection Machine is designed to abolish this time-consuming traffic between memory and CPU.

The intention is to give every cons cell its own processing power. 'Imagine that you have a tiny little processor within each of these cells, and that the little processor within each of these cells is capable of doing a few simple things,' says Knight.

The machine will have a single instruction, multiple data stream architecture. All processsors will execute the same instruction at the same time. For example, all cells which point to a letter 'A' might be instructed to set a particular bit in one of their registers. This architecture is expected to speed up the process of searching the database for a particular structure.

The plan is to build a prototype machine with 4000 processor chips. Each chip will contain 64 simple processors. Each processor will have registers for the two forward pointers, and a few local 'scratchpad' registers. Each processor will also have a register holding a 'back pointer', so that the data structure can be traversed in the reverse direction, from leaf to root.

The machine's other key component will be a switching chip which functions something like a telephone exchange. A number of these chips will allow signals to be routed from any processor to any other. The design allows for 3300 signal paths between processors to be active at any one moment. Most conventional computers, of course, have only one bus or data path. But with a quarter of a million processors trying to talk to each other, Knight admits that even 3300 paths may prove to be too few.

Since communication is known to be the major problem in highly parallel computers, it may be wrong to expect a prototype machine to abolish the communication bottleneck in one fell swoop. The machine will not, initially, be engineered to run at high clock rates. Later on, there may be a tenfold gain in speed to he harvested by tightening up the system timing.

Often a new computer design is simulated on an existing computer before any hardware is built. But no attempt has been made to simulate the Connection Machine. 'If it were easy to simulate on a von Neumann architecture we wouldn't need to build it,' says Knight. He feels that a simulation would be of little value if it ran 10,000 times slower than the real thing. He also believes there is a 'sociological' problem: people are unwilling, he feels, to think seriously about programming a machine which exists only as a simulation.

The likely uses of the machine fall into two categories loosely described as 'robotic' and 'cognitive'. A major concern in the robotic area is the control and planning of physical actions, but similar importance is attached to the machine perception of sounds and images.

Machine vision systems often operate in two stages. In the first stage, the image is represented by a grid-like array of picture points. Contrast is enhanced, noise is reduced, and edges are located, by signal processing operations. The same operations are performed for every picture point, so time can be saved by processing many points in parallel.

The second stage of processing uses a symbolic representation of the scene, and may bring knowledge-based programming techniques to bear. A typical task is to identify a known three-dimensional object in an unknown orientation. 'That's a hard problem, and you want to be able to do it in parallel,' says Knight.

His machine will support both stages of the vision process. The main routeing network will come into play later on, in the symbolic stage of vision processing. To support the early, signal processing stages, there will be additional connections which link the processors into a two-dimensional grid. One processor would be allocated to each picture point, and for signal processing purposes it would only communicate with its immediate neighbours.

Work in the 'cognitive' area is likely to focus on artificial intelligence databases, reasoning by analogy, commonsense reasoning, and language processing. Knight comments, 'The problem that this machine is really designed to address is the problem of large AI databases.'

Current MIT thinking on the representation of knowledge says that exceptions are as important as rules, beliefs are more useful than certainties, and contradictions are part of the very fabric of knowledge. Marvin Minsky, the head of the AI laboratory, holds strong views on this. (This accounts, in part, for the sceptical attitude of MIT people towards logic programming, as represented by the language Prolog. But Prolog's advocates understand the problem. They are working on it too.)

Says Knight: 'It's completely clear to everyone here that there is no hope of constructing or maintaining a logically consistent database, and that if you had one it would be harmful.' He considers that an AI database should be able to produce justifications for the beliefs it holds. It should be able to retract beliefs which are found to be false, and the effects of the retraction should propagate through the whole belief system.

Most work, he feels, has been on small databases of 100 to 1000 facts. 'That simply isn't enough to capture knowledge, even in a limited domain such as an expert system,' he maintains.

As far as the hardware is concerned, the toughest technical problems revolve around the design and performance of the machine's interconnection network. Here, MIT computer theorists including Ronald Rivest have contributed their insights.

There is a new prospect of industrial collaboration. Knight hopes that a dozen scientists and engineers at General Electric's corporate research centre in Schenectady will join the project

The Defense Advanced Research Projects Agency (DARPA) has been asked to fund the construction of MIT's Connection Machine. But if DARPA refuses, the project's whole future could be in doubt.

The machine as described here was never funded and never built. DARPA placed an order with Thinking Machines Corporation and was unwilling to support the construction of a very similar computer at MIT. Thinking Machines launched its Connection Machine in April 1986. Meanwhile Tom Knight has been working for Symbolics, and it is likely that some of his ideas for parallel processing will eventually emerge in Symbolics products.

Further reading

Fahlman, S.E. (1979). *NETL: A System for Representing and Using Real-world Knowledge*. Cambridge Mass.: MIT Press. (An influential early investigation of ways of representing knowledge in hardware.)

Hillis, D. (1985). *The Connection Machine.* Cambridge, Mass.: MIT Press. (Describes the machine built and marketed by Thinking Machines, lucidly presents some of the major issues in parallel computing, and presents Hillis's view that computation should be more like physics.)

57
Reaching data faster

Imagine an unlit wine cellar full of cobwebs. The butler, searching for a particular vintage, carries a bottle carefully upstairs, examines the label in the daylight, finds it is the wrong bottle, and tramps back down the stairs to try the next one.

That is the procedure that computers must sometimes resort to, in order to find a particular piece of information. Maybe a butler who could run upstairs in 50 nanoseconds would do the same. But the obvious course is to put a lamp in the cellar and examine the bottles down there, where they are stored.

This profound piece of wisdom is at last being heeded by computer designers. A great deal of to-ing and fro-ing can be saved, if the memory itself contains mechanisms for certain kinds of inference or pattern matching. In some designs, such as those of Danny Hillis or Tom Knight, most of the machine's computing power is placed close to memory. In other designs the memory units and processing units may be placed on opposite sides of a communication network, but the memory has a repertoire of actions and the processors can send it more elaborate requests than the usual simple 'read' and 'write'.

Britain's Alvey Directorate calls such memories 'knowledge manipulation engines'. Others would just call them smart memories. They are likely to be an important component of systems for vision, language processing, and other applications where large bodies of knowledge must be sifted through in a short time.

9 May 1985

Much research in artificial intelligence has been concerned with ways of representing knowledge. One could argue that this has also been the major concern of the designers of database management systems, though their priorities have naturally been different from those of AI workers. But the advent of large commercial knowledge-based systems has focused attention on the common ground. Luckily it turns out that both lines of research have led to very similar models of data, which may broadly be classified as relational.

Consider that old AI favourite, the semantic network. The nodes of the network represent entities known to the system. Some nodes will represent individuals like 'Jane' or 'Scotland', and they will be linked by arcs which represent relations such as 'lives in' or 'visits'.

Most semantic net schemes also allow a node to represent a class such as 'person', 'professor' or 'country'. One can now introduce two particularly useful relations: membership of a class (Jane is a professor) and inclusion of one class in another (all professors are persons). This provides a framework for logical deduction. For example one can deduce that Jane is a person, even though the network has no direct link between the 'Jane' and 'person' nodes. Jane will inherit properties that are associated with the classes she belongs to. If all professors are clever, we have no need to represent explicitly the fact that Jane is clever.

Semantic nets, and the related 'frame'-based representations, were initially explored in software, but in the late 1970s people began to think about translating these data models into hardware. It dawned on them that with very large scale integration of silicon circuits, processing and memory need no longer be physically separated. If processing power were spread throughout memory, a database could be searched rapidly without clever indexing. And perhaps quite complex logical inferences could be performed as part of the same process.

Scott Fahlman explored the possibilities in his doctoral thesis, written in 1979 at the Massachusetts Institute of Technology. That led to MIT's 'Connection Machine' project (see Chapter 56). Several members of that project left to set up Thinking Machines Corporation in Cambridge, Massachusetts. This company is developing a 64,000-processor machine which is a more or less direct translation into silicon of the semantic net model.

Meanwhile, Scotland's own connection machine is taking shape at Strathclyde University under the supervision of Douglas McGregor and John Malone. Its patented technology is blindingly fast and kick-yourself simple. McGregor demonstrates the principle with a Heath Robinson lash-up of lamps, batteries, diodes and crocodile clips. This contraption is strictly for public relations. The real machine will reproduce the same circuits at microscopic scale and in astronomic numbers, perhaps on unbroken four-inch diameter wafers of silicon.

Imagine building a physical model of a semantic network, with diodes representing the 'is a' links. A diode is a device which passes current in one direction only. Now suppose you wish to find all the persons known to the system. You simply apply a voltage to the 'person' node. Current will flow down the class hierarchy to the 'professor' node, and on to the 'Jane' node. Current will also flow to all the nodes for butchers, bakers, candlestick makers and other classes of person. It will flow on to every node representing an individual who belongs to one of those classes and must therefore be a person. Because diodes are one-way conductors, no current flows upwards from the 'person' node to the 'living-thing' node or any other node representing a class which includes all persons.

Current will flow 'up' the tangled hierarchy, however, if the voltage is reversed. By applying a reverse voltage to the 'Jane' node, one can discover all the classes to which Jane belongs: not only 'professor', 'person' and 'living-thing' but 'mother', 'woman', 'cyclist' and probably many others.

Wiring diodes by hand is not the ideal way to enter facts into a database. The chips designed at Strathclyde have diodes already in position for every possible connection. So an 8-node chip has 56 diodes, laid out on a square matrix and criss-crossed by conductors. It works like a crossbar switch in a telephone exchange. Each diode is associated with a one-bit memory cell. Writing a '1' to this cell switches the diode into circuit and establishes a link in the semantic network. Writing a '0' erases the link.

The remarkable thing about this arrangement is its speed. It can perform hundreds of logical inferences, in parallel, within one microsecond. The current fans out almost instantaneously through long chains of diodes and switches. This contrasts with similar designs where, according to McGregor, signals can only propagate at a rate of one link per machine cycle.

The Strathclyde group is designing a series of increasingly complex 'generic associative memory' chips. The first was an eight by eight matrix, which worked. The second was a 32 by 32 matrix, which did not. A new attempt at the 32 by 32 chip is being made, before the group tries anything more complicated.

Practical networks are expected to have upwards of 10,000 nodes. It is not feasible to construct a 10,000 by 10,000 matrix. Fortunately it is not necessary either. Software simulations have shown that a number of smaller matrices, with relatively few connections between them, will serve. The natural 'clustering' of data comes to the rescue.

Each new data item is assigned a 'token', a unique address in one of the matrices. The item itself will typically, but not necessarily, be a character string such as 'John Smith'. (It is not quite that simple. The system may know of several entities called 'John Smith' in different contexts.) The system delays assigning a token until it knows what class of things John Smith belongs to. If John Smith is a person, it looks for a free line in that matrix which already has a 'person' line. Setting one bit in that matrix records the fact that John Smith is a person. John Smith may later prove to belong to a number of other classes, but he will definitely not be a company or a motor vehicle. He will belong to the classes that persons usually belong to. And those classes will usually have tokens close to that of 'person' itself. Most of John Smith's associations are local, and fall within a single matrix.

'One of the interesting things is how well such a simple clustering strategy actually works,' says McGregor. On the relatively rare occasions when a long-distance link is required, it can be set up through a series of matrix-to-matrix connections, just like a trunk call in the telephone system.

The associative memory is a truly connectionist machine, since it stores all its information in the connections between nodes, and none in the nodes themselves. Of course, something must keep track of what each node or token stands for. This is done by software at present. Later, a fast hardware unit might take over this task.

How would one retrieve all the records of people who are professors AND enjoy cycling OR jogging? Since finding the tokens of all professors (or cyclists, or joggers) is as quick as finding one, Boolean queries of this kind are handled by retrieving entire classes and then intersecting or uniting them as necessary. Latch circuits will be provided along the edges of the matrix chips, to store the result of one search while the next is carried out. For more complex queries, single-bit latches would be insufficient, and the appropriate temporary storage would be a stack several bits deep.

As a database machine, the diode memory could act as an intelligent index to a large disk store. 'The data which goes in this is a rather small, specialized subset of the total data in the database,' explains McGregor. 'You can manage with this small percentage in this fast device, and use it to access very much larger volumes.'

In this case, some tokens would be associated (through links in the associative store itself) with the addresses of blocks of disk memory. Suppose you wished to search for all piano-tuners in Willesden. Querying the 'piano-tuners' node would return the addresses of all blocks containing any data on piano-tuners. Querying the 'Willesden' node would return the addresses of a second set of blocks. Those blocks which occurred in both sets would then be read out from disk and scanned (by software in the host computer, initially) for the relevant records.

If the 'Willesden' node did not point directly to any disk blocks, the system could search for a node higher up the tree such as 'north-west London' which did. One would normally search first up the hierarchy, and then (reversing the current to the diodes) down the hierarchy to find the relevant disk block addresses.

With only a single kind of link – the diode – the associative memory can only represent one kind of relation. Normally this would be the 'is a' relation, which stands both for class membership and the subtly different concept of inclusion of one class within another. So this is not a true 'semantic network' machine, capable of performing complex inferences on data related in many ways. However, any amount of relational data, including colossal semantic networks if required, could be held in backing store. By speeding up retrieval of such data, the associative memory could help AI programs to run faster, even though it is not really an 'AI processor' itself.

Working 32 by 32 chips were produced soon afterwards. Part of an Alvey grant of £460,000 has gone towards the development of a further improved chip in CMOS (complementary metal oxide silicon) technology.

McGregor has also developed a logical model of data which he calls the FACT system. The intention is to implement this on the GAM hardware. Meanwhile, software implementations are available from Deductive Systems, a company set up by McGregor and others to market the technology.

In 1985 there were reasons to suppose that Thinking Machines was building a Fahlman-style semantic net machine as stated above. As more details of the Connection Machine emerged, it became clear that it had evolved towards a more generalized design. Knowledge can be, and has been represented in the Connection Machine as a semantic net. But the machine can also be used in many other ways.

58

Four steps to the sugar-cube supercomputer?

There is nothing implausible in the idea that biological processes and materials should be used to construct computing devices on a scale 100 or 1000 times smaller than today's VLSI chips. But that is not to say that it will ever happen. Even the most carefully imagined scenarios have large gaps in them. For instance, there is as yet no candidate for the role of a biological transistor.

And for another, more mundane reason it may never come to pass. To fit a great deal of computing power into a very small space is clearly a desirable achievement. But no one will care whether these nanocomputers are biological, or constructed in some other way – for example by micromanipulators based on the technology of the scanning tunnelling electron microscope. If we get there first by some other route, then the weeds will grow on the biological path we might have travelled.

Our lives are dominated by implausible technologies, while plausible ones fade into oblivion. Who would have backed the heavier-than-air machine against the obviously serviceable airship? Who would have thought that we would ride in relative quiet and comfort in vehicles driven by a series of explosions? Ernest Rutherford dismissed atomic energy as 'moonshine', and his judgement was absolutely sound. He died just before the implausible discovery of nuclear fission which changed everything. We had no right to expect that the fission of uranium 235 nuclei would release enough neutrons, on average, to support a chain reaction.

J.B.S. Haldane warned that the future would be vastly more surprising than anything he could imagine. If a scenario for something like the biochip seems too plausible, that's probably a bad sign.

---

25 October 1984

'If you took all the information in all the computers existing in the world today and used biomolecular technology, it would fit into one sugar cube,'

James McAlear told an airline magazine last year.

McAlear is the biochip's most exuberant publicist. He is one of a growing number of scientists who believe that silicon may be replaced by organic and biological materials in the computers of the future.

It is good attention-getting stuff. In 1983 and the first half of 1984, 100 articles on the biochip appeared in the press, and most of them must have mentioned McAlear, his partner John Wehrung, and their tiny company Gentronix.

Gentronix has a staff of six, and occupies an unostentatious unit on a high-tech industrial estate in Rockville, Maryland, 14 miles north of Washington, D.C. The company started in the early 1970s, offering electron microscopy and microanalysis services to industry. The biochip research developed gradually. A couple of patents were filed in 1976. The US Government showed interest. Gentronix has had four grants from the National Science Foundation, totalling approximately $300,000.

The Department of Defense is supporting work on biochips at the Naval Research Laboratory. It is thought that biochips, particularly those which use light radiation rather than electricity, may be resistant to the destructive electromagnetic pulse generated by nuclear explosions.

IBM was one of the first big companies in the area, but it has kept a low profile recently. McAlear says that in the US, General Electric, General Telephone and Electric, Rockwell and Westinghouse are involved in research on biomolecular electronics. He adds that American Cyanamid, Du Pont and Tektronix have shown interest in joint ventures with Gentronix.

Japan is the other centre of biochip fever. Matsushita, Mitsubishi, Sharp, Suntory and Toshiba are among the companies there that have entered the field, says McAlear.

Several US universities are working in biochip-related areas. Robert Birge recently set up a laboratory for biomolecular electronics at Carnegie-Mellon University.

Molecular electronics is one of the areas targeted in the West German government programme of advanced information technology research. The UK's Alvey programme has avoided the subject, but UK government programmes on biotechnology and optoelectronics provide alternative routes for funding biochip-related work.

Market studies by the Mitre Corporation and by Technical Insights have focused attention on the biochip. And a multi-client study by Gorham International of Portland, Maine will be published next February at a price of $7,500 (with reductions for early subscribers).

Project director Hugh Olmstead has hired McAlear and Wehrung as prime investigators, and sceptics may use this fact to question the Gorham study's objectivity. But McAlear believes the study will help to separate the hype from the genuine commercial possibilities. Biochip research has lost credibility, he believes, when reporters have mixed up current research with near-science-fiction predictions.

It is a long road from today's very large scale integrated circuits, with a feature size of one micrometre, to the ultimate three-dimensional computer with atom-sized components. 'We are dealing with an increase in density which is much greater than that which occurred between the vacuum tube and VLSI,' McAlear told a conference in Australia in September 1983. Recently he and Wehrung have been emphasizing that this phenomenal transformation will not be achieved in one go.

'It simply is not reasonable to assume that one can make circuits in the near future which are going to connect down to a structure of molecules,' says McAlear. In discussions with Albert Lawrence of Hughes Aircraft, and Alwyn Scott of the Los Alamos national laboratory, he has worked out a four-stage scenario leading from today's technology to the ultimate biocomputer. This scenario will be reflected in the forthcoming Gorham study.

Stage 1 devices, the scenario suggests, will be electronic in the conventional sense. Signals will be carried by comparatively large numbers of electrons flowing in conductors and semiconductors. The conductors will be metallic, deposited on protein by staining techniques like those that biologists use to show up the internal details of cells under the electron microscope.

Eventually, stage one technology is expected to pack devices into one thousandth of the space required by today's silicon technology. That assumes that three-dimensional chips can be made with sub-micron feature sizes.

Gentronix already has a rudimentary 'stage one' process which has been tried out at a feature size of four microns. It uses a film of a synthetic protein called polylysine, deposited on a substrate and covered with a conventional resist material: polymethyl methacrylate, better known as Perspex (Lucite in the US).

An electron beam writes patterns in the resist, under computer control. Resist is then dissolved away from the exposed areas. The composite is then treated with further reagents which deposit metallic silver wherever the protein layer is exposed. There is no need to remove the remaining resist, and McAlear says that the silver can be built up until it more or less fills the troughs in the resist layer. The result, he claims, is an almost flat surface which should provide a good base for further layers of protein and resist.

He sees this as an alternative route to the three-dimensional chips that other laboratories are trying to make out of silicon. But those laboratories are spared one very important worry: they already know how to make transistors out of silicon.

The first generation of biochips could include genuine computing elements, if someone can invent an organic transistor or logic gate. This has not happened yet, so it is possible that stage one devices will perform little or no information processing. But McAlear foresees other intriguing possibilities: capacious optical memories, solid-state 'retinas' for robot vision, and thin-film TV screens. He suggests that a three-dimensional TV or data display could be made by depositing an array of light-emitting cells on a flexible membrane that vibrates like a drumhead.

Even these applications have no guarantee of success, since they will need organic materials with special optical properties. Phthalocyanine dyes are seen as a likely material for erasable laser disks and may also have suitable properties for some types of biochip.

Biosensors are devices which respond to biochemical stimuli with electrical signals. Biosensors sensitive to oxygen, glucose and other substances of medical significance have been developed for diagnostic tests. Others are likely to be used to control industrial processes and to warn soldiers of chemical or biological attack. Today's biosensors are hybrid components. They rely on biological materials such as enzymes or antibodies for their sensitivity and specificity, but their electronic parts are made of silicon or another inorganic semiconductor. Biosensors that are fully organic (apart from metal 'wires') may emerge from 'stage one' technology.

Stage two technology is expected to achieve feature sizes as small as 0.1 micron. This is also regarded as about the theoretical limit for silicon technology. Stage two rests on the idea that protein molecules can assemble themselves into predetermined structures. Many of the working parts of cells, for example the intracellular 'muscles' called microtubules, will reassemble themselves if they are deliberately broken up in the laboratory. The protein coats of viruses can do the same trick.

Most molecules crystallize into regular and potentially infinite arrays, but the self-assembling molecules of life 'crystallize' into objects of particular shapes and sizes. This observation has led to the idea that proteins could be designed, by computer, to assemble themselves spontaneously into useful biochip structures. Antibody molecules, or active fragments of them, might be suitable.

McAlear accepts that it would be difficult to design a biochip that assembled itself in ready-to-work condition. At the moment he is thinking of more modest schemes in which the protein serves as scaffolding. Other materials would be added later. Polymethyl methacrylate could be used to form optical waveguides within the chip. The whole device might use light, rather than electricity, to transmit and process information.

Once again there is a need for an organic switch or logic gate, this time an optical one. Once again, the state of the art with inorganic materials is more advanced. Optical logic gates exist, but they are made of indium antimonide and similar compounds.

Stage three, McAlear says, 'Would involve the fabrication of devices at the next order of dimension down, which would be 1/100th micron.' When they met McAlear in San Diego in November 1983, Albert Lawrence and Alwyn Scott suggested a method of signalling along 'wires' less than a hundred atoms wide. Signals would be carried by packets of energy called excitons. Lawrence suggested that excitons might be conducted along columns of phthalocyanine molecules stacked like plates. The molecules are flat, square, and have a hole in their middle, which in this case would be occupied by a rare earth metal ion.

Exciton conductors probably cannot be directly interfaced with ordinary electronics, but light can be converted into excitons and vice versa, so an exciton-based chip might communicate optically with other components. Excitons travel at about one-tenth the speed of light, rather slower than electrical signals.

The proposed stage 4 technology relies on wave-like disturbances called solitons which propagate, in theory, without losing any energy. Power would probably still be needed for logical and switching operations involving solitons, however these are achieved.

The boundary between stages 3 and 4 is blurred. Soliton phenomena occur in many areas of physics. A solitary water wave in a canal, and a ripple in a protein helix, can both be described as solitons. And the excitons of stage 3 may prove to propagate in solitonic fashion. Also, feature sizes in stages 3 and 4 may not be all that different. The phthalocyanine 'wires' envisaged for stage 3 would be about one nanometre – roughly ten atoms – wide. Long polyacetylene molecules only two or three atoms wide have been proposed as soliton conductors for stage 4. But now McAlear says that very few people take a polyacetylene single chain seriously as a conductor of solitons or similar phenomena.

First estimates must therefore be revised. It may not be possible to squeeze the world's computing power into a sugar cube: ten cubes, perhaps.

59

Landscape gardening in hyperspace

Certain ways of thinking about problems crop up repeatedly: satisfying multiple constraints; searching a multidimensional space; climbing hills or following valleys in a landscape. Metaphors like these have inspired new computing architectures; they also help researchers to get a mental grasp of what is going on, as these novel machines solve problems and improve their performance through learning.

---

31 January 1985

A molecular biologist wondered why we dream. An H-bomb inventor improved his calculations by leaving things to chance. Both contributed, indirectly, to the development of machines which are wired like the brain, which follow the same statistical laws as collections of molecules, and which (a recent discovery) can learn.

Edward Teller, the 'father of the H-bomb', was one of the authors of an influential 1953 paper in the *Journal of Chemical Physics*. The paper presented a new 'Monte Carlo' method of solving optimization problems.

Problems where the 'goodness' of a solution can be measured directly include the well-known one about a travelling salesman who has to visit a large number of cities. A good solution is simply a route with a low total mileage. It sounds simple, but in this and similar problems the search space can be enormous and good solutions are surprisingly hard to find.

One way to tackle the salesman problem is to start with a random route and try to improve it progressively by small changes. But you may get stuck in a 'local minimum' of the search space which is nowhere near the best solution. This is a common hazard in optimization problems. To avoid it, Teller with four colleagues developed the method which is known (after the 1953 paper's leading author) as the Metropolis algorithm. Instead of hanging on to every improvement it achieved, the new algorithm occasionally, on a chance basis, sacrificed a short-term gain in the hope that this would lead to a long-term advantage.

Something very similar happens among atoms and molecules. Occasionally a particle will acquire enough energy to climb over some energy barrier and drop into a state of lower energy than the one it started in. Its chance of acquiring the necessary energy rises sharply with temperature. One of the parameters in the Metropolis algorithm plays a similar role to temperature.

If the 'temperature' is too low, the algorithm may get trapped in local energy minima. If the temperature is too high, the system never settles on a solution at all. Choosing an intermediate temperature will help. But it is even better to start at a high temperature and gradually 'cool' the system down. This technique is called 'simulated annealing', by analogy with the heat treatment used to relax stresses in metals and glass.

The key paper on simulated annealing is by Kirkpatrick, Gelatt and Vecchi, and appeared in *Science* in May 1983. Scott Kirkpatrick (an IBM research scientist) and his colleagues demonstrated the power of the method by redesigning part of the IBM 3081 mainframe computer.

The problem was to arrange 98 chips on a 10 by 10 ceramic module, so that the interconnecting wires would be neither too long nor too crowded. The exercise started with the original 3081 design, and 'annealed' it by swapping pairs of chips. In 12 minutes of computer time, the chips were completely rearranged, and the total wire length was reduced by 10 per cent.

The possible uses of annealing are many and various. It is probably not the best way of solving the salesman problem. But it handles the chip placement problem rather well, and could probably be applied more generally to the design of complex systems. Annealing has also attracted considerable interest among researchers in machine vision and speech recognition.

All these problems have something in common. A solution can be expressed as a large number of simple yes/no decisions, each of which interacts positively or negatively with others. The problem can be presented as a network of constraints. This network need not be an abstract entity. One can easily imagine a network of physical units, each of which is either 'on' or 'off', and each of which is influenced by excitatory or inhibitory inputs from other units. The kind of unit required behaves in important respects like the well-known McCullough and Pitts model of the neurone.

In the brain, of course, all the units operate in parallel. Whether they do anything that corresponds to simulated annealing has yet to be determined. But at least three groups have been trying to see what can be achieved by introducing parallelism into the annealing process.

Stuart and Donald Geman, respectively at Brown University and the University of Massachusetts, have been using annealing to remove noise from images. Paul Smolensky of the University of California, San Diego, is investigating annealing search, knowledge representation and learning in networks.

Geoff Hinton and Scott Fahlman of Carnegie-Mellon University, and Terry Sejnowski of Johns Hopkins University, are studying the theory of what they call 'Boltzmann machines'. They have built a semi-parallel machine with seven 68000 microprocessors, and they envisage future machines with much more parallelism and much greater speeds.

The Pittsburgh and Baltimore based group is interested in artificial intelligence applications, including vision. One of their most important discoveries is an algorithm which enables the Boltzmann machine to learn. The algorithm trains the network in a general sense to model its environment. Specifically, the network is taught to respond with an appropriate output, for each of a set of possible inputs.

The units themselves are simple threshold devices with no memory. Information is stored in the connections between them. Learning is achieved by modifying the strengths of these connections. The basic idea is that the strength of a connection between two units is increased a little, each time both units are 'on' together. The neurophysiologist Donald Hebb suggested that the brain learns in this way.

But Hinton and Sejnowski decided that the network also needs an opportunity to weaken certain connections. The purpose of this is to suppress spurious responses which arise spontaneously in the network. The network's output should reflect its input, and not its own internal peculiarities. So learning proceeds in two phases: a 'positive' phase when both inputs and outputs are 'clamped' in training patterns; and a 'negative' phase when the inputs are clamped but the outputs are left free.

The inspiration for this two-phase learning algorithm came directly from the theory of dreams proposed in 1983 by Francis Crick and Graeme Mitchison, both of whom were then at the Salk Institute in California. Crick's fame as co-discoverer of the structure of DNA ensured that the theory was widely reported in the newspapers.

We all spend around two hours dreaming every night. Crick and Mitchison proposed that the function of dreams was to erase spurious memory traces formed when new memories were deposited over old ones. Crick discovered that a friend at the California Institute of Technology, John Hopfield, had tested a similar mechanism in a computer-simulated neural network. Mitchison repeated Hopfield's experiments.

'We knew about the Crick–Mitchison work and the idea of what they called 'unlearning', and that was one of the things that prompted us to look for a learning algorithm of the kind we looked for,' says Hinton.

A psychologist who gained his experience in artificial intelligence at Edinburgh and Sussex, Hinton is particularly interested in vision. Many vision problems involve a search for a 'most plausible' hypothesis which, as far as possible, satisfies a large number of constraints simultaneously.

One such problem is to find a plausible combination of surface orientations and lighting to account for the shading in an image. Another is stereo fusion – the extraction of depth information from the views seen by two eyes or cameras. Similar approaches may be used to deduce that separated line segments in an image belong to the same edge; and to identify groups of edges which could be the boundaries of solid objects.

Hinton hopes that the Boltzmann machine approach can be extended into other areas of artificial intelligence research. Already his group has shown that a machine of this kind can represent knowledge in the form of a production system – a set of 'if this, do that' rules. But Hinton stresses that this is not yet a practical way to implement a production system.

No one has yet done a detailed comparison between the Boltzmann machine learning algorithm and the established learning algorithms such as Ross Quinlan's ID3. This is one area where the bottom-up 'connectionist' approach could fuse creatively with conventional top-down artificial intelligence. And despite considerable mathematical analysis, there is still much to be learned about the 'energy landscapes' that Boltzmann machines traverse as they seek the deep valleys of minimum energy.

'We have very little grasp of what the energy landscapes are really like,' says Hinton. An energy surface occupies a multi-dimensional space, and Hinton points out that any two-dimensional representation is bound to be misleading. Nonetheless, any graphical representation is better than none, and some of the group's future work may be on a better ways of visualizing energy surfaces on the computer screen.

Some landscapes are easy to search, and some are difficult. Hinton hopes to find out why. He has already done some work on techniques which mould the surface so it is easier to search – a process that he describes as 'landscape gardening the energy surface'.

The Boltzmann machine has not altogether fulfilled its promise. Though small ones perform adequately, the concept does not scale up well to large networks. But there are many other kinds of network to try, and this is becoming an increasingly lively area of research. A promising learning algorithm for multi-layer nets, known as error back-propagation, has been developed at the University of California at San Diego. David Rumelhart's group at UCSD has been a focus for research on 'parallel distributed processing' (to use the UCSD terminology). Crick is a member of the group. Hinton and Sejnowski both worked there before moving East.

Further reading

Hinton, G.E., Sejnowski, T.J. and Ackley, D.H. (1984). *Boltzmann Machines: Constraint Satisfaction Networks that Learn.* Technical Report CMU-CS-84-119, Carnegie-Mellon University Department of Computer Science.

Kirkpatrick, S., Gelatt, C.D. and Vecchi, M.P. (1983). 'Optimization by simulated annealing' *Science*, **220**, 671–680.

Rumelhart, D.E., McLelland, J.L. and the PDP Research Group (1986). Eds. *Parallel Distributed Processing*. 2 vols. Cambridge, Mass.: MIT Press. (A major collection, edited at UCSD. More notable for its wealth of technical detail than for reflective discussion of the issues.)

60

Bits, beliefs and Boltzmann

Discussions of biochips and protein computers inevitably appeal to any remnant of vitalism that survives in our belief systems. The overt reason for turning to biotechnology is that it offers a means of creating extremely small engineered structures. The scientifically unmentionable implication, with its resonances of myth and witchcraft, is that a biological computer might in some sense come to life. It might have a real mind, whatever that means.

The connectionists and 'bottom-up' AI researchers cannot be accused of witchcraft or vitalism since they start with a logical model of a neurone rather than the biological material itself. There is an enormous difference.

Nevertheless an air of mystery surrounds these brain-like models of computation which depend on emergent phenomena. Do they in some absolute sense have powers that are denied to conventional algorithmic programming? Or are they merely more efficient at certain kinds of task? The latter seems to be the case, since in truth most of the research has not been done with novel hardware at all, but with simulations on conventional computers.

Theoretically, a simulation is just as good as the real thing, if you do not mind waiting for the results. But the practical prospects for research are transformed if the hardware, when built, runs a hundred, a thousand or maybe a million times faster than the simulation. This might be what is needed to get artificial intelligence research out of its real or imagined impasse. It is important to grasp that the new massively parallel architectures are not just offering more of the same old brute computing power. They suggest new ways of solving problems, which may turn out to capture more of what we regard as intelligence.

The danger is loss of insight. If we rely on emergent properties of hardware or software, we risk never understanding the processes from which those properties emerge. It would be sad if the art of understanding whole systems, which has made so many gains in the field of software engineering, were forced onto the retreat in the closely related discipline of artificial intelligence.

Luckily this fear seems unfounded. The work of the connectionists revives a tradition of mathematical rigour, the like of which is rarely seen these days in mainstream AI research.

---

10 January 1985

John Searle's BBC Reith Lectures on 'Mind, brain and science' hit at least one crack in the armour of artificial intelligence researchers.

Searle seized on a supposed claim by John McCarthy that even a thermostat has beliefs. Most people have some trouble with the idea that the closure of two contacts in a thermostat constitutes a 'belief' that the room is too cool. Why, then, should we say that a computer program 'believes' something when all that has happened is the setting of one bit in the computer's memory?

Searle further argues that human minds possess a quality of 'intentionality' that no computer program can reproduce. He has yet to explain what, in the structure of the brain, could account for such a difference.

Many artificial intelligence workers would not yield the intentionality point to Searle. But most would accept that computer models of belief, desire, reason and other mental phenomena have so far failed to reproduce the richness and subtlety of their equivalents in the human mind.

The whole AI enterprise has been based on abstractions. Details have deliberately been ignored. But what Searle sees as a fatal flaw has in fact been the secret of AI's success. No one really thought that a belief was a binary digit stored somewhere in the brain. AI researchers deliberately chose simple-minded representations of mental states because they had to start somewhere. Later on, they hoped to have the chance to investigate the rich and complex thing that a belief or a concept really is.

Whatever Searle says, this top-down approach has been successful. And this success extends beyond the well-publicized expert systems, most of which operate in areas where knowledge can easily be compartmentalized.

Among the many researchers who have made progress in more problematic areas of knowledge are Roger Schank at Yale, and Douglas Lenat at Stanford University. Schank and his colleagues have modelled the network of relationships between concepts, which they believe underlies language.

Lenat's program Eurisko improves its own strategies for learning, reasoning by analogy, and problem-solving. Of course, Eurisko's concept of 'two' does not have all the rich associations (two eyes, two ears, two's company, tea for two, two-finger salute . . .) that surround 'two' in a human mind. But Eurisko demonstrates that a good deal of serious reasoning can be performed with deliberately simplified versions of human concepts.

In a *Scientific American* article, Lenat pointed out that even when it has run for weeks at a time, Eurisko's experiences are not nearly as varied as those of a human infant. He suggested that the way to improve the program's analogical reasoning would be to expand its knowledge base.

'More knowledge' is the solution often proposed by the top-down school of artificial intelligence. It could be a very powerful way of increasing the subtlety, richness and general wisdom of AI programs, since the added knowledge may include knowledge about knowledge, and knowledge about thinking. Even if this meta-knowledge is not supplied, perhaps because humans have difficulty in making it explicit, there is still the hope that given the chance, learning programs like Eurisko will bootstrap themselves to higher levels of performance.

Lenat is perhaps in a minority when he doubts whether parallel processing will greatly increase the power of programs like Eurisko. By contrast Japan's fifth generation computer project, deeply committed to the 'more knowledge' thesis, assumes that as knowledge bases grow there will be a corresponding need for highly parallel machine architectures.

Both Schank and Lenat have been attacked for using *ad hoc* devices, and working without formal theories. What no one questions is that they have achieved results.

Japan's fifth generation architectures, in common with most of the parallel architectures proposed in Europe and the US, are born of 'top-down' thinking. The details of the hardware are determined by the need to run Prolog or Lisp or a group of similar languages. And those languages are modelled on the way logicians or computer scientists believe knowledge can be manipulated.

But there is now a resurgence of interest in 'bottom-up' architectures, inspired by the nervous system or other complex systems with interesting 'emergent' properties. Neural nets, Boltzmann machines and cellular automata fall in this category.

In these architectures, stability and instability, rather than logical truth and falsehood, are the important issues. Knowledge is never represented by the setting of a single bit of memory. Instead, subtle changes occur throughout the system whenever an item is added to its knowledge.

In theory any parallel machine can be simulated on a sequential machine. But if the simulation runs a million times slower than the real thing, it becomes essential to build some hardware.

Proponents of these alternative architectures believe that though the quantity of knowledge stored in a given amount of hardware may appear to be less, in some sense its quality is improved. And hardware, they point out, is cheap in the age of the 256-kilobit memory chip.

Propositional representations of knowledge, based on truth and falsehood, have lost their charm even among some practitioners of top-down AI.

In 1969 Marvin Minsky and Seymour Papert of the Massachusetts Institute of Technology proved that single layer neural nets or 'perceptrons' could not do such simple things as counting objects. Their proof helped to discredit bottom-up architectures for a decade or more. But now Minsky tells his students that the idea of 'truth' is dangerous. He is working on a model of learning and memory which does not use symbols or representations.

In developing his concept of 'K lines', Minsky has tried to find a way of reactivating processes that were going on when something deemed to be 'interesting' happened, without falling into the trap of crude stimulus-response behaviourism.

Alan Kay of Apple Computer admires the work of Schank and Lenat. Schank, he says, 'is closer to having his finger on what needs to be done, than anybody I've seen.' His main reservation about Schank's work is that it still uses symbols. 'I don't think that representation based on symbols, in the sense that they're used in computer science, has any bearing whatsoever on the kinds of memory structure that these systems will use in the future,' says Kay, a former biologist whose work in computer science has often been inspired by biological models.

It is one thing to suggest that biology can provide models for artificial minds. It is another to say, as Searle does, that mind is an intrinsically biological phenomenon, 'along with growth, reproduction, the secretion of bile, and digestion'.

Searle's lectures contained hints that he does not really believe that wet protein has magical properties absent from silicon or green slime. However he was adamant that mind is rooted in the physical structure of the brain. He attacked artificial intelligence and the whole 'cognitive science' approach, which seeks to understand the mind in terms of the logical structure of brain or computer, rather than its physical implementation.

This was the approach of the English mathematician and computer pioneer Alan Turing, as Andrew Hodges stresses in his biography *Alan Turing: the enigma*. Turing produced the first precise logical description of a general purpose computer, some years before anyone physically built such a machine.

Anyone who attempts to model mental processes with digital electronics of any kind, bows to Turing's belief. If it is logical structure that counts, a mind could be based on electronics. If physical implementation is crucial, then we have no reason to suppose that anything other than living neurones can do the job.

Even those who work with electronic models of the neurone, like Geoffrey Hinton at Carnegie-Mellon University, have broken with Searle and joined Turing. Hinton plans to build a machine made of many small units which are logical models, but not physical models, of the neurone.

Igor Aleksander of Imperial College, London, and his colleagues at Brunel University, are probably the first people in the world to commercialize a bottom-up parallel processing system capable of performing non-trivial tasks. Their Wisard system can learn to recognize a human face in five seconds. It can learn to recognize a class of patterns, given a few well-chosen examples.

Wisard's randomly connected single-layer net has led some people to suppose that the people who designed the device do not know how it works. 'We have a complete and developed theory of how this works,' Aleksander counters. 'The only problem about this theory is that it is probabilistic.'

But this is not a new problem for science. At the microscopic level, the steam engine and the laser are also based on probabilistic theories. Hinton's group at Carnegie-Mellon call their proposed architecture the 'Boltzmann machine' after the scientist who produced a statistical theory of thermodynamics.

Aleksander is now seeking ways of grafting knowledge based programming onto unconventional architectures similar to Wisard. 'There has been this crazy division between top-down and bottom-up approaches,' he says, 'which isn't a correct division anyway, because nobody works entirely top down and nobody works entirely bottom up.'

Boltzmann machines and neural nets with feedback tend to settle down in stable states. Each stable state lies at the bottom of an 'energy well' in the space of all possible states. Training the system creates a new energy wells. An energy well can represent a learned concept. Networks of wells, linked by valleys, might represent semantic nets, decision trees or other data structures used in artificial intelligence. Such ideas may sound exotic, but with very large scale integrated circuits it may at last be possible to put them to the test.

Further reading

Dennett, D. and Hofstadter, D.R. (1981). Eds. *The Mind's I.* Brighton: Harvester Press. (Includes a famous article by Searle, with whom the editors disagree.)

Grabiner, J.V. (1986). 'Computers and the nature of man: a historian's perspective on controversies about artificial intelligence' Bulletin *(new series) of the American Mathematical Society*, **15**, no. 2, October, 113–126. (AI programs do less than their authors claim.)

Lenat, D.B. (1984). 'Computer software for intelligent systems' *Scientific American*, September, 152. (Accessible account of AM and Eurisko.)

Lenat, D.B. and Seely Brown, J. (1984). 'Why AM and Eurisko appear to work' *Artificial Intelligence*, **23**, 269–294. (Lenat's contrite reply to criticisms.)

Ritchie, G.D. and Hanna, F.K. (1984). 'AM: a case study in AI methodology' *Artificial Intelligence*, **23**, 249–268. (One of AI's greatest 'successes' debunked.)

Searle, J.R. (1985). *Mind, Brain and Science*. London: BBC Publications.

Sloman, A. (1978). *The Computer Revolution in Philosophy*. Hassocks, Sussex: Harvester Press.